T0326872

"This Is Jerusalem Calling"

"This Is Jerusalem Calling"

State Radio in Mandate Palestine

BY ANDREA L. STANTON

University of Texas Press ⟵⟶ *Austin*

Requests for permission to reproduce material from this work should be sent to:
Permissions
University of Texas Press
P.O. Box 7819
Austin, TX 78713-7819
http://utpress.utexas.edu/index.php/rp-form

♾ The paper used in this book meets the minimum requirements of
ANSI/NISO Z39.48-1992 (R1997) (Permanence of Paper).

Library of Congress Cataloging-in-Publication Data
Stanton, Andrea L.
    This is Jerusalem calling : state radio in mandate Palestine / by Andrea L.
Stanton. — 1st ed.
        p.   cm.
    Includes bibliographical references and index.
    ISBN 978-0-292-74749-4 (cloth : alk. paper)
    ISBN 978-1-4773-0223-1 (paperback)
    1. Palestine Broadcasting Service—History.   2. Radio broadcasting—
Palestine—History.   3. Radio—Palestine—History.   I. Title.
    HE8699.P32S73   2013
    384.54095694′09041—dc23   2012044365

doi: 10.7560/747494

Contents

Acknowledgments   vii

Introduction: Tuning in to Palestine's Radio History   1

1. Selling Radio, Selling Radios: Advertising Sets in
    Mandate Palestine   29

2. Peasants into Palestinians: Rural and School Broadcasting   76

3. Broadcasting a Nationalist Modernity: The PBS Arabic Section   123

4. Putting Religion on the Radio   152

5. Claiming the PBS: Whose National Radio?   168

Conclusion: The Multiple Afterlives of the PBS   195

Timeline   201

Notes   203

Bibliography   235

Index   247

Acknowledgments

This project was a pleasure from beginning to end. I am deeply grateful to the many people and institutions who helped bring this project to life—starting with former Palestine Broadcasting Service Assistant Director Rex Keating, whose memoirs were my first indication that mandate-era radio in Palestine might be a subject worth investigating.

During my years of research, the staff at numerous archives went out of their way to track down archival files and suggest additional materials. Debbie Usher of St. Antony's Middle East Center Archive welcomed a very green researcher with warmth, tea, and numerous useful tips for future searches. At the Israel State Archives, Michal Saft was particularly kind, cheerfully accommodating everything from a tight travel schedule to a loud digital camera. Staff at the British Library and the British National Archives (formerly the Public Records Office) were equally helpful. The microfilm room staff at both New York and Columbia Universities charitably overlooked my hogging the super-high-resolution magnifying lenses as well as my tendency to cart enough bags into their rooms to make it appear as if I might move in permanently.

Other people helped in less direct ways. Eddie Palmer opened the door to a rich archival treasure trove—the Boutagy family collection of photographs, papers, and family memoirs, as well as the Boutagy family website. Kevin Martin sent chapters of his dissertation on modernity in 1950s Syria for comparative purposes. They also proved a rich source of inspiration, for which I am grateful. Amos Nadan sent relevant portions of his then-manuscript—those dealing with agricultural programming on the PBS—which helped flesh out the tricky issue of audience response (or lack thereof) to this programming. Relli Shechter helped refine my thinking on advertising, as did Victoria de Grazia. Sherene Seikaly welcomed me as a fellow sojourner at the Israeli State Archive and uttered my favorite characterization of academic work: "This is hard." Kira von Ostenfeld, Jon Webster, and Kristen Brainard provided good company in New York, while Andrew Tabler, Melody Russell, and Kristin Shamas, as well as Habib Battah, Charles Chuman, and Tsolin Nalbantian did the same in Damascus and Beirut. Ted Kerr has been a constant fount of encouragement in Denver.

Several organizations kindly provided venues to present chapters in paper form: the annual Middle East Studies Association (MESA) conference; the annual American Historical Association (AHA) conference; the World Congress for Middle Eastern Studies (WOCMES); the Roger Williams University Conference on Religion and the State; and the Center for Arab and Middle Eastern Studies' (CAMES) faculty and visiting scholars' research seminar at the American University of Beirut. The questions, comments and suggestions that audience members and participants made at these conferences and seminars added depth and richness to the research that went into this project. Similarly, I would like to thank Salim Tamari for publishing an excerpt of Chapter 1 in the *Jerusalem Quarterly*'s 50th anniversary issue, and the University of Texas Press for granting permission to do so.

During the research for this project, I was a grateful recipient of much Columbia University funding: a multi-year fellowship and summer funds that the History Department provided, a Graduate School of Arts and Sciences' (GSAS) Reid Hall research grant and a Middle East Institute summer regional travel research grant. The Department of Education supported my language training with an academic year and summer FLAS. I appreciated the financial support that each grant provided, and was grateful for the 'vote of confidence' in my work that each represented. I would also like to thank the History Department, GSAS and Middle East Institute staff—particularly the inestimable Astrid Benedek.

As this book grew out of my doctoral dissertation, I am most grateful for the intellectual support that Richard Bulliet, Rashid Khalidi and Anupama Rao provided during my days in graduate school. They suggested avenues of conceptualizing and problematizing 'radio' as a subject that would never have occurred to me and showed me the forest whenever I became too bogged down in the many trees of this project. They asked questions about radio technology, commodity culture, listening practices, audience reception and how the PBS intersected with mandate politics that opened up new ways of thinking about the material I uncovered.

I would also like to thank two 'families': my own family—my parents Darlene and Jerry, sister Brianna and brother-in-law Bill, and extended family, including my khalto Patricia—who have been long-standing and at times long-suffering supporters, and who have provided me with love, support, and my favorite nephew and niece. I have also had the very good fortune to find a home at the University of Denver, where my colleagues—Sandy Dixon, Ginni Ishimatsu, Luis Leon, Carl Raschke, Greg Robbins, Alison Schofield, and Nicole Willock—as well as other DU luminaries, including Consuelo Bennett and Eleanor McNees, have been enthusiastic cheerleaders for this project. May every assistant professor receive bear hugs when announcing her first book contract.

I would especially like to thank my friend from Columbia days, Ramzi Rouighi, for what has been nearly a decade of encouragement and support. He soldiered through some truly awful draft chapters, tactfully suggesting improvements without even one grimace. When it came time to revise the dissertation for publication, he graciously did it all again, and reviewed my book proposal to boot. Thank you.

Finally, my sincere and multiple thanks to the University of Texas Press, particularly Senior Editor Jim Burr, Manuscript Editor Victoria Davis, and copyeditor Sheila Berg, as well as the two anonymous (but greatly appreciated) manuscript reviewers. After I presented at WOCMES in 2006, an older Jordanian man of Palestinian descent approached me with a frown. "Why are you spending so much time on something so unimportant?" he asked. Thank you all for considering the story of the PBS an important part of mandate Palestine's history, and for bringing it to print.

Needless to say, all factual and conceptual errors are mine and mine alone.

"This Is Jerusalem Calling"

Tuning in to Palestine's Radio History

On the penultimate day of March 1936, as Palestine was moving from the pale gray of winter into the lush green of spring, the Palestine Broadcasting Service (PBS) began radio broadcasts from a new transmitter in Ramallah. The mandate state was well into its second decade, with the contours of British governance and Arab and Zionist contestation firmly and clearly established. The territory of Palestine—mentioned in the Bible, central to the three Abrahamic faiths, and ruled by the Ottoman Empire for centuries as part of its "Arab provinces"—was given after World War I to Great Britain to govern under a League of Nations mandate. Like the rest of the Ottoman Empire and the colonial territories controlled by the losing countries of World War I, Palestine was considered currently unfit for self-governance; unlike the African lands, whose mandates were issued almost in perpetuity, Palestine and the other Arab provinces were considered "Class A" mandates—requiring only minimal tutelage to prepare them for self-governance.

However, the terms of the mandate for Palestine as ultimately approved at the San Remo conference in 1922 differed in several crucial ways from those for Iraq, Lebanon, and Syria. The text of the mandate authorization included that of the Balfour Declaration, an ex officio "declaration of sympathy" issued in 1917 as a letter from Arthur Balfour, British foreign secretary, to Baron Nathan Rothschild. "His Majesty's Government view with favor," it stated, "the establishment in Palestine of a national home for the Jewish people, and will use their best endeavors to facilitate the achievement of this object." The text continued, "it being understood that nothing shall be done which may prejudice the civil and religious rights of non-Jewish communities in

Palestine . . . or the rights and political status enjoyed by Jews in any country." In the letter that framed the declaration, Balfour noted that it had been approved by the British cabinet and asked Rothschild to forward it to the World Zionist Federation.[1]

The Balfour Declaration made no mention of the independent Arab state that Great Britain had already promised to Husayn, Sharif of Mecca, and his sons.[2] Nor did it mention the political rights of the people of Palestine. Yet the declaration was merely that. The original document had no binding force; its authority derived from Britain's position as one of the most powerful empires in the world. Once inserted in the San Remo resolution, however, the Balfour Declaration became an actionable part of the mandate; as the text stated, "The Mandatory will be responsible for putting into effect the declaration originally made on November 8, 1917."[3] With this text, the British government committed itself not only to governing Palestine (which British officials considered desirable for a number of reasons, political, imperial, and religious) but also to supporting the aims of the global Zionist community.

In consequence, mandate Palestine suffered not only the two-way, nationalist/colonizer clashes of any colonial state; it also endured the three-way conflict produced by splitting the Palestinian population into Jew and Arab—a three-way conflict that further encouraged the political separatism of the Zionist movement. The result was a deeply contentious environment in which mandate state institutions faced from each community both attempts to discredit them and attempts to claim or co-opt them. The situation was made more contentious by the striking demographic shifts taking place throughout the territory and within each community. As Assaf Likhovski notes, the mandate years "saw accelerated economic and demographic growth that resulted, to a large extent, from the massive influx of Jewish capital and immigration."[4] These interventions did not have an equal impact on all people or across all parts of the territory. They were as much a destabilizing force as a generative one, but they did spur the massive political, economic, social, and cultural shifts already taking place in Palestine. They did so, further, in the context of major population growth: the overall population increased from 750,000 in the early 1920s to nearly 1.9 million by the end of the mandate. Again, the larger shift came from the Jewish population: from about 83,000 to 90,000 in the early 1920s to 530,000 to 550,000 by 1944.[5] In other words, within twenty years the number of Jews had increased from roughly 10 percent to roughly 30 percent of the overall population, while the overall population had increased

250 percent. The Palestine Broadcasting Service, a state institution that operated from March 1936 through the end of the mandate, was born into this environment.

Inaugurating the PBS

The PBS's inaugural broadcast—held near the Ramallah transmitter rather than in the Jerusalem-based broadcasting offices in order to minimize technical problems—was attended by an array of dignitaries and numerous mandate government figures. High Commissioner Arthur Wauchope—governor-general of mandate Palestine and the highest representative of British power there—himself gave one of the opening speeches, which were broadcast live. "For some years I have been greatly impressed by the benefits that a well directed Broadcasting Service can bring to the mind and spirit of any people who enjoy its advantages," he stated, adding that in Palestine "broadcasting will be directed for the advantage of all classes of all communities." Wauchope's comments about advantages fit neatly within mid-1930s European understandings of radio broadcasting, and in particular reflected bureaucratic conceptions of radio as a public good intended to benefit listeners. Yet as his comment about "all communities" indicated, his speech was delivered not to a group of European broadcasters or bureaucrats but in the highly charged political context of mandate Palestine. What advantages could radio broadcasting provide for listeners in this context, and how would a government-operated radio station address the religiously inflected nationalist tensions of Palestine's two primary communities?

In his speech Wauchope stated that the station would not cover politics but instead focus on "knowledge and culture." With this statement and what followed, he laid out both the promise and the limitation of radio broadcasting in mandate Palestine. At the same time he gave voice to the British bureaucratic perspective on the territory and its biggest challenges: how to bring its rural Arab "peasant" population into the twentieth century while providing sufficient cultural stimulation for its urban Jewish "professional" population. He made only an oblique, brief reference to what Palestinians might have considered their biggest challenges—the political and religious contestation over the nature and identity of the mandate territory—suggesting the bureaucratic "modernization first" perspective brought about by the temporary calm of the mid-1930s. Wauchope's speech suggested that modernizing Pales-

Figure 0.1. Sir Arthur Wauchope, high commissioner of Palestine, delivering the inaugural address for the Palestine Broadcasting Service from Ramallah, March 30, 1936. Source: G. Eric and Edith Matson Photograph Collection, Prints and Photographs Division, Library of Congress, LC-DIG-matpc-16766.

tine would inherently resolve the problem of Palestine, somehow harmonizing the competing aims of its two populations.

While assuring listeners that the station would reach out to all people in Palestine, Wauchope described two groups that he hoped the station would reach, farmers and music lovers, "in both of which," he said, "I have deep interest." "We shall try to stimulate new interests and make all forms of knowledge more widespread," he promised. For example:

> There are thousands of farmers in this country who are striving to improve their methods of agriculture. I hope we shall find ways and means to help these farmers and assist them to increase the yield of the soil, improve the quality of their produce, and explain the advantages of various forms of cooperation.
>
> There are thousands of people in Palestine who have a natural love of music, but who experience difficulty in finding the means whereby they may enjoy the many pleasures that music gives. The Broadcasting Service will endeavor to fill this need and stimulate musical life in Palestine, so that we may see both Oriental and Western music grow in strength, side by side, each true to its own tradition.[6]

Why these two groups above others? Wauchope's focus on them suggested both the mandate government's chief interest and some of its blind spots. In part, the mandate government's position echoed the British Empire's experience in India, which transferred to Palestine along with the many British officials who served in both places. Mandate government officials (with support from British officials in the United Kingdom) saw rural Palestinians as a backward population that needed modernizing. Without modernization, officials worried, farmers—more often described as "peasants"—might serve as a dangerous, destabilizing force.

While farmers were described in Wauchope's speech as benefiting from pedagogical broadcasts explaining cooperative farming or soil yield, music lovers were described in terms of pleasure. Wauchope suggested that for them the crucial issue was not improving their work productivity but the quality of their leisure pursuits. For them, the station would provide a more "stimulating" musical culture, encouraging "Oriental" and "Western" musical traditions to flourish—but to do so separately. Wauchope's image of two traditions developing "side by side" rather than in conversation with one another is a striking illustration of how deeply embedded the narrative of "East" and "West" had become.

What is equally striking about the groups Wauchope highlighted was their ostensibly nonsectarian nature. But those listening to his speech would have recognized these two groups as religiously marked. Farmers would have been understood as Arab "peasants"—cited in newspaper and government accounts as the paradigm of backwardness in Palestine and later targeted with specific PBS radio programs and free radio sets. Music lovers would have been understood as the Zionist immigrants from Central and Eastern Europe, whose numbers included a high percentage of amateur and professional classical musicians and who later complained effusively about the quality of the music (recorded and live) that the PBS broadcast. Together, these two groups—and Wauchope's focus on them—foreshadowed two primary foci of PBS programming.

Wauchope closed by reading a congratulatory message from the chairman of the British Broadcasting Corporation (BBC), thanking the postmaster general and assorted other government departments. He expressed confidence that the PBS, "founded upon the solid rocks of high aim and public interest, will play an increasing part in the social life and entertainment of the people."[7] Wauchope's mention of the BBC and other mandate officials signaled the formative relationship between the BBC and the PBS in its early days, as well as the close collaboration of government branches with regard to station operation and governance. At the same time the extensive coverage given Wauchope's speech in

Palestinian newspapers highlighted the importance of the station to various Palestinians' national aspirations, as well as its importance to the mandate government.

The PBS then began broadcasting, going on air as the national, state-run radio station of British-controlled mandate Palestine. Modeled on the BBC, the PBS was a noncommercial public station that enjoyed a broadcasting monopoly in Palestine. It was funded primarily by government allocations, with additional revenues coming from the annual license fees required of radio set owners; and its programming was intended to "educate and elevate" listeners as citizens rather than to entertain them as consumers. The inauguration of the PBS also connected Palestine to a much broader set of developments, stretching from Europe through Africa, Asia, and the Middle East. The early 1930s had been a golden era for state-run radio throughout Europe. By the mid-1930s it was becoming a golden era for Middle Eastern and North African state radio as well, as the European countries that governed from Morocco to the Gulf claimed frequencies on behalf of their colonies and mandate territories.[8] Radio was the premier mass medium of the early and mid-twentieth century, and people and governments alike believed in its power—which made state-run stations a locus of anxiety and excitement at the state and popular levels.

The PBS: A History

This book tells the forgotten story of the Palestine Broadcasting Service, the government-operated national radio station of mandate Palestine that operated from 1936 until the end of the mandate in 1948. At that point its Jerusalem headquarters was rechristened Kol Israel, the nascent Israeli national station, and its Ramallah transmission tower was used for a newly created Jordanian station. The story of radio in the Middle East conventionally begins with Gamal Abdel Nasser's Voice of the Arabs in the mid-1950s. But what this book shows, using mandate Palestine as a case study, is the importance of radio to the political and social life of the Arab world in the 1930s and 1940s. More specifically, it argues that radio broadcasting in mandate Palestine took a separatist approach to Hebrew- and Arabic-language programming that reinforced the profound dis-integration that the mandate state facilitated at the political level. While the PBS did not create the conflict between Arab Palestinians and Zionists, it reflected and magnified it, becoming an outlet for the articulation of Palestinian and Zionist national identities. Radio broadcasting as a communication form, and the PBS as an institution, pushed these expressions of national identity and the expression of the conflict over Palestine in new directions.

Radio broadcasting has been little addressed in scholarship on Middle Eastern history. Although there is a relatively mature literature on the political, social, and technological history of radio in Great Britain, France, and the United States, scholars have not connected these metropolitan histories to the history of radio broadcasting in their former colonies, protectorates, or mandate states. The literature that does cover radio in the Middle East tends to treat it as a minor part of a broader issue—propaganda under Gamal Abdel Nasser or development in the postcolonial Maghreb.[9] Yet stations in the Middle East did not appear ex nihilo or only after independence: their creation was intimately connected to colonial or mandate politics and to European states' experiences with radio broadcasting at home.

This book highlights the close connections between the Palestine Broadcasting Service and the British Broadcasting Corporation—connections that were manifested at the level of organization and programming and included BBC personnel seconded to run the station in its early years.[10] At the same time this book highlights the degree to which the PBS took on a life of its own, with local hires exercising tremendous influence over programming choices and competing for station control. This work also notes the importance of considering radio broadcasting in terms of technology as much as in terms of news and entertainment broadcasting. Radio is often understood as a vehicle for transmitting communications of various kinds, but it must also be recognized as an infrastructure and an apparatus. The collection of broadcasting and transmitting technologies, which ranged from microphones and wires to transmission towers, is as crucial to radio's success as a transmitter as the programming it transmits—just as radio receiving sets, each with its own capacities and limitations, were crucial to listeners' ability to access broadcasts. This book acknowledges that understanding the radio technologies of the period is crucial for understanding the PBS and its audience's listening experiences—and hence its ultimate success.[11]

"This Is Jerusalem Calling" draws on three years of research in two sets of multisited archives and aims to understand the extensive reach and understudied effects of radio, which as a communicative medium became a key element in an emergent middle-class culture of consumption and display in mandate Palestine. It analyzes the development of

radio there as both a highly politicized broadcasting medium and a commodity closely tied to the maturation of an urban, self-consciously modern Arab middle class. Focusing on the Arabic-speaking community but considering the Hebrew-speaking community as well, it uses the PBS as the lens through which to narrate radio's role and influence, as a broadcasting medium and as a physical object, within these Palestinian communities.

This is the history of an institution—the radio station created by the British mandate government and staffed by a mixture of British civil officials and Arab Palestinian and Jewish personnel. As such, it is very much a colonial history, or a contribution to histories of colonial and mandatory regimes. But it is also the history of a medium (radio broadcasting) and of a commodity (radio sets) whose intersection in mandate Palestine produced an important set of social effects. These effects had an impact on the development of the Arab community both internally and in its relations with the British mandate state and the Zionist community.

More broadly, this work's underlying argument has implications for the study of non-Western media and class formation, particularly with reference to consumption and gender. More specifically, it reframes the narrative of the Palestinian mandate, placing debates about political determination, cultural identity, religious practice, and gender relations in the context of the most powerful mass medium of the interwar era, radio. While mandate studies is a growing field, the study of mandate Palestine has been dominated by political history. Looking at "softer" forms of power and at this crucial development of media infrastructure—as well as at its use as an ideological apparatus—expands the field of debate. By recovering the PBS's history, it also helps connect two strands of scholarship on mandate Palestine, bringing together political and social history by demonstrating how culture became a government management project.

Mandate Radio: Colonial Propaganda or National Institution?

By the late 1930s the Levant had a number of government-operated broadcasting stations, including Radio Damascus, the Egyptian State Broadcasting Service (Radio Cairo), Beirut's Radio Orient, and the Palestine Broadcasting Service, as well as an intermittently broadcasting station in Mosul. Yet to the extent that scholars have considered these stations, they have dismissed them as vehicles for government propaganda—and unsuccessful ones at that. They assume that radio sets' high cost combined with the popular perception of the stations' "taintedness" as colonial mouthpieces to discourage most people from tuning in. Yet the historical evidence says otherwise. Period documents, personal memoirs, and newspapers from Palestine all suggest that people *were* listening—that the PBS and, by extension, other stations became an integral part of Levantine life, especially in urban areas.

Although the mandate government exercised tight control over news broadcasts, locally hired staff at the PBS (and other stations) enjoyed great autonomy in developing the musical, theatrical, ethical, children's, and women's programs that constituted 70 to 80 percent of broadcasting hours. These programs reflected and reinforced post–World War I cultural developments circulating throughout the Arab world: changes in musical composition, the popularity of "foreign" tunes like the tango and the foxtrot, emergent theatrical forms, new pedagogies, and discussions of culture, ethics, and national identity. When they tuned in, listeners heard the sounds of a particular urban modernity, featuring locally prominent lecturers, regionally famous *firqas* (musical ensembles usually having eight or nine musicians and Western instruments), new takes on familiar *taqasims* (instrumental improvisations using the modal scales of Arabic music), and women from local elite families discussing the topics "The Arab Mother" or "The Muslim Woman during Ramadan." Without making a heavy-handed argument about the role of radio in producing national identity, this work highlights the PBS's influence in giving Palestinians an image of what kind of persons, culturally speaking, they should be.

Limited Audiences, Large Impact

The Palestine Broadcasting Service, while created to serve and to reach all Palestinians, almost certainly never reached the majority of the population. The same would have been true of most radio stations broadcasting in this period, due either to the limited territorial coverage that any station—even when supplemented by relay towers—could provide or to the relatively high cost of many radio sets. Yet just as radio stations in the United States, Canada, France, Italy, Germany, and Russia in the 1930s and 1940s are considered to have played a crucial role in the cultural, political, religious, and even economic developments of the interwar period, so stations like the Palestine Broadcasting Service did in the territories of the Middle East. For a station to have a major impact in this era did not require that the majority of the population tune in. Yet knowing the number of listeners would help in assessing the specific importance of the PBS.

The only solid numbers regarding the PBS's listenership come from the mandate government statistics on the number of radio set licenses that it sold each year. This number was taken by some Palestinians as a gauge of the PBS's popularity, and yet what it indicated was only the number of legally licensed radio set holders—not which stations they or other members of their household listened to. The radio license requirement was modeled on the "user pays" approach taken in Great Britain: those who used the services of the BBC, it was argued, should be the ones who paid for it. The model did not transfer perfectly: Great Britain's much larger and more urbanized population base meant that the BBC was able to run itself as a self-supporting, nonprofit corporation independent of the British government.

From the earliest planning stages, mandate officials acknowledged that Palestine's much smaller population would prevent a Palestine station from supporting itself on fees alone. Yet government officials appear to have concluded that the "user pays" principle was worth maintaining—even before a station existed. The government appears to have begun requiring radio set licenses in 1926, a year before the founding of the BBC; that year the government sold 80 licenses. By the end of 1929 Palestinians took out approximately 240 licenses; from the end of 1932 to the end of 1933, the number jumped from 900 to 2,500. In absolute numbers radio set license holders were a tiny percentage of Palestine's population, but the rapid percentile growth from year to year suggests the fascination of radio in this early period.

In Palestine radio set licenses sold for 500 mils (approximately half a British pound) for most of the life of the mandate, with the price rising gradually to one pound by World War II. Licenses were sold by the set and were good for one year; like the radio station, they were overseen by the Post Office, as part of its broader directive to govern and regulate the territory's communication networks. Because licenses tracked the number of radio sets operating in the country rather than the number of listeners, they do not accurately reflect the radio listening audience in Palestine. In part, this was due to contemporary cultural assumptions, which echoed European and North American listening practices, about radio set ownership and use. Radio sets in this era were relatively expensive, and they were big. Except in the wealth-

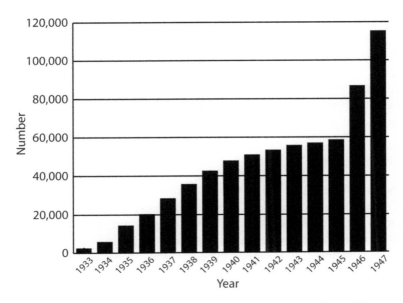

Chart 0.1. Total number of radio set receiver licenses held in Palestine from 1935 (one year before the PBS began broadcasting) through 1947. Government statistics are not available for 1948 or 1949.

iest families, it was unlikely that a radio set would have been a casual or discretionary purchase made by someone other than the head of the household—or that a household would have more than one set. Consequently, the number of radio set licenses held in any year reflected only a fraction of the actual number of people listening to radio broadcasting on that set. As discussed in later chapters, estimates for the number of listeners per radio set for any given broadcast range from two to three in a home to ten or more in a rural setting or public venue like a café. Even these numbers, however, do not account for the number of people who might listen to a particular set over the course of a week. But they do suggest the degree to which radio set ownership grew from year to year.

Chart 0.1 indicates that Palestine saw steady and significant growth in the number of radio set licenses from 1935 through 1941, with the number of licenses taken out annually increasing by 5,000 to 8,000 per year. This growth slowed dramatically during the central years of World War I, but the number of licenses still increased by 2,400 to 3,100 license holders per year from 1941 through 1945. By 1947 the mandate government recorded more than 115,000 radio set license holders, or roughly 9 to 11 percent of the total population. (Palestine's population figures are frequently contested; Jacob Metzer uses 1.34 million as the population in 1947.)[12] Even with a conservative three-listeners-per-set multiplier, radio set licenses suggest that 27 to 33 percent of Palestinians tuned in to the radio—many of them to the Palestine Broadcasting Service. This book argues that such listener projections speak not to the station's failure to reach Palestinian listeners but to its success.

Press Comparisons

Beyond license statistics, the most substantive indication of the importance of radio broadcasting for mandate Palestine came from another mass medium, the newspaper. As the scholars Ami Ayalon and Mustafa Kabha have shown for Arabic periodicals, the press in mandate Palestine was a thriving institution with a growing readership—one that itself might be productively compared to radio.[13] Newspapers were unlikely to have reached a majority of the population in any Middle Eastern country during the mandate period: although literacy rates and living standards increased during the mandate, Arabic newspapers reached only a minority of the adult Arabic-speaking population. (Readership rates in the Jewish community were higher, although they were distributed across several publication languages.) Overall, circulation statistics appear low relative to the size of the population: even in 1946 a government survey put the circulation of three major newspapers, *Falastin*, *al-Dif'a*, and the *Palestine Post*, at 8,000, 13,000, and 20,000 respectively, in a population of roughly 1.9 million. These numbers suggest that the PBS reached a far larger audience than the combined circulations of all Palestinian newspapers, yet newspapers are recognized as having played an important role in the political and social life of the mandate.

What these statistics suggest is a need to problematize assumptions about mass media reaching the majority of a given population, in addition to problematizing assumptions about the transparency of license or circulation statistics. These statistics obscure the importance of both newspapers and radio in Palestine, by suggesting a one-to-one correlation between licensee and listener or subscriber and reader. As Ayalon and others have argued, scholars need to see beyond these numbers in order to account for group listening and group reading practices. Doing so opens up the more realistic possibility that newspapers and radio reached 30 or 40 percent of Palestine's populations—making them both mass media, although not necessarily media that the majority of the population could access on a regular basis. These statistics suggest the contours and the character of newspapers' and radio's importance in mandate Palestine. They do not depreciate them. Similarly, they highlight Palestinians' uneven access to both media—access limited by disposable income, distribution networks, and reception issues. Palestinian newspapers formed a public sphere but one that favored the prosperous, the literate, and the urban. Radio broadcasting reached a similar audience—although possibly with a less urban skew. Yet newspapers of all languages and all political and religious affiliations attracted readers with lively discussions of political and social issues in Palestine and abroad.[14] Radio, in the form of the PBS, would do the same.

Press Coverage

Palestine's newspapers frequently reported on the PBS, treating it as a news subject as well as an issue for debate and discussion. News articles, programming schedules, and editorial pieces all addressed the station, its programming, and its administration, passionately critiquing everything from the political leanings of station administrators to the frequency with which certain records were played during the classical music hour. The degree of scrutiny that these papers gave the station helps indicate what it meant to them and to their Palestinian audience. In particular, the establishment of the PBS created a new space for the ongoing contestations between Palestine's Arab and Zionist populations, facilitating debates over what language the station would use, which times and days it would be on air, who would be in charge of its administration, and who would shape its political and cultural identity.

While the PBS would become the radio station of greatest importance to Palestine's newspapers, radio broadcasting was not a new subject for them. When the PBS began broadcasts in 1936, the press had already become accustomed to treating radio as a news object—and a news source. Radio in the 1930s was for many a symbol of modernity—of the advances of the modern world—and as such it was newsworthy. The Palestine press reported on the progress of numerous stations, charting the construction and establishment of stations around the region and in Europe and covering special broadcasts and technical malfunctions as news items. They even found radio sets newsworthy, as in a May 1935 article in *Falastin* that covered the Yemeni government's purchase of three radio sets and three telegraph machines.[15] In doing so *Falastin* drew a distinction between Palestine, where radio set purchasing was an ordinary activity, and countries like Yemen, where radio sets remained a novelty.

Palestine's papers treated foreign and especially European stations as credible sources for global news and news on Palestine, particularly given the tight censorship regime under which mandate-era newspapers operated. When local officials refused to comment on news regarding Palestine, the papers turned to foreign radio stations. Numerous headlines and articles began "Radio London [i.e., the BBC] reports . . ." or "Last night, Radio Paris stated . . ." While mandate government officials rather than any popular groundswell drove the establishment of the PBS, the newspapers' existing practices of covering radio broadcasting as a news source and a news story helped the PBS gain local significance.

The Birth of the PBS

The British mandate government's interest in establishing a broadcasting station in Palestine in the early 1930s reflected a broader trend in radio broadcasting evident throughout the world: a move toward state control of frequencies and broadcasting apparatuses and an emerging idea of radio as a scarce public good, both of which intersected with Britain's responsibility to lead its mandate territories toward self-governance. The early 1930s witnessed a key moment in the development of radio broadcasting: the creation of government-operated state radio stations throughout Europe and European colonies around the world.[16] The introduction of state radios marked the end of the "golden age" of amateur wireless broadcasting, which in the 1920s had peppered the world's airwaves with numerous privately owned and operated stations.[17]

However, the very freedom that initially encouraged amateur broadcasters ultimately undermined them. The popularity of amateur broadcasting and the ease of getting on the air had produced airwave congestion. Station interference became an increasingly common problem, irritating amateur broadcasters and concerning governments, which used radio broadcasts for military communications. In addition to military communications, governments were increasingly aware of the powerful new possibilities radio offered for them to shape their national communities through news, education, and entertainment programming. In the 1920s few governments had seen these possibilities or considered them worth the technical headaches. By 1930 technical advancements and an increased awareness of the power of radio to reach and influence people had turned governments around the world into eager players, ready to transform broadcasting into a vehicle for serving state objectives.

The Palestine Broadcasting Service was a product of this period, when government bureaucrats around the world looked to harness the power of broadcasting to shape their citizens in particular ways. In Palestine the mandate government initially seemed to welcome private radio stations, issuing a medium-wave broadcasting license to Mendel Abramovitch in 1932. Radio Tel Aviv, Abramovitch's station, conducted its first broadcast at the government-sponsored Levant Fair.[18] However, the mandate government soon began plans to establish its own station. These plans coincided with a broader international initiative to clean up Europe's crowded airwaves, which left Palestine only one broadcasting frequency. The mandate government soon revoked Abramovitch's license, despite his protests; Radio Tel Aviv went off the air in 1935, as planning for the Palestine Broadcasting Service intensified.

International Governance

The idea of international governance for communications media dated to the nineteenth century, when disagreements over telegraph procedures (language of transmission, secrecy, rates, etc.) were resolved through a series of international conferences. These conferences produced international governing bodies with the authority to manage conflicts and punish violations.[19] Starting in the mid-1920s, radio was handled in a similar manner. To address the problem of crowded European airwaves, in May 1933 the International Broadcasting Union met in Lucerne. Broadcasting interference complaints had increased since the previous conference, held in Prague in 1929—as had the number and reach of European stations. Stations now outnumbered available wavelengths; the phenomenon of unrestricted broadcasting, which had worked well in radio's early days, had produced a free-for-all in which stations broadcast with little regard for their potential to disrupt, interfere with, or overpower other stations using the same frequency. The Lucerne conference resolved the interference issue by assigning specific wavelengths to each country and by assigning shared wavelength only to countries sufficiently distant to preclude interference.

For Palestine and the rest of the Middle East, the Lucerne conference's most significant decision was geographical. The conference was intended to address issues relating to European broadcasting. However, it defined the "European Zone" to include Palestine, Syria, Lebanon, Turkey, and all of North Africa. (The Arab Gulf, Iraq, and Trans-Jordan were at the time considered unlikely to start radio broadcasting and so were neither discussed nor assigned wavelengths.) The conference defined them as part of the European zone because—depending on transmitter strength and weather conditions—any station broadcasting within this zone was likely to be heard elsewhere within the zone. In other words, because a station broadcasting from Palestine could cause interference if broadcasting on the same wavelength as an Italian or other European station, Palestine was included in the European zone.

The extension of "Europe" to the Middle East was a concession to technological limitations, not a statement of equality. In fact, including the Middle East worsened the situation, for it increased the number of entities fighting over slices of the same wavelength pie. Further, allocating wavelength by country placed mandate territories and colonies on the same plane as their French and British custodians, granting them the same right to a wavelength and a national broadcasting station. At the same time the list of conference participants made it evident who held the reins of power in these territories: the mandate government's postmaster general (and lieutenant colonel), William Hudson, for example, represented Palestine.[20] As a result, wavelengths became tools for colonial powers like Britain and France to use to protect their own broadcasting interests, and broadcasting stations could be understood as vehicles for extending colonial control.

While mandate officials claimed a wavelength for Palestine, support for a national radio station began building at home. This raises the question, why did Palestinians of various backgrounds and political commitments support the idea of a broadcasting station? I suggest that it reflects a general understanding of radio stations as symbols of sovereignty, that radio stations in the 1930s should be considered one of the twentieth century's "signs of statehood." Assessing nation-states and other politico-territorial entities for signs of statehood is an analytic approach used by historians, political scientists, journalists, and others. The signs used to scrutinize modern states have generally been internal, including such domestic concerns as a head of state, a national anthem, a functional political system operative throughout the territory, one or more functionally national languages, a functional national currency, manned borders, passport control, and so on. Yet they have also included different forms of international recognition—which in this era would have included recognition by the League of Nations, the International Broadcasting Union, and similar organizations. Establishing a radio station in Palestine was a visible sign of progress toward the mandatory goals, which the British government could highlight in its annual report to the League of Nations Mandates Commission but which Palestinians themselves could similarly use to argue to the League of Nations and other organizations for greater autonomy or full independence. While rarely phrased in such stark terms, this contrast should serve as a useful reminder of just how powerful radio broadcasting—in its content and as a symbol—was in this period.

Establishing the PBS

Although the British home government supported Palestine's right to a wavelength, it did not take an active role in planning the anticipated broadcasting station. Mandate government officials drove the creation of the PBS. After the Lucerne conference Postmaster General Hudson drew up a proposal for the station, laying out several of its ultimate characteristics. For example, he recommended that the station broadcast in the mandate's three official languages—Arabic, Hebrew, and English—but allot hours proportionally with the population. The government then established a broadcasting committee, whose members included Hudson, Jerusalem District Commissioner Michael (M. F.) Abcarius, Director of Education Humphrey Bowman, and Assistant Treasurer J. E. F. Campbell, to review Hudson's proposal and estimate the costs involved. In other words, the station was government supported from the beginning, and British mandate officials shaped its contours.

The Broadcasting Committee's report, submitted in December 1933, envisioned a station modeled closely on the BBC: a nonprofit station funded by government subsidies and radio receiver license fees, with programming intended to improve as well as entertain the listening public. It presumed a ready interest among urbanites, in particular European Jews and British subjects resident in Palestine. It forecast rising Arab interest in radio, stemming from the inauguration of the Egyptian State Broadcasting Service in early 1934 and Lebanon's planned Radio Orient. It anticipated that rural listening would increase as electrification made it possible to operate electric radios. To encourage Arab listening, the committee recommended that the station broad-cast on medium wave, as medium-wave radio sets were less expensive than shortwave.

The report proposed one hour of broadcasting each day in each lan-guage, with Arabic in the earliest slot and English in the latest, from late afternoon to early evening. In the later evening an "international program" would provide entertainment accessible to all, regardless of language. To minimize production costs, the committee suggested in-corporating news and entertainment relays from the BBC, as well as gramophone recordings—avoiding more expensive live broadcasts. The committee described recent improvements in recorded music as a cru-cial factor in making the station financially feasible. "The transmission of gramophone records has been so improved that the quality is now in-distinguishable from direct production," it reported. "Thus orchestral and vocal musical items and, in fact, whole programs are now largely produced from gramophone records," which, it noted, "can be read-ily and cheaply obtained" from the BBC and similar sources. (The com-mittee here appears to have meant European music and programs, as the BBC did not broadcast in Hebrew or in Arabic in the early 1930s.)[21]

While entertainment, even recorded, would seem to have been a happy subject, the Broadcasting Committee's report closed on a melan-choly note. The year 1933 had been a relatively quiet one in Palestine, but the committee stressed that the station should not exacerbate ex-isting tensions. "Controversial opinions and biased views should be es-chewed, especially on political and religious subjects," it stated, outlin-ing what would become its policy of favoring entertainment broadcasts, limiting news broadcasts, and prohibiting political discussions. Further, it suggested, radio broadcasting could play an important role in uplift-ing spirits around the region. "Much could be done to widen interests and to add to the gaiety of life, in order to counteract a morbid outlook which appears to be endemic in the Near East," the committee stated. In its members' views, radio's importance in Palestine was not its ability to convey news but its ability to add cheer.[22]

Perhaps the most surprising aspect of the report was the recommen-dation to proceed with plans for the station, given the small numbers of projected listeners. The report itself noted that only 2,313 radio li-censes were recorded in 1933, with 3,500 estimated for early 1935. Each license presumably served more than one person, and the num-ber of licenses was increasing. However, the listening audience was still a tiny percentage of the population, estimated at just over one million in 1931.[23] For most Palestinians, regular radio listening up to this point had been a largely unknown experience. The Palestine Broadcasting Service planned to make radio a much more important part of people's lives.

Press Interest

News of the proposed station reached most Palestinians several months after the Broadcasting Committee's report, meeting an enthusiastic reception in the English-language, Jewish-owned *Palestine Post* in summer 1934, with a slower response from the Arabic papers. Often critical of the mandate government, the *Post*'s editorial staff waxed rhapsodic about its foresight in establishing a broadcasting station: "The Palestine Government in announcing the early establishment of a Broadcasting Service is conferring upon the country what may be a veritable boon. . . . By introducing this very modern amenity, the Administration deserves the gratitude of the public."[24] It praised radio's capacity to bring news and entertainment from around the world and to reach out to rural and urban inhabitants alike.

In late 1934 the *Palestine Post* published the first of a three-part series assessing the new station's structure, organization, and programming. (The Arabic papers began covering the station with smaller articles, although the numerous advertisements for radio sets make it clear that publishers were not unaware of radio's interest for their readers.) Staff editor E. D. Goitein's "This Is Jerusalem Calling" focused on language, suggesting that the station broadcast Arabic lessons in Hebrew and vice versa and praising its potential to foster a standard, modern version of both languages.[25] His second article, "Free Expression of Opinion," asked that the Palestine station, like the BBC, be made an independent entity rather than a subdepartment of the Post Office. He advocated freedom of expression, with limits on inflammatory language but not on the opinions expressed. He further asked the station to "build up a picture of Palestine bigger than Jewish Palestine or Arab Palestine," each community including the other, envisioning the station as breaking down rather than reinforcing the separatism that other mandate departments facilitated.[26] Goitein's third piece, "A Well-Run Broadcasting Station: Music, Drama, and Entertainment," emphasized the importance of entertainment programming. He praised local Jewish classical music, theater, and music hall groups, encouraging the use of local talent and Arab ensembles. He endorsed the use of broadcasting for entertainment rather than pedagogic purposes, noting that listeners might turn their sets off—or tune in to another station—when the Palestine station grew didactic.[27]

While public figures like Goitein expressed their vision of the station, government preparations continued—with little evidence to suggest their incorporation of these visions or any particular interest in popular opinions of the planned station. By mid-1935 preparations were well under way. In July the government released a communiqué describing construction progress and outlining the station's programming. The station would broadcast for five hours each evening, with programs in Arabic, English, and Hebrew and entertainment intended for general interest provided by relays, gramophone recordings, and local productions. The communiqué highlighted mandate officials' assumption that community would follow language: Arabs would listen to the Arabic section, Jews would listen to the Hebrew section, and everyone would enjoy light classical music. With no public outcry, it appeared that Palestinian communities accepted the linkage of community, language, and listening hours. This was one of the station's most lasting impacts on mandate Palestine: the use of language to reinforce the idea of two separate communities rather than to promote the development of two interpenetrating and interconnected communities.

The communiqué closed with a paragraph on "loud speakers for villages," indicating the importance that the government assigned to rural broadcasting and its anxieties about Palestine's rural populations.

> His Excellency the High Commissioner is particularly anxious that the benefits of broadcasting shall be enjoyed by the rural, as well as by the urban population and is therefore arranging for the experimental installation of loud speakers of special design at 100 villages and settlements. The programs of the Jerusalem station will contain items (e.g., short talks on agriculture, education, health, etc.) intended to be of practical value to rural listeners.[28]

Practicality for rural listeners and entertainment for urbanites: government officials imagined rural and urban listeners as discrete communities. Palestine's listening public was divided first by language and second by location. Like the language division, this reflected other assumptions: rural listeners were often described as peasants, uneducated and Arab. They were described in mandate and British home officials' correspondence as a potential source of danger if not carefully managed, educated, and domesticated—a task that the Palestine station could now undertake.

Meanwhile, public interest in radio listening appeared to be growing, with 5,900 radio licenses reported throughout the territory by mid-1935. The more Palestinians who owned a set, the larger the potential audience the Palestine station would have. As the *Post* noted, this equated to 5.7 sets per 1,000 people (roughly one for every 175 inhabitants), on par with "Hong Kong, Indonesia, and Spain," less than Great Britain's 147.45 per 1,000 but far more than Egypt's 0.73 per 1,000 ratio.[29] Undaunted, the Egyptian State Broadcasting Service had recently begun operations; its success in attracting listeners lent credibility to the idea that a Palestine station could be successful. At the same time, Radio Cairo reminded mandate officials that Palestinians with radio sets already had a number of broadcasting stations to choose from—some of which might be broadcasting news and opinions hostile to British interests. Tuning in to a Palestine station would mean not tuning in to a station broadcasting German, Italian, or other unfriendly views.

BBC Connections

The hiring patterns of the Palestine station reinforced its British flavor. Several BBC administrators were seconded to Palestine to see the station through its early stages, at least in part because of mandate officials' perception of "the lack of suitable persons available" in Palestine in terms of radio administrative and program experience.[30] The most prominent was R. A. "Tony" Rendall, BBC west regional program director, who was named PBS director in September 1935.[31] The BBC provided the station with administrative staff through the late 1930s; not until the early 1940s was the station director chosen in-country. Stephen Fry, who came from BBC Outside Broadcasts, succeeded Rendall as director and was replaced by Crawford McNair, deputy conductor of the BBC Northern Orchestra, in 1938. (McNair served until October 1941, when wartime restrictions changed the PBS's administrative structure.)[32]

Most of these "BBC men" were relatively young and not yet at the peak of their careers, making a stint in Palestine perhaps more appealing. That they were seconded rather than hired outright suggests the degree of BBC involvement in the new station: indirect but substantial. Seconded staffers brought a BBC sensibility to Palestine, and PBS administrative staff members were sent to the BBC for training during

Figure 0.2. Subdirector of Arabic music Yahya Lababidi and subdirector of Arabic broadcasting Ibrahim Tuqan, April 20, 1940, at a PBS reception. Source: G. Eric and Edith Matson Photograph Collection, Prints and Photographs Division, Library of Congress, LC-DIG-matpc-20590.

summer holidays.[33] Yet it is not entirely clear from extant station documents that BBC personnel were able to successfully execute their own vision for the station. Mandate government documents suggest dissatisfaction with Fry and McNair in particular—a dissatisfaction supported by the often-critical tone that local newspapers took when discussing the station. The BBC in the 1930s enjoyed a much greater degree of independence from the British government than the PBS did from the mandate government, which may have made the situation more difficult for BBC personnel working at the PBS.

British staffers filled the station's top administrative posts; there was no discussion of Palestinians of any background serving as director or deputy director. However, the station did make numerous local hires at the section-head level and below. Evidence from memoirs and newspapers suggests that the selection of local Palestinians to head the Arabic, Hebrew, and Music sections was a delicate process. Mandate government officials wanted section heads of sufficient stature to lend credibility to the broadcasting station; at the same time officials feared that well-known figures would use the station for their own purposes. In December Eliezer Lubrani and Karl Salomon, recently arrived from Germany, were hired as subdirectors of the Hebrew and "European and Hebrew" Music sections, respectively;[34] the well-known poet Ibrahim Tuqan was hired to head the Arabic section in mid-February 1936, with Yahya Lababidi hired as subdirector for Arabic music.[35] Lubrani had worked as an editor at the Hebrew-language *Davar*; Salomon was a well-respected conductor. Only Tuqan had a reputation as a nationalist agitator and, like many Palestinian men of his generation, had an arrest record.

Early Days on the Air

At the inaugural broadcast of the Palestine Broadcasting Service in March 1936, High Commissioner Wauchope included one further caveat in his speech. "The Broadcasting Service in Palestine will not be concerned with politics," he stated. "Its main object will be the spread of knowledge and culture," he continued, adding, "nor, I can assure you, will the claims of religion be neglected."[36] While Wauchope mentioned only two groups—farmers and music lovers—in his description of those who might benefit from the station's programming, here he outlined the station's primary features: an avoidance of politics, a focus on education and entertainment, and a tempered willingness to respect the "claims" of religion. These features affected programming in various ways. In practical terms, the broadcasting day consisted of parallel programming, divided by language. Each included two news broadcasts, with music, theatrical works, educational talks ("The History of the Arabic Printing Press," "Folk Culture among Yemeni Jews," etc.), children's hours, women's programs, and the occasional scriptural reading. Most programs lasted either fifteen or thirty minutes, with language programming in blocks: two Arabic programs followed by two Hebrew programs, for example. The Arabic section received the most on-air time, with the Hebrew section receiving slightly less and the English section roughly half the on-air hours allotted the other sections.

The opening of the PBS marked a tremendous development for Palestine. Yet beneath the welcoming words and visions of progress lurked tremendous potential for controversy. Within weeks the station was caught up in a larger crisis: the beginning of the three-year Arab revolt.

The PBS and the General Strike

Tensions between Palestinian Arabs and Zionists had been worsening throughout 1935, forming a two- and three-way field of contestation with British authorities. In mid-April 1936 followers of Izz al-Din al-Qassam, a charismatic Syrian fighter killed in late 1935 during a shootout with British soldiers, ambushed a group of Palestinian Jews near Tulkarm. On April 19 nationalist uprisings broke out in Jaffa—forty kilometers southeast of Tulkarm—and, despite British attempts at containment, soon spread, with leadership committees forming in Jaffa and other cities. On April 24 the Jaffan committee called for a general strike—the closure of shops and businesses operating across all industries—with the goal of paralyzing Palestine's economy. While the strike caught most Palestinian elites—the historic leadership class—off guard, Grand Mufti Hajj Amin al-Husseini moved to found the Arab Higher Committee, claiming control over the revolt and ensnaring it in many of the factional politics characteristic of Palestinian elite politics.[37]

The general strike began three years of uprisings and "disturbances" in urban and rural areas alike—known to history as the Arab Revolt.[38] The strike itself lasted until mid-October, ended by a combination of heavy British military suppression and the diplomacy of a Saudi, Egyptian, Iraqi, Jordanian, and Yemeni delegation.[39] Yet as the mandate government reneged on negotiated promises and ordinary Palestinians pushed the leadership to focus on the British rather than the Zionists, nonurban Palestine became the site of a general armed revolt. With the strike and boycott together hurting the Arab economy, guerrilla fighting throughout Palestine, and great animosity toward the mandate government expressed by Jewish and Arab Palestinians, it was not an auspicious time for a government broadcasting station to begin operating.

Or was it? The Permanent Mandates Commission met for its annual examination of the mandatory progress reports in May 1936, one month into the strike.[40] During this meeting the British representative argued that the PBS was providing a vital and appreciated public service by providing reliable information during the chaos. "Since the disturbances, regular use has been made of the Broadcasting Service to broadcast all official communiqués, and different sections of the population are reported to have expressed appreciation of this method of issuing authoritative statements of fact," he said.[41] Back in Palestine, a mandate government committee in October praised the PBS and described it as offering political benefits during crises. "The political value to Government of a well-established service in time of crisis as well as in times of normal development has been made abundantly clear," the report stated.[42] Similarly, a 1938 letter written by High Commissioner Wauchope noted, "During the disturbances of 1936 there was an organized movement to boycott the radio, but it seems that the boycott was more honored in the breach than in the observance."[43] The radio could reach people when newspapers and communiqués, blocked by road closures or guerrilla warfare, could not. And when it did, it provided them with the government's point of view.

The PBS's broadcasts during the general strike reflected the possibilities and limitations of a government station in this situation. On the one hand, the mandate government tightly restricted news broadcasts during this period, and mandate officials criticized the BBC Arabic service for broadcasting news of violence and government reprisals. On the other hand, the government tried to use the station to reach out to listeners and calm the situation. High Commissioner Wauchope himself made several broadcasts in 1936. The *Palestine Post* described his July broadcast as "obviously directed to the villages," with Arabic translation, and noted, "though he was addressing peasants, and addressing them over the heads of a leadership which had lost the way, there was no condescension."[44] Yet in speaking to Arab "peasants," Wauchope signaled that the mandate government had given up on the possibility of reaching an accord with the Palestinian leadership. He had previously used the PBS to address them; now, the newspaper suggested, Wauchope "tried to translate the disaster into terms which would bring the damage home to the peasant," mentioning higher taxes and ruined harvests.[45] As he had mentioned during the station's inauguration, Wauchope continued to hope that the PBS could influence Palestine's rural Arab population.

Conclusion

Wauchope's broadcasts appear to have done little to persuade rural Palestinians to lay down their arms; what persuaded them was three years of increasingly severe British military repression. Yet the general strike marked a definitive moment in the early history of the Palestine Broadcasting Service. The station could have fallen into irrelevance or seen its budget reappropriated for military exercises. Instead it continued broadcasting despite many challenges—logistical, technical, political, and more. Surviving the Arab Revolt allowed the PBS to become a crucial institution and a crucible in which ideas of national and cultural identity, religious affiliation, and rural-urban distinctions were forged.

The story of the PBS continued through the end of the Palestine mandate, yet its importance has been little appreciated in subsequent scholarship. As a mandate government radio station, the story of the

PBS is that of a semicolonial institution. But it is also the story of a station whose broadcasts in mandate Palestine produced an important set of social effects. These effects influenced the development of the Arab community both internally and in its relationships with the mandate state and the Zionist community. Paying more attention to the PBS helps reframe the narrative of the Palestinian mandate, placing debates about political determination, cultural identity, religious practice, and gender relations in the context of the most powerful mass medium of the interwar era. This work examines five areas in which the PBS played an important role for Palestine.

The first chapter, "Selling Radio, Selling Radios: Advertising Sets in Mandate Palestine," connects the creation of the PBS to the dramatic rise in the number of radio sets purchased throughout Palestine—a rise due in large part to the growing number of other stations receivable in Palestine, including Egyptian State Broadcasting's Radio Cairo. More crucially, it connects radio as a broadcasting medium to radio sets as symbolically rich commodities, which together instituted new social, familial, and work behaviors collectively described as "listening practices." It examines the proliferation of newspaper advertisements of radio sets, arguing that radio sets came second only to Kiwi shoe polish as the most frequently advertised commodity. It analyzes these advertisements, noting their innovative blend of manufacturer boilerplate (generally an image, brand name, and slogan in English or French) and Palestinian dealers' Arabic text. It further analyzes the role of radio sets in middle-class urban Palestine, describing them as highly visible entry-level luxury goods that strongly communicated "modern" and "cosmopolitan" to friends and neighbors. In doing so, it highlights the importance of the 30 to 34 percent of Palestinians who lived in urban areas, whose role in defining a Palestinian national identity has been underplayed since 1948 in favor of a rural nationalist self.[46]

Chapter 2, "Peasants into Palestinians: Rural and School Broadcasting," examines the British mandate government's efforts to shape two key communities in Arab Palestine: fellahin—rural farmers or, as British officials termed them, peasants—and schoolchildren. The British government had grown increasingly concerned about rural Palestinians after the 1929 riots, which they felt were sparked in large part by economic desperation and alienation from Palestine's urban modernization. Starting in 1930, government officials initiated several programs designed to anchor rural Arabs to the land and improve the quality of their lives. Once the PBS started its broadcasts, these officials turned to radio as well. They saw radio as a vehicle for bringing rural Arabs into the modern age through educational and entertainment programs, including school broadcasts and the "Talks to Farmers" series. At the same time, the government's radio set distribution program engendered fears that rural Palestinians would listen to the "wrong" stations— Italy's Radio Bari and Germany's Radio Zeesen. This chapter concludes by turning to the private sector, examining Arabic-language radio set advertisements aimed at rural consumers and using them to show rural Palestinians in a different light.

Chapter 3, "Broadcasting a Nationalist Modernity: The PBS Arabic Section," examines how Palestine's Arab community engaged the PBS's Arabic section to promote a self-consciously modern Palestinian nationalism that connected with the broader Arab region. The station's Palestinian employees included representatives from most of Jerusalem's old elite families, as well as "new men" from bourgeois and other less elite families—most of whom, like Ibrahim Tuqan and ʿAzmi Nashashibi, came from urban backgrounds. These men (and some women) maneuvered within the operating framework of British colonial modernity, working through the PBS to build and strengthen an Arab Palestinian modernity. The tension produced by the interplay of the competing agendas of the British mandate government and the Arab Palestinian nationalists it employed conditioned many of the pushes and pulls affecting Arabic programming at the station. This chapter highlights a moment within this larger process—ʿAjaj Nuwayhid's singular tenure as head of Arabic programming—as an illustration of the station's capacity to serve as the vehicle of a Palestinian nationalist modernity.

Chapter 4, "Putting Religion on the Radio: Religious Broadcasting," examines the inclusion of religious programming on the state-run PBS, arguing that the negotiations this engendered with Palestine's numerous faith communities helped foster a regional legacy of government management of on-air religious expression. The British mandate government had modeled the PBS on the BBC, translating the latter's commitment to spreading morality through Christian broadcasts into a promise to respect the "claims of religion" for Palestine's faiths. While this produced little controversy in the 1930s, a post–World War II restructuring led to complaints regarding the choice of texts, prebroadcast censorship of sermons, and staffing during weekly services. PBS and other mandate government personnel devoted increasing efforts to managing these complaints and in doing so helped solidify what would become a regional practice: state control of broadcast media, including religious programming. This chapter draws two contrasts with the previous chapter. First, it shows the PBS's British administrators as taking a leading role in the station's commitment to religious broadcasting—at times causing more controversy than if programming decisions had been made by locals more attuned to sectarian nuance—as in the case of an "ecumenical" Bible reading. Second, it shows a contrast between 'Ajaj Nuwayhid's vision of Islam as a common cultural reference—and hence means of unification—for Arab Palestinians and British administrators' conception of Palestinians as defined and divided by religion.

Chapter 5, "Claiming the PBS: Whose National Radio?," examines the tensions between the Arabic and Hebrew sections of the PBS, which increased as the years passed and escalated into open hostility during the mandate's final two years. In doing so, it also demonstrates the extent to which both communities identified with and laid claim to the PBS as a national station. The station became the site of critical tensions four times, reflecting larger concerns over the state, and fate, of Palestine. Issues of "whose national radio" started with the station's name, continued with the playing of "national" anthems and the use of audience statistics, and ended with the physical carving up of the station as the mandate state collapsed.

The work concludes by tracing the disavowal and recuperation of the PBS over the past six decades. In the immediate aftermath of the mandate, Israelis and Palestinians alike derided and dismissed the PBS as a colonial institution. Recent decades have witnessed efforts by both the Israeli Broadcasting Authority and the Palestinian Broadcasting Corporation to reclaim the PBS as a protonational station. The Palestinians have recuperated the PBS by honoring it as the predecessor of the post-Oslo Palestinian Broadcasting Corporation. Since the mid-1970s, the Israel Broadcasting Authority has similarly worked to link Kol Israel with the PBS, starting with a 1976 television special, *Forty Years of Kol Israel*. Whether the use of the PBS in this manner will provide common ground for cooperation—or for further conflict—between Palestinian and Israeli broadcasting authorities in the years to come remains to be seen.

CHAPTER 1

Selling Radio, Selling Radios: Advertising Sets in Mandate Palestine

The radio was still a fairly new invention at that time, and not everyone possessed one. We were among those who did not have a radio at home, and in spite of our insistence my father never consented to bring the radio home because, he claimed, it would distract us from our lessons. We finally got one through the good favors of electrical engineer Farah Halaby, a relative and close friend who was a radio and electrical supplies dealer. . . . Farah offered us a radio set, and my father had to accept the offer. Like all radios at that time, it looked like a beautiful piece of wooden furniture. Many friends of ours who didn't possess a radio used to visit us in order to listen to the news. It became a habit for some of my teachers to call at our house every Wednesday to spend the evening with us and listen to the radio.

JOHN TLEEL[1]

The Strange Commodity Form of the Radio

In order to answer the question why radio merits study as a historical subject it is necessary to resuscitate an awareness of the strangeness of radio—an awareness that has been lost in the seven decades since its widespread introduction throughout the world. "Radio" refers both to the object and to the broadcasting phenomena accessible through it. In earlier decades the two were often but not always distinguished by employing the term *radio set* for the object; *alat al-idhāʿa* was used in Arabic. (These may seem obvious points—after all, the same blurring occurs with the word *television*. But the language and concepts used today with reference to television are not sui generis but derive from those used in previous decades for radio—a derivation now largely forgotten.) "Radio" is distinguished both by its physicality—by the peculiar nature of the radio set as an object—and its sociality—by which radio the object serves as the means to another end, access to a different type of community and a different type of experience than that available in the preradio era.

Physicality

What made radios distinguishable as objects, as physical things that attracted consumer interest of such a kind that their purchase was made after conscious deliberation ("I have decided to buy one of these") rather than on impulse ("Why not get one of these?") or automatically ("Of course I need another of these")? First, they were big. In the 1920s radios were often sold in furniture shops as furniture; they took up the space of a two-door buffet or side cabinet. Their rectangular bodies were solidly fashioned out of wood, reinforcing their position as "furniture." Radios in the 1930s and 1940s were smaller but not small, roughly $3' \times 2' \times 1.5'$. They could now sit atop a side cabinet but would leave little room for any other object. While still most often constructed of wood, their knobs and, increasingly, parts of their frames were constructed from the latest man-made materials (plastic and Bakelite)—keeping pace with similar trends in the furniture industry. Radios of this generation shared another characteristic with furniture: expense. Their construction—the work involved in crafting the frame and constructing the receiver—and status as one-time purchases made them, much like other home appliances sold in the same period, relatively expensive commodities.

Beyond differences in size and construction material, radio sets of the 1930s and 1940s called for labor far beyond today's plug-and-play sets. They required the installation of an aerial—the ancestor of the metal antennas or covered wires sold with some of today's portable stereos, which one tapes or otherwise attaches to a wall or out through a window for improved reception. The weaker powers of reception of 1930s radios required that an aerial—a pole with antenna attached—be physically erected near the house or building in which the radio was installed. This was neither an easy nor a foolproof task, as the instruction manual for the 1936 His Masters' Voice radio model 149 suggests.

Poor construction of or a badly chosen location for a radio set's aerial

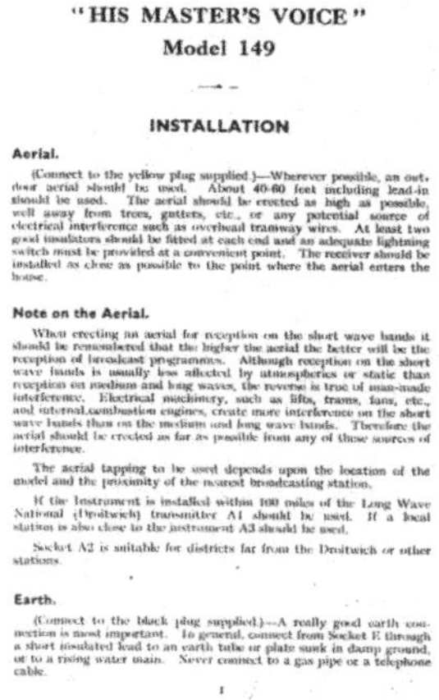

"HIS MASTER'S VOICE"
Model 149

INSTALLATION

Aerial.

(Connect to the yellow plug supplied.)—Wherever possible, an outdoor aerial should be used. About 40-60 feet including lead-in should be used. The aerial should be erected as high as possible, well away from trees, gutters, etc., or any potential source of electrical interference such as overhead tramway wires. At least two good insulators should be fitted at each end and an adequate lightning switch must be provided at a convenient point. The receiver should be installed as close as possible to the point where the aerial enters the house.

Note on the Aerial.

When erecting an aerial for reception on the short wave bands it should be remembered that the higher the aerial the better will be the reception of broadcast programmes. Although reception on the short wave bands is usually less affected by atmospherics or static than reception on medium and long waves, the reverse is true of man-made interference. Electrical machinery, such as lifts, trams, fans, etc., and internal-combustion engines, create more interference on the short wave bands than on the medium and long wave bands. Therefore the aerial should be erected as far as possible from any of these sources of interference.

The aerial tapping to be used depends upon the location of the model and the proximity of the nearest broadcasting station.

If the Instrument is installed within 100 miles of the Long Wave National (Droitwich) transmitter A1 should be used. If a local station is also close to the instrument A3 should be used.

Socket A2 is suitable for districts far from the Droitwich or other stations.

Earth.

(Connect to the black plug supplied.)—A really good earth connection is most important. In general, connect from Socket E through a short insulated lead to an earth tube or plate sunk in damp ground, or to a rising water main. Never connect to a gas pipe or a telephone cable.

1

Figure 1.1. Page 1 of user's manual for the 1936 HMV 149, a tri-band radio. This manual accompanied the version of the radio set manufactured for the British market, hence the reference to Droitwich. Technical concerns such as the one mentioned here limited manufacturers' abilities to produce one set and one manual for universal distribution. Source: Paul's Radio Museum, www.paulplu.demon.co.uk.

could doom its owners to a lifetime of listening to broadcasts obscured by static. Even a properly installed aerial did not guarantee clear reception. Especially in the 1930s, tuning was a difficult and never-finished process, partly due to the limited sensitivities of 1930s radio sets and partly due to the tendency of many stations to wander from their assigned frequencies. Although both were great improvements on sets and stations of the late 1920s, tuning still required both skill and practice on the part of the radio owner.

By the 1940s the introduction of the "spread band" and manufacturer-installed station presets as well as other technical improvements had made tuning a less involved process. Most radio sets were also now sufficiently powerful to require only a wall- or window-mounted aerial, allowing their owners greater though still not total flexibility in deciding where to place them. This also allowed owners the option of moving their radios to other locations within a room or even to other rooms within the house or building, making radios, like furniture and other movable objects, amenable to redecoration schemes.

In short, despite the constant flow of technological improvements, radio sets of this generation were not objects made invisible by their small size, portability, ease of use, and minimal expense. The contemporary idea of turning on a radio for background noise when one enters a room had little relevance in this period, not least because houses and businesses did not have a radio for each room but *one* radio in toto. Hence its location in a central, semipublic space: a living room rather than a bedroom, or the customer side of a restaurant or coffee shop rather than its kitchen. Hence also the listening practices described in anecdotal accounts taken from around the world: people sat, in groups, and listened attentively to radio broadcasts. If they did not literally "watch" the radio set, it was nonetheless a central object of visual attention.

Sociality

These listening practices point to the second aspect of radio: its sociality. Through their ability to receive broadcasts from stations near and far, radio sets opened the way to a new kind of experience and made possible the knitting together of different forms of community. This kind of experience and these forms of community were based neither on the orality of direct interpersonal exchange nor on the visuality of print but on the aurality of listening. In order to fully comprehend this, we must, as Susan Douglas argues, "historicize" listening. "Radio listening is such a mundane, effortless act that we have become oblivious to its complexities," she notes. "Yet radio has taught us, socialized us how to listen to different things, and how to feel during different modes of listening"—listening practices that have not only been taught and learned, but changed with the decades. We must dissociate ourselves both from today's casual listening practices and from an overemphasis on the magical aspects of radio in its early days.[2] The way in which this sociality manifested itself should not be confused with the "oooh ahhh" experience of radio that prevailed in the early 1920s, although that may have been the case for more rural areas in the 1930s—particularly in Arab Gulf territories like Yemen.[3]

By the 1930s listeners' expectations for radio listening had shifted. They had exchanged a willingness to wonder at the magic of receiving sound through one's radio set, regardless of how poor the quality or how ephemeral the existence of the broadcaster, with the desire for the pleasure of hearing the scheduled broadcasts of institutionalized stations—broadcasts whose schedules were regularly printed in the local newspaper or listeners' journal. If the amateur broadcasting of the 1920s had produced a sociality based on the spontaneous experience of connecting with other people in other places by tuning fortuitously to their broadcasts, the regularization of the airwaves in the late 1920s and early 1930s replaced spontaneity with consistency. Schedules and stations introduced the possibility of a different kind of community—one based on focused listening to news, music, educational, or entertainment programming. The PBS was established in this latter period, and scheduling, consistency, and a concern with reaching listeners dominated its programming decisions.

Learning to Listen

Before the PBS began broadcasting, Palestine's residents had limited radio options linking them to listening communities outside Palestine. Listening communities—the "imagined communities" that formed around radio—included the physical communities created by group listening and the broader imagined community of fellow listeners. In both cases, several factors helped shape the community—starting with language. Those interested in Arabic-language programming could tune in to Egyptian State Broadcasting. Those interested in English-language programming could tune in to the BBC's Empire Service. And those interested in other European programs could tune in to stations from France to Russia. Reception for these stations, however, could be poor, and their news and weather broadcasts had little relevance to those in Palestine.[4]

By tuning in to the PBS, people joined a new listening community—one oriented to a national space, reinforced by news, weather, and entertainment broadcasts. Listening communities had two aspects: the physical presence of others in group listening contexts and the imagined presence of a community of fellow listeners, often reinforced by the broadcaster addressing them as a group. In both cases, the community was largely time, language, and program dependent, with further differentiation by gender. PBS station programmers imagined several listening contexts: women at home alone, children in school, men relaxing together in coffee shops, men working together in factories, villagers gathered in the village guest house, children in family groups at home, men and women together at home, men at home either alone or with other men, and families together at home. They constructed daytime household how-to programs and light entertainment for women working alone in their homes; educational broadcasts for schoolchildren; afternoon news and music for families gathered at home for lunch or groups of men socializing in local cafés; evening current events digests and ethical talks for the man of the family as he relaxed at home; and theatrical productions and music for the family to enjoy. Although it is difficult to quantify the degree to which people's listening practices matched the programmers' visions using available sources, a qualitative analysis drawn from memoirs, consular reports, and similar sources suggests that aside from greater gender mixing in the evening, the portrait was not inaccurate.[5]

These listening communities were also divided by language. Although the Arabic and Hebrew and secondarily the English sections all had similar programming slots, each section filled its programming hours with different content. Only the news and government communiqués were broadcast word for word in Palestine's three languages. Consequently, listeners were split by language, limiting the opportunities for Arabic and Hebrew speakers to listen to the same program together as well as the opportunities for those who listened to the same program in different languages to discuss it afterward. The presumption from which PBS programmers began—that Palestine was composed of discrete, nonoverlapping listening communities—precluded intercommunal conversations sparked by questions like "Did you catch such-and-such on the radio last night?" Imagined listening communities reinforced rather than challenged the established division of the country into Arab and Jew.

At the same time, listeners in Palestine could join other imagined communities beyond the mandate state's borders. Most if not all Middle Eastern and European stations could be heard on medium wave or shortwave. For Arabic speakers, this primarily opened up access to an imagined community of listeners to the Egyptian State Broadcasting Service, the largest station in the region. They also had access to Radio Orient (broadcasting from Beirut) as well as the North African stations and the changing array of smaller, more ephemeral Levantine stations (most notably Damascus and Baghdad). For the many recently arrived European Jews, the supra-Palestine listening communities included the stations of central and Eastern Europe. As time went on and Europe seemed increasingly a space hostile to Jewish communities of any kind, these stations appear to have receded in importance.

Beyond the question of language, broadcasters themselves did much of the work of creating these imagined communities. By addressing listeners as members of a larger group, with shared interests and attitudes, broadcasters fostered a sense of immediacy and intimacy that made the clichéd image of their entry into the listeners' living room not an invasion but a cozy gathering of friends. This phenomenon echoed the use of "Dear Reader" and other invocations of community that advice columnists, editorial writers, and others had made in the press and other print media—but, as Douglas argues, the visceral immediacy of listening made broadcasters' appeals much more compelling. Rather than merely see early midcentury (American) radio as a nation-building tool, she suggests, "radio's role in constructing imagined communities—including those that are oppositional to or uneasy with 'the nation'— [is] much more powerful than what print can do. This has to do in part with the act of listening itself, with the knowledge that you and other listeners are experiencing that very moment of your lives in exactly the same way."[6] Her words echo Benedict Anderson's, pointing to the ways in which radio and the act of listening could provide a far more potent base for the formation of communities of all types—not only the national.

Consumption

Radio's two aspects, the physical and the social, together conditioned its entry into the circuits of consumption operating in mandate Palestine. Radio sets and radio broadcasting occupied an equally peculiar position within these circuits, a peculiarity occasioned partly by radio's status as an imported good and partly by the bias of the models used for understanding consumption. In her work on the connections between sex, gender, consumption, and consumerism, Victoria de Grazia has pointed to both a "Euro-American model" and the need for countermodels as explanatory frameworks for these phenomena. She adopts the term *consumer society*

> to identify the emergence of a peculiar type of market society, the
> Western capitalist system of exchange, and especially to probe the ever
> more identifiable *modern* aspects of its development. This modernity
> lies first in carrying out acts of consumption within capitalist exchange
> networks and then in the organization of institutions, resources, and
> values around ever-larger flows and accumulations of commodities.
> It also lies in the transformation of goods from being relatively static
> symbols around which hierarchies were ordered to being more directly
> constitutive of class, social status, and personal identity.[7]

Elizabeth Frierson has similarly argued that the most compelling model for framing the historical evolution of patterns of consumption may also be the most limited, geographically and temporally. Frierson's work on the late Ottoman women's press indicates the emergence of "a modernized but not entirely Westernized commercial sphere." She suggests that the production, distribution, regulation, and consumption norms that developed in the Hamidian and Committee of Union and Progress (CUP) eras may differ sufficiently from those of the Euro-American model, putting late Ottoman scholars "in a position to argue forcefully for disaggregating the categories 'Western' and 'modern' and remixing them in a more analytically productive way."[8]

Three decades separated the late Ottoman era of Frierson's research from that of mandate Palestine—decades that brought momentous changes in the political, economic, and social arenas. However, Frierson's reservations regarding whether this or any other European- or American-centered model can be easily employed to explain consumption in capitalist societies are still useful. It is not that the modernization of areas outside Europe and the United States was aggressively non-Western or took entirely alien forms. On the contrary, the flow of capital and finished goods from Western countries to Palestine and other places, as well as the regulation of such flows by colonial or mandate governments, meant that their economic modernization took place in conversation with European and/or American production, consumption, and distribution structures and behaviors. However, to say that European and particularly British economic modes influenced Palestine's modernization is not to say that it can explained as a derivative phenomenon and judged by the degree to which it "succeeded" or "failed" to faithfully mimic a European model. Examining how radio sets were distributed and marketed in mandate Palestine illustrates this kind of economic modernization.

It might be helpful here to point to Timothy Burke's work on the consumption and marketing of soap and other toiletries in early- and mid-twentieth-century Zimbabwe. Burke takes Marx's notion of the commodity fetish and focuses on the second term, adopting it for use as a rigorous theoretical concept for explaining the circulation and significance of goods in late-capitalizing societies: "Fetishism, then, is more than (but includes) the meanings invested in goods; it is also the accumulated power of commodities to actually constitute, organize, and relate to people, institutions, and discourses."[9] Unlike Marx, Burke sees fetishism as constructing real needs for people and real relations between people, making the utility and meaning of any given commodity the result of a kind of dialogue between different social classes rather than the imposition of one on another. Drawing on Foucault, he argues that "the uses and understandings inherent within a commodity in a given time and place are likely to be the result of the intersections of macro powers and micro powers, the partial and challenged hegemony of rulers and the episodic creativity of the ruled, the logics and disjunctures of everyday life."[10]

Considering radio in mandate Palestine as a commodity fetish in this sense may open a way to a better understanding of the prominence of radio sets in period advertisements, of radio broadcasting as news sources and news items in the local press, and (in another sphere) of radio broadcasting as a powerful specter haunting mandate government officials. Ultimately, it may also suggest reasons why the contemporary significance of radio both as commodity and as vehicle largely disappeared from popular memories of this period.

Consumers

Generally speaking, more people around the world in the 1930s and 1940s were interested in radio listening and radio set ownership than were able to afford a radio set. Moreover, while the rhetoric of radio stations and broadcasting visionaries in this period assumed mass audiences, contemporary notions of the mass consumption of radio *broadcasts* required only mass access to those broadcasts, not mass consumption of radio sets as purchased commodities. To what extent was the radio set market in mandate Palestine a "mass" market? Relli Shechter argues that in the Middle East mass markets for manufactured goods developed later than in Western Europe and North America:

> At the risk of oversimplification, Western consumer societies have developed largely as a result of internal historical dynamics in which the first, and especially the second "Industrial Revolution," coupled with increase in demand, promoted acceleration in production and the creation of nation-wide markets. In contrast, most novel commodities in non-Western countries initially arrived from abroad (or were inspired by commodities first produced in the West), a process associated with the peripheralization of these countries in the European world economy. Their consumption in such environments was more exclusive than in core countries—only small and relatively affluent groups of consumers could purchase imported commodities. The mass market in colonial/developing settings was slower to arrive, and commodities had to go through long processes of "trickle down" adoption, and adaptation, before a sizeable demand was established in the receiving countries.[11]

Shechter argues further that the development of true mass markets, which he defines as "democratized" markets in which "most consumers could purchase similar commodities, albeit with distinct difference in quality," in the Middle East occurred just after World War II or even later.[12]

While Shechter's periodization may be correct for certain commodities, as applied to radio set purchases it risks making the Middle East a more "special" case than the evidence merits. Mass markets for radio sets developed slowly in Europe as well. The market in most European states remained elite or semielite until after World War II. As de Grazia notes in her study of mass organization as a means of building popular consent in fascist Italy,

> in Italy, as in Western Europe generally, advances in broadcasting technology and mass production methods during the interwar years had transformed the radio from a specialty item with a limited audience into a major commodity of industrial production and one of the most important sources of popular entertainment. During the fascist era, the number of radio subscribers increased from an estimated 27,000 in 1926 to over one million at the end of 1939. Yet for all this, the radio was by no means a household item in Italy—the cheapest Marelli radio, advertised at 600 lira with a 114 lira annual government tax, was priced well above the average monthly wage of an industrial worker.[13]

Although addressing a slightly earlier moment in American consumer history, Marchand's tracing of the emergence of the term *mass* as it developed in opposition to the advertising industry's presumed earlier focus on "class"—the tiny stratum of wealthy Americans who regularly purchased (luxury) manufactured goods in the late nineteenth and early twentieth centuries—might be useful here. While increasing use of the term *mass* reflected merchants' and advertisers' interest in broadening their reach beyond this limited consumer base, the expansion was limited to those middle- and upper-middle-class Americans with the regular disposable income to spend on manufactured convenience, lifestyle, and luxury goods. Marchand cautions that the "term 'mass audience' referred primarily to those Americans with higher-than-average incomes" rather than to the mass of Americans. "'Mass' was defined not in terms of the population as a whole but in relation to the narrow elite that had preoccupied the attention of many advertisers before the economic changes of the 1920s."[14]

Without suggesting a perfect parallel, Marchand's definition of *mass* in 1920s and 1930s America in effect describes the situation among the Arab population of mandate Palestine in terms of the vision of advertising merchants and the actual expansion of Arab Palestine's consuming classes, which grew in conjunction with the emergence of a consumerist urban middle and upper middle class. (It also highlights the sometimes-forgotten fact that Arab Palestinians—Christian and Muslim—constituted the majority in Palestine's cities for most of the mandate period.)[15] It also resonates to a certain degree with the "diffusion of innovations" model proposed by Everett Rogers.[16] Rogers suggested people take up new "things"—behaviors, ideas, technologies—in stages and that societies' rate of adoption proceeds in the shape of a bell curve. Rogers may be best known for his argument that people often do *not* flock to the new. As the opening line of his well-known work states, "Getting a new idea adopted, even when it has obvious advantages, is often very difficult."[17] By 1936, when the PBS began broadcasting, however, radio broadcasting was no longer "new" to most of Arab Palestine—even if relatively few had the means to purchase a radio set.

Without statistical data it is difficult to determine precisely when the consuming classes of Arab Palestine were at what point along Rogers's diffusion curve with respect to radio set purchasing. However, it might be reasonable to sketch out an "innovator" (the 2.5 percent tiny minority of risk-friendly, first adopters) period for the early 1930s and an "early adopter" (the 13.5 percent substantial minority who function as opinion leaders and role models) period starting shortly after Radio Cairo went on the air in 1934—most of whom would have lived in urban areas. The late 1930s and 1940s could be understood as a time of early majority (the 34 percent who fall in line with early adopter endorsements, leading to what has been more recently termed the "tipping point")[18] radio set adoption for Arab Palestinians, suggesting its spread through the middle and upper middle classes—those eager to fit in with modern life and possessed of the disposable income to act on their desires—and the extension of radio purchasing to rural areas. The phenomenon of early majority adopters made the radio set market a type of mass enterprise.

Of course, Marchand's use of the term *mass market* referred more to the expansion of the narrow elite market that had previously existed and thus encompassed the growing but still minority consuming middle and upper middle classes. Understanding the 1930s and 1940s radio set market in Arab Palestine as a mass market, even if a restricted one, makes it easier to understand the consumer desires and aspirations reflected—or at least projected—by radio set advertisements. One might reasonably say that for much of Europe and the Middle East, the 1930s and 1940s saw the expansion of the radio set market toward larger percentages of the population without yet including the majority. At the same time, this expansion made radio a more "visible" commodity, for many consumers bringing it well within the range of imaginable consumption or consumption to which they could aspire.

Radio Sellers in Mandate Palestine: A System of Licensed Agents

The history of radio set sales in Palestine encompassed the development of a consumerist Arab urban middle class, the formation of a distinct market supported by the particular production and distribution structure that prevailed between international manufacturers and Palestinian distributors, and the changing relationship between Arab and Jewish communities in the late 1930s and early 1940s. To elicit this history, this section considers several interrelated questions. On the supply side, who was making, marketing, and retailing the radio sets for sale in mandate Palestine? On the consumer side, who was purchasing radio sets, and what did it mean to buy a radio, in cultural as well as financial terms?

If little work has been done on tracing the history of the sales and marketing of manufactured goods in mandate Palestine, almost none has been done on the sale of radio sets. It is safe to say that sets were being sold there regularly by the early 1930s, and likely during the late 1920s as well, although to a much smaller, more economically and culturally elite consumer base than would later emerge. The increase in sales from the 1920s to the 1930s reflected the growing number of European and regional stations received in Palestine, as well as technological changes that made radio sets more affordable and thus more attractive to domestic consumers as well as international distributors. D. L. LeMahieu notes that the impact of these developments was particularly apparent in Britain, perhaps the "fastest-adopting" European country with respect to radio and one of the two major countries of manufacture for the radio sets sold in Palestine. He writes, "As components became standardized and manufacturers practiced new economies of scale, good-quality radio sets became affordable through hire-purchase plans for many working-class families." LeMahieu also credits new features like "automatic volume controls, push-button tuning, multiple wavebands, static reducing devices, better calibration dials" with increasing radio's appeal.[19] Other European countries saw a similar broadening of the radio-buying public to include a greater (but not yet *the* greater) part of the population, although this was more quickly evident in northern and western countries in Europe like France and Germany than southern and eastern ones like Italy and Spain.

While technological developments broadened the radio market in Palestine by making sets both more affordable and more widely available, they remained sufficiently expensive in local terms to make it questionable whether a truly "mass" market for radio sets emerged during the mandate. This is perhaps largely due to the almost total absence of radio set production in Palestine at this time. Although a few local entrepreneurs made isolated attempts to develop an indigenous radio manufacturing industry, their efforts bore little fruit until they obtained the support of the Israeli state in the 1950s. Almost all radio sets sold in Palestine (and throughout the non-Western world) were manufactured by American, British, Dutch, and French corporations, which added shipping costs and import duties to the already high price of foreign-made sets relative to the Palestinian economy. Consequently, like the other big-ticket items—refrigerators, air conditioners, and automobiles—advertised in newspapers during this period, imported radio sets were luxury items.

The minimal presence of a manufacturing industry in Palestine, combined with a relatively immature and limited market for the sale of manufactured goods, produced a sales and distribution system perhaps particular to non-Western, so-called late-developing (at least in manufacture and market terms) areas. As Kevin Martin has noted for a slightly later period in Syrian history, the most striking thing about advertisements in mandate Palestine's Arabic press generally is the predominance of imported, foreign-manufactured goods sold by local sales and distribution agents—in Arabic, the *wakil*.[20] In his study of 1950s Syrian periodicals, Martin observes that "few advertisements appear to be placed directly by foreign manufacturers. Most are for the product *and* the merchant/distributor, who almost always proclaims his status as 'exclusive agent' for the product on offer."[21]

This licensing "system" operated as a series of concession agreements between international corporations and local businessmen for exclusive sales rights in a specified territory. Sales and distribution agents tended to be either merchants with import and/or trade goods shops or technical specialists (e.g., engineers) with some kind of specialized knowledge of the product over which they held a monopoly. A number of these men appear to have capitalized on such knowledge by obtaining concessions for a stable of products, often combining their sales offices with repair shops. Thus, for example, T. Golender of Tel Aviv held sales concessions for the Atwater Kent and Pilot brands. In addition, agents could subcontract distribution rights to other sellers operating in that territory—as a Jerusalem shop owner holding a concession for General Electric products for Palestine and Trans-Jordan, for example, might have done by hiring a man to sell GE washing machines in Nablus. Such subagents worked with the licensed agent as employees or partners; they had little or no direct contact with the foreign manufacturer. They operated purely as sales agents, selling the products that the concessionary agent had ordered from the manufacturer, at prices and with payment terms the agreement between the two had stipulated.

False Agents

The phenomenon of agents selling multiple brands, as well as the hierarchies of control established by subcontracting distribution rights, suggests that the "exclusivity" of an agent's contract with any one brand served the agent by preventing other vendors from cannibalizing sales of that brand instead of serving the brand's manufacturer by limiting the sales of other, competing brands. The preventive function of such contracts might represent what Frierson would see as a modern but non-Western intervention in existing circuits of production and distribution. Similar attempts at prevention are apparent in agents' fear of and consequent efforts to police what might be termed "false agents."

The problem of false agents—vendors selling radio sets without first obtaining a distribution agreement with the manufacturer—appears to have arisen in the later 1930s, caused indirectly by the introduction of new radio stations in the region and in Europe. The burgeoning interest in radio listening and thus in radio set purchasing led to market growth that attracted opportunists as well as bona fide sellers. A rather dire warning was published on January 29, 1937, in the *Palestine Post* by the Camden, New Jersey–based Radio Corporation of America (RCA). The announcement ran with RCA's corporate name and location as the headline and continued:

> NOTICE / It has been brought to our attention that unauthorized persons import RCA Victor radios into Palestine through chan-

nels other than those established by the factory. The public is, therefore, warned to abstain from buying these sets which are manufactured for the American market only and are not suitable for use in tropical climates. Our sole authorized distributors for Palestine and Trans-Jordan are Messrs. Palestine Radio Co. and it is strongly recommended that all RCA Victor Radios should be purchased through their local agents only. No guarantee will be extended on sets which have not been imported through the above-mentioned authorized distributors. / RCA Victor Division / Radio Corporation of America[22]

The warning was striking for two reasons: its placement by the American manufacturer, signifying the gravity of the offense committed by such "unauthorized persons," and the equally chilling implication that RCA radios purchased through them would (a) break down quickly and (b) be quickly identified as illegally imported "American market" radios when taken in to the Palestine Radio Company for the necessary repairs. Of course, it is impossible to determine merely from looking at the newspaper advertisement whether it was truly placed directly by the manufacturer or by the agent with the manufacturer's consent. Regardless, the impression given the newspaper reader was that the matter was of sufficient import to prompt the manufacturer's direct and unmediated communication with its public—an impression that intentionally or unintentionally served the interest of its authorized agents in maintaining their positions as mediators of the channels of RCA radio distribution.

The problem seems to have continued for some time: a notice placed in the same newspaper three months later, on April 1, 1937, was still striving to identify the legal RCA vendors to the buying public:

To all radio buyers in Jerusalem and suburbs / we beg to inform the public that / Moses Kashioff (American Radio Agency) / 6 King George Ave., Jerusalem / is associated with us in the sale of original RCA Victor Radios. All persons who purchase radios through the above firm may be assured that they are getting the right radio for this semi-tropical climate. / Every radio sold by the above-mentioned firm is shipped by arrangement with the RCA Victor and bears their guarantee. / (Signed) Palestine Radio Co / RCA Victor Representatives for Palestine and Trans-Jordan. / IMPORTANT: Please note that we are in no way connected with D. Kashioff who has a place of business elsewhere in Jerusalem. Our address is: King George Ave., Telephone 1174.[23]

The problem of false agents—whether considered real or the product of manufacturer or at least agent anxiety—seems to have peaked in 1937. The Philco Radio & Television Corporation was also placing notices in the *Palestine Post* at this time, promising similarly dire consequences for anyone so foolish as to buy from an unauthorized vendor. On April 1 and April 6, 1937, the company ran this notice:

> Philco Radio & Television Corporation / Philadelphia, Pennsylvania, USA / NOTICE / It has been brought to our attention that unauthorized persons import Philco Radios into Palestine other than through the proper channels established by the factory. The public is therefore warned to abstain from buying these sets which are manufactured for the American climate only and are not suitable for use in tropical climates. / OUR SOLE AUTHORIZED DISTRIBUTORS FOR PALESTINE ARE The INTERNATIONAL RADIO & MUSIC STORES, LTD. AND IT IS STRONGLY RECOMMENDED THAT ALL PHILCO RADIOS SHOLD BE PURCHASED ONLY FROM THEM OR Their AUTHORIZED DEALERS AND AGENTS / NO GUARANTEE IN RESPECT OF SERVICE WILL BE EXTENDED ON PHILCO RADIOS WHICH HAVE BEEN IMPORTED THROGUH OTHER THAN The ABOVE-MENTIONED AUTHORIZED DISTRIBUTORS, FURTHERMORE NO GUARANTEE CAN BE GIVEN THAT The REQUISITE PARTS FOR The REPAIR OF SETS MANUFACTURERD ONLY FOR The AMERICAN MARKET WILL BE AVAILABLE IN PALESTINE. / Philco Radio & Television Corporation. (Capitalization in the original.)

After this loud warning, the ad closed by identifying International Radio & Music Stores as the licensed agent and listing their locations. For Philco Radio, this print equivalent of yelling appears to have been successful: no further warnings appeared in the newspaper.

In 1939 the specter of false agents and unauthorized selling resurfaced—this time in the pages of *Falastin*. On May 30 and June 2, the American Household Equipment Company of Belgium, international distributors for Airline Radio, placed warning notices on behalf of Matalon Brothers, the company's distribution agent in Palestine. These notices advised consumers that anyone who had purchased an Airline radio from Shukri Rizk should pay the debt owed to the Matalon Brothers account at Barclays, the Arab Bank, or the Banca di Roma. Moreover, the notice cautioned that neither Badiʿ Musa nor Khalil Mazin were authorized to collect moneys owed for Airline radio purchases and that Mata-lon Brothers would not recognize the claims of any consumers who had "paid" via those men.[24] The company's agreements with these three men, whose names appeared in newspaper ads for Airline radios in 1937 and 1938, had evidently been terminated.[25] A similar issue had been raised the previous year in the *Palestine Post*, relating to the repair of ra-dio sets using techniques and "original parts" provided exclusively to the agent by the set manufacturer. J L & B Haissman, the Philips Radio concessionaires, advised consumers:

> WARNING / We hereby warn all owners of PHILIPS wireless sets that in case of defects they have to send in their sets for repair to / OUR LABORATORIES ONLY / as we alone are in possession of the original PHILIPS spare parts which cannot be obtained anywhere else. / We shall not be responsible for sets which have been repaired other than in our laboratories and advise the public to apply to our laboratories only at TEL AVIV 24, Nachlat Benyamin St. (2nd floor); Jerusalem: Jaffa Road, near Egged; Haifa: 53 Kingsway; and all our branches in the colonies./ J L & B Haissman / sole distributors in Pal-estine of PHILIPS RADIO.[26]

The connections drawn in this advertisement between the agent's ex-clusive relationship with the manufacturer and his enterprise's expertise in set repair and servicing played a role in the copy of many advertise-ments. Here, however, that expertise was used as a warning: those cus-tomers who took their sets elsewhere for servicing would be (1) dissat-isfied with the repairs of those using non-Philips-brand parts; (2) found out when, having recognized the wisdom of "expert" servicing, the technicians in J L & B Haissman's shop identified the offending spare parts; and (3) rejected by both shop and technicians as owners of sets no longer eligible for branded repairs.

These rare references to false agents might be understood as impor-tant primarily for indicating that the licensed agent system generally functioned well. The strength of the system rested on the work done by the agents themselves to construct meaning and value for the relation-ship they had established with product manufacturers. While the phe-nomenon of unauthorized agents chastised in the local newspapers fo-cuses attention on the problem of illegitimacy, the real issue is the ways in which legitimacy and the related concepts of authorization and exclu-sivity were produced as meaningful. The number of agents who explicitly announced their status as "exclusive agent" or "possessor of the monopoly" for particular brands in their advertisements appears to speak both to the manufacturers' confidence in them (as evidenced by hiring them to represent their brand and their products) and to the consumers' trust in them. But they might also suggest agents' interest in building both consumer trust and consumer preference for branded goods from authorized sellers.

Markets

Agents obtained concessions to sell particular brands or product ranges over a specified territory rather than for selling specifically to an Arab, Jewish, or even British market. This led, especially in the years before the 1936 general strike, to "cross-advertising" by agents who were members of one community (whose names and/or business addresses made this evident) in the presses of another. The earliest appearances of this in *Falastin* were the ads for Minerva Radio placed in 1934 by Kovalsky & Sons, agents with shops in Jerusalem, Tel Aviv, and Haifa.[27] The first week of January 1936, for example, Rabinowicz, the Siera Super radio agent, with shops in Tel Aviv and Jerusalem, ran Arabic-language ads in *Falastin* and English-language ads in the *Palestine Post*, both following the "Silence! Listen to the Siera Super" / "Listen the Siera Super Is Playing" ad campaign.[28]

In the early to mid-1930s one could even find a sprinkling of advertisements for various products printed in Arabic newspapers that used both Hebrew and Arabic text. Although not a regular occurrence, these advertisements suggest that little stigma in terms of consumer avoidance attached to the overt identification of a particular shop with a Jewish clientele or of a particular product with a Jewish agent. The relatively high number of advertisements for smaller brands—Atwater Kent, Minerva, Siera Super, Zenith—also indicates the relative openness of the radio set market in the mid-1930s, which supported competition among a large number of brands from manufacturers of varying sizes and international stature.

After the general strike of April–October 1936, the number of identifiably "Jewish" agents placing ads for the sale of radio sets in the Arabic newspapers declined. As the mandate era proceeded, agents appear to have focused increasingly on intracommunity consumer markets. In some cases, a brand appears to have switched markets from the Arabic-speaking to the (English-speaking) Jewish one, perhaps influenced by changes in selling agents. The same Zenith radio that under Kumayko advertised in *Falastin* in 1934 had by 1937 disappeared from its pages and reappeared in the *Palestine Post* as the concession of the Svislotzky Brothers of Tel Aviv.[29] Similarly, Westinghouse Radio ads appeared in *Falastin* in 1934 under the agency of the "National Electricity Shop [owned by] Snobar and Abu Khadra."[30] The brand then disappeared from *Falastin*, though for the rest of the mandate period advertisements appeared regularly in the *Palestine Post*, courtesy of its new agents, Alexander Salkind and the Levinson Brothers, both of Tel Aviv.[31]

On the other hand, some agents appear to have focused on intracommunity sales from the beginning. The Palestine Radio Company, which had the monopoly over the very large RCA concession, never placed an ad in *Falastin*. Nor did Rabiner Electrical, J L & B Haissman, or the International Music Stores—the three concessionaires for Philips radios. This produced a very different branding situation in Palestine from that in Lebanon and Syria, where Philips radios were marketed to the Arabic-speaking populations. The two companies that did seem to split the difference, with Arab and Jewish agents throughout Palestine selling to segregated audiences, were Airline and Pye. In both cases the concession was held by a "Jewish" company that subcontracted to various distributing agents, who appear to have sold the brand strictly intracommunally.

Airline was a subsidiary brand of the U.S. Montgomery Ward Company; it first appeared in the *Palestine Post* in a September 4, 1935, announcement by Montgomery Ward congratulating Hochberg Radio Service (Jerusalem), Matalon Brothers (Tel Aviv), and Rabiner's Electrical Store (Haifa) for taking the Airline concession.[32] In April 1937 the brand began appearing in *Falastin*, with Badiʿ Musa and Ramadan ʿAkila listed as agents.[33] Although Musa appears to have had a run-in with Airline's Belgian distributor in 1939, by 1940 Badiʿ Musa and Shukri Rizk were again listed in Arabic newspaper advertisements. For the Airline radio concessionaires, the division of markets by community and language appears to have been total: the Arabic-language advertisements mentioned only Musa and Rizk; the English-language advertisements in the *Palestine Post* mentioned only Hochberg Radio Service, Matalon Brothers, and Rabiner's Electrical Store.[34] Pye was an English brand that entered the Palestinian market in December 1938 under an exclusive contract with Matalon Brothers.[35] Advertisements published in 1939–1940 listed Matalon Brothers as the distributing agent in the English press and the ubiquitous Badiʿ Musa in advertisements placed in *Falastin*.[36] This system prevailed through the next decade, despite the war and a change in licensed agent: 1946 and 1947 advertisements listed P. Schiglik of Tel Aviv as the "general distributor for Palestine," with subagents such as Fritz Friedlaender, who was licensed as the sole seller of Pye sets in Jerusalem.[37] The advertisements printed in *Falastin* listed only Shihada Su'ada of Jaffa as the Pye agent.

One might assume that by 1946, if not by 1939, dividing distribution by language and community was the only way to effectively sell any brand to Palestine's Arab and Jewish populations. However, the sales success enjoyed by one Arab company throughout the life of the mandate suggests that with enough effort, as well as perhaps the "right" combination of religious and civic affiliations, one could sell radio sets across communities. That company, T. S. Boutagy & Sons, was in many ways a singular operation, far surpassing most other firms in terms of sales volume, product diversification, and sophistication in sales and marketing. It will be considered here as a case study: in many ways it was the ultimate radio set agent.

Radio Sellers in Arab Palestine: T. S. Boutagy & Sons

Although numerous radio set agents advertised their respective brands in the pages of *Falastin*, one agent and one brand dominated, with advertisements that appeared more frequently, took more page space, and employed more creative ad copy. For regular readers of *Falastin*, it must have been difficult to avoid conflating the generic term *radio set* with the His Master's Voice (HMV) radios for which T. S. Boutagy & Sons had the sole sales and distribution concession. Thanks to this concession and Boutagy's stores' marketing efforts, the company had become the most prominent purveyors of radio sets in Arab Palestine—but the company's presence extended far more broadly into Palestine's commercial and social life.

T. S. Boutagy & Sons was a family-owned trading goods store chain based in Haifa, mandate Palestine's center of Arab commerce; Boutagy had additional storefronts in Jaffa, Jerusalem, and Amman. The stores' founder, Théophile Seraphim Boutagy, a member of Palestine's small Anglican community, was born in 1870 in a small town outside of Haifa.[38] His father was the Reverend Seraphim Boutagy, a minister of the Anglican Church in Palestine. His parents, Boutros and Francesca, both Catholic, had emigrated from Port Said and settled in Acre in 1836, the year of Seraphim's birth; Seraphim was the youngest of six and the only one born in Palestine. Seraphim married Afifeh Khairallah in 1855 in Haifa and sometime later converted to Anglicanism. (The marriage caused a permanent rift between Seraphim and his father, as Afifeh was the eldest daughter of the family's plantation manager and thus, at least in Boutros's opinion, a social inferior.) The couple had nine children, of whom T. S. was the fifth.[39]

T. S. Boutagy studied at the Anglican schools in Nazareth and Haifa before matriculating at the American University of Beirut (AUB), where at his father's direction he studied pharmacy in order to work with Shukri, his older brother and a practicing doctor. T. S. preferred craft-work, however, and as a teenager apprenticed himself for a time to a local carpenter; he also learned how to make violins. After finishing at AUB, he went on a Grand Tour through Europe, the United States, and Africa. After returning to Palestine, T. S. married Sophia Dimishki (al-Dimashqi), whose father was the Reverend Hanna, or Yuhanna Dimishki, a refugee from Damascus. Reverend Dimishki was employed in Palestine by the Anglican missionaries and served as a preacher in Lydda.[40] T. S. and Sophia had eight children.

Thanks to the success of T. S. Boutagy & Sons, as well as the family's various civic and religious activities, the Boutagys became prominent members of a cosmopolitan, relatively affluent community of Palestinian Protestants. The family features in May Seikaly's study of Haifa in the decades between the two world wars: she introduces them as "the richest Protestant family [in Haifa], whose wealth was greatly enhanced by British influence."[41] While the degree of the Boutagys' commercial success was singular, their position as a Haifa-based family of Arab importing agents was not. The Boutagys merely weathered better what Seikaly sees as the rise and decline that these families experienced during this period. Seikaly sees the mid-1920s as a period of growth and prosperity for these families, who capitalized on the increased discretionary income among Arab consumers (brought about by good harvests and market prices) and the purchasing power of newly arrived Jewish immigrants. The Boutagys were one of several trading families to "expand their businesses by catering to the tastes of the Jewish and British population," which meant seeking import agent agreements with European manufacturers whose products this population desired.[42]

However, the first flush of profitability was followed by a period of "fierce competition between importers of personal and household goods, and of goods destined for the [British mandate] administration"—

Figure 1.2. Boutagy's Stores made the company's imports a selling point, as in this 1936 advertisement that says the company founded a "new institute of radio and music" in Palestine. Source: "The New Institute of Radio and Music That Was Founded in Palestine by Boutagy," Boutagy's Stores advertisement, *Falastin*, Nov. 18, 1936, p. 7.

a competition that Seikaly says Jewish firms had won by 1933. Those Arab firms that remained active as importing agents survived by turning to niche markets and specializing in particular types or brands of goods. "By the late 1920s," Seikaly writes, "such firms as Boutagy began to specialize in imports of medium-sized household goods, musical equipment and clothes, almost all imported direct from England."[43] This specialization allowed Boutagy's Stores to thrive in the 1930s and 1940s.

The Boutagys' cosmopolitanism took the form of an orientation to European culture, which was reflected in the names they gave their children (Charles, Elizabeth, Émile, Gordon, Hilda, Olivia, Wanda, and William), the schools they attended (private Protestant schools and AUB), the languages they spoke (English, French, German, and Italian), their travel destinations (Europe, the United States, the Caribbean), the imported goods they purchased, and the activities in which they participated (for T. S. these included serving as the grand master of the Haifa Freemasons' lodge and as the honorary consul of Finland).[44] This orientation in turn may have given the Boutagys an edge in obtaining concessions for imported products and successfully marketing them to Arab Palestine's consuming classes.

Although T. S. Boutagy's name and photograph were prominently displayed on company material, Émile was perhaps the most involved in the family business, serving as Boutagy's Stores' general director in the 1930s and taking over entirely in 1940 on his father's retirement. The 1947 edition of *Palestine Personalia* identified him as "Bey, Merchant"—an indication of the family's social as well as mercantile prominence.[45] The family's third son, Gordon Boutagy, ran the Jerusalem branch of Boutagy's Stores. (Judging from the Boutagy's Stores ads, which differentiated between the Jerusalem branch and the others, Gordon's store was run as a semiautonomous operation.) The second eldest, Charles V. Boutagy, branched out into the hotel and summer resort market as proprietor of the Windsor Hotel in Haifa and the Jerusalem Hotel in Jaffa. It was Palestinians like the Boutagys that the Foreign Office's Overseas Planning Committee had in mind when both praising and faulting Arab Palestine's urban bourgeoisie:

> A notable development of the war years has been the growth of something like a national consciousness among Palestinian Arabs, especially in the towns. The town Arab regards himself as on a cultural level with any of his neighbors. Unlike the Egyptians or the Iraqis, Palestinian Arabs are not markedly divided into rich and poor, masters and men; they are a middle-class bourgeoisie with strong family ties. It is from the newly-conscious middle class that the future leaders of Palestinian Arab thought are likely to come. Arab industry has made headway during the war . . . [but] the Arabs tend to regard trade developments in terms of increased imports of consumer goods rather than the initiation of new enterprises. They see themselves easily outstripped by the Jews, but it is difficult to make them mend their old trading habits.[46]

Figure 1.3. T. S. Boutagy & Sons paper. Notice the strikingly modern building, which appears to be wholly dedicated to professional use (while in fact the Émile Boutagys lived above the ground floor store) and includes none of the smaller, older buildings that in reality surrounded the main building and were used by T. S. Boutagy & Sons for repairs and warehousing. Notice also the number of radio aerials included in this depiction of the building, reinforcing the modernity of the building and the company itself. Source: Private collection.

Figure 1.4. J. Gordon Boutagy's professional stationery suggests that despite the range of imported goods sold through Boutagy's Stores at this time, HMV was if not its most prominent then at least the one with which it was most closely linked. Source: ISA RG 103 (Edwin Samuel Papers) 667 3.

The Boutagys elevated those "trade habits" to an art form, starting with the Boutagy's HMV licensed agent agreement. They also appear to have operated a fairly religion- and ethnicity-blind business. Not only did Boutagy's Stores advertise regularly in the *Palestine Post*, whose pages were filled with advertisements addressed to Palestine's Jewish community, but their advertisements in *Falastin* seamlessly adapted their product sales pitches to whatever holiday was approaching, whether Eid or Easter. The company's staffing policies were apparently equally open. In January 1940 Émile Boutagy sent a letter to the Chief Secretary and the High Commissioner soliciting the government's village radio set business. He closed with a "support local businesses" message with a twist: "the Palestine Government may like to give support to local industries maintaining a large mixed staff of both Arabs and Jews."[47]

The HMV monopoly was not T. S. Boutagy & Sons' only concession; on the contrary, *Palestine Personalia 1947* described Émile Boutagy as "represent[ing] a number of world famous factories."[48] However, it was the brand most often featured in Boutagy's newspaper advertisements, making it if not the company's most significant monopoly, at least the one with which Boutagy's was most closely associated in *Falastin*-reading Palestinian consumers' minds. Nor was this an association that Boutagy's Stores discouraged. As the above illustration indicates, the stationery that J. Gordon Boutagy was using professionally in the late 1930s blended the Boutagy's Stores name, his name, his role as "agent, importer & distributor," and the HMV logo of a dog listening to his master's voice played on a gramophone.

Like many advertisements of the time, Gordon Boutagy's stationery illustrates the ways in which the product brand and the agent's "brand" often blended together, at least for marquee product lines. At times the connection between Boutagy and HMV seems to have been so strong as to overwhelm customers' awareness of the store's other products. Thus a June 1938 advertisement placed in *Falastin* reminded consumers that "[Boutagy's Stores] are not just [for] radios but [for] cars as well."[49]

T. S. Boutagy & Sons was perhaps the major advertiser in *Falastin* throughout the 1930s and continued to be a regular advertiser through the 1940s. In the mid- and late 1930s, a half- or three-quarter-page Boutagy's Stores ad was a staple element of most issues. Most Boutagy's HMV ads followed the pattern, mixing generic HMV ad plates and copy with Arabic narrative text. Boutagy's regularly included narrative photographs of its HMV radios, photographs that told stories of in-home listening or of the radio set's development in a scientific factory. Even when Boutagy's advertisements were built around product photographs—beauty shots of radio sets floating in the white space of the newspaper page—their ad copy stood out. A Boutagy's HMV ad was textually dense, with lengthy, storytelling text that wrapped itself above, beside, and below the radio set photograph. This density made it immediately recognizable on the page.

While other radio set sellers also included product photography and Arabic text, they limited themselves to communicating product attributes and store information. Boutagy's Arabic ad copy was more engaging and more locally focused. Its HMV advertisements presented sophisticated narratives that promoted radio sets as dowry or wedding gifts, commented on current world events, lauded a performer scheduled to appear on the Cairo or Jerusalem radio station, followed an African explorer on his travels, or referred specifically to developments in Palestine. Whereas competitors were content to list the number of vacuum tubes, promise superior sound quality, or invite consumers to view "the newest model," Boutagy's HMV advertisements exemplified what Marchand in his study of developments in the American advertising industry between the world wars calls the evolution to "selling the benefit instead of the product"[50]—in this case, the enjoyment of radio listening, the physical proof of one's position as an urbane member of modern culture, and the connection to the wider world—whether geographic or cultural—that radio afforded.

When contrasted with its other advertisements, the attention Boutagy's Stores paid to its HMV radio advertisements was striking. On days that Boutagy's advertisements did not focus exclusively on HMV products, the company ran similarly sized ads promoting its many other items: men's dress coats and dress shoes, baby carriages, air conditioners, refrigerators, motorcycles, barber's chairs (for professional use), hunting rifles, and so on. The accompanying copy was functional, describing the products rather than telling a story about the experience of purchasing or using them. Presumably, HMV radio sets were highlighted in Boutagy's advertisements because they sold in sufficient quantities to be profitable and because the HMV brand communicated a midlevel luxury position consistent with the store's "brand."

The first point distinguished radio sets from air conditioners or motorcycles, two commodities with consumer cachet but each too expensive to sell in large enough quantities to justify the expense of regular advertising. The second distinguished radio sets from shaving cream or shoe polish, imported products advertised elsewhere in *Falastin* but both too affordable to communicate an upper-middle-class consumer identity. Situated along this continuum of products, radio sets in 1930s and 1940s Palestine might be considered just-affordable luxuries: entry-level luxury goods whose purchase price brought them just within economic reach of consumers for whom refrigerators, automobiles, heaters, and air-conditioning remained either impossibly expensive or impossibly dependent on electricity.[51] While a 20LP radio set represented roughly four weeks' wages for an unskilled Palestinian laborer, it might have represented three for skilled construction workers or two for a government clerk.[52] Radio sets were not cheap, but they were within reach for those with the ability to save—or to buy on installment.

Radio Selling: Print Advertisements Placed in the Arabic Press

For all agents involved in the sale and distribution of radio sets, the production and sales restrictions that governed radio sets during World War II coupled with the chaotic situation of the final years of the mandate resulted in a tighter market, generating fewer and less elaborate radio set advertisements. Consequently, this section focuses on advertisements of the 1930s. Boutagy's Stores advertisements form the bulk of the advertisements published in this decade, dominating the field in sheer quantity as well as setting the standard for ad production, including copy and taglines. However, advertisements of other agents and brands are included where appropriate to give a comprehensive portrait of the state of radio set advertising in this period.[53]

Advertisements in the Mandate Press

Advertisements took up more limited space in mandate papers than readers familiar with 1930s and 1940s newspapers in Western Europe and the United States might expect. The three major newspapers publishing in mandate Palestine—the Arabic-language *Falastin* (founded in 1911, Christian-owned), the Arabic-language *al-Dif'a* (founded in 1934, Sunni-owned), and the English-language *Palestine Post* (founded in 1932, Jewish-owned)—published fewer than ten advertisements on most days. Many pages had no advertisements, and a page with more than two advertisements was quite unusual, particularly for the Arabic newspapers. As a result each individual advertisement was perhaps more eye-catching, since it competed with few if any other advertisements on the page. Yet these few advertisements showcased a wide variety of products and services.

Advertisements in *Falastin*: A Survey

By the mid-1930s *Falastin*'s pages were sprinkled with advertisements for a wide range of consumable goods and services: local products, travel, insurance, imported goods. By articulating notions of modernity filtered through certain imported products, these advertisements helped forge a cosmopolitan, middle- and aspiring upper-middle-class identity for Arabic-speaking Palestinians. *Falastin* was not the only Arabic-language paper, but its decades of experience gave it a professionalism and sophistication that exceeded those of its competitors. In particular, *Falastin* stood in contrast to *al-Difa'*, which by the 1940s became Palestine's highest-circulation Arabic newspaper, with *Falastin* in second place. For much of the 1930s, *al-Difa'* faced various start-up issues: widely varying print quality, typos, ugly fonts, smeared print runs, and so on. It also had trouble maintaining a consistent length; although most papers varied in length between weekday and weekend editions, *al-Difa'* seemed to vary more randomly. Finally, it had a very low number of advertisements, both in absolute terms and compared with other Palestinian papers, especially *Falastin*. Even when *al-Dif'a* matured—which happened during the challenging war years—it continued to publish a relatively low number of advertisements, with a similarly low level of sophistication.

Ads for local products tended to be small and simple, often merely stating the name of a firm or product and where to find it. Ramallah Arak Company was a relatively typical local advertiser. The company advertised in *Falastin* on an occasional basis, promoting its *araq* (a clear, anise-flavored liquor similar to ouzo and usually mixed with water) as healthful and describing itself as a "registered brand"—analogous to a registered trademark. Ramallah Arak was one of the few companies promoting alcohol in *Falastin* and other period newspapers. However, its advertisements were representative of many local products, demonstrating both the company's professionalism (shown in its having a logo, a registered brand, a benefit claim, and contact information) and the small scale of its operations.[54] In addition to local product advertisements, local firms and branches of international service companies, in particular insurance and travel, advertised their services. Steamship companies like Messageries Maritimes, tourist companies like Thomas Cook, hotels like the Continental in Jaffa, and related firms promoted travel both within Palestine and around the region as well as to Europe and the Americas.

Ads for imported products were generally larger and more sophisticated than local product or service ads. They typically included the logo of the product in its proprietary font. They often included an image—usually of the product being advertised but sometimes a drawing or photograph of a sample customer, with or without the product. Palmolive Soap advertised in *Falastin* from time to time, with medium-sized advertisements that included an image of a Palmolive bar of soap and sometimes also an image of a satisfied user. Palmolive ads represented slightly more sophisticated, textually dense imported-goods advertisements, promising users a "schoolgirl's" complexion.[55] Radio set ads generally fit into this latter category, although—as described below—they appeared far more frequently and often with more elaborate ad copy.

Marketing Radios and the Problem of Consumer Desire

The sales agreements joining American and European radio set manufacturers and Palestinian agents licensed the agent to sell the manufacturer's products; they did not actively involve the manufacturer in sales efforts. To make a concession profitable, the licensed agent needed to market and advertise the products he was authorized to sell—or, in some cases, to create a market for them. It was his task to not only promote the brand image of the products under his control but also and more fundamentally to develop the market for such goods by fostering consumer desires for them in both their generic and branded forms.

The determination of consumer desire is as difficult for the historian or social analyst as it has historically been for vendors and advertisers. Advertisements and marketing campaigns might most productively be considered to reflect the latter's best guess about the content and direction of consumer desire circulating around particular products. Crudely put, their advertisements focused on the fulfillment of this desire as distilled through one of two categories: desire for the product and desire for what Marchand calls the "benefit" enabled by that product. With radio, the product was the set, while the benefit included both the experience of listening to radio and what might be understood as a set of associations linked to radio set ownership. (These included product specifications such as "new 1937 model," "tri-band receiver," "superhet[erodyne]," "9 tube," and "spread-band" in the "radio set" product category and distinguishing them from "easier tuning," "better reception," and "clearest sound" as auxiliary members of the "listening experience" benefit category.) The pages of *Falastin* in the 1930s were filled with a relatively even mix of product and benefit radio set advertisements, as well as those that blurred distinctions between the two.

It would be unfair to dismiss product-focused radio set advertisements as transparent and thus rhetorically inert. Certainly these ads did work to evoke or stimulate consumer desire for the radio set showcased by text such as "the new RCA model." However, the focus here is on advertisements seeking to highlight benefits: those that linked consumer desire with the experience of radio listening as well as the associations or experience of radio set ownership. Advertisements that mentioned specific stations or programs engaged with the literal benefit: access to radio broadcasts and the physical possibility of listening to radio. Other advertisements—those that photographically or textually depicted people listening to their radios—suggested the community-building aspects of the sociality of radio. At the same time, the rich visual or textual descriptions of these latter advertisements promoted the association of certain qualities with radio ownership, in particular, domestic radio ownership.

Such associated qualities derived first and foremost from the connection between radio sets as imported goods and the American or European contexts in which they originated. These connections were reinforced by the languages (English, French, German, Dutch) in which the cities listed on the sets' spread-bands were printed, as well as by manufacturer-produced promotional photographs that showed the radio set surrounded by listeners or technicians in its country of origin.

The presence of a radio set in a home suggested that its owners enjoyed the affluence, sophistication, and urbanity linked to a certain kind of cosmopolitan modern life. (Specific iterations of such associations varied, ranging from a technical familiarity with modern electrical appliances to a connoisseur's appreciation of classical music.) Those advertisements able to communicate both the associative and experiential aspects of radio set ownership were those that most fully addressed consumer desires.

Before offering too tidy a correlation between radio set advertisements' stimulation and satisfaction of consumer desire, it may be useful to consider the qualification that Martin makes regarding consumer desire. He describes the Syrian advertisements he analyzes as evoking not only desire but also anxiety. In his assessment, advertisements for imported "modern" products communicated two messages to would-be consumers: "this is who you can be" but also "this is who you should be." If the first spoke to consumer desire as aspiration, sending a positive (at least from the viewpoint of those in favor of consumerist modernities) "you too can achieve this" message, the second spoke to consumer anxiety, sending a prescriptive "you should achieve this" message with a negative "but are you able?" undertone.[56] The advertisements' confirmation of the presence of radio sets in Palestine reminded consumers that the purchase and utilization of such sets was now among the available or, speaking prescriptively, requisite ways of exhibiting modern behavior. By the 1930s the general population was familiar with the fact of radio sets—with their existence as objects and as vehicles to radio broadcasts. This familiarity coupled with their continued economic inaccessibility for the majority of people helped them signify modernity for both their purchasers and the many Palestinians who saw or heard radio sets only in the homes and businesses of others.

Advertisement Formats

Like those for other big-ticket items, advertisements for radio sets in the Palestinian Arabic press shared a similar and noticeably hybrid format. (Advertisements placed for similar items in the *Palestine Post* were much less hybrid, tending either to be entirely "locally produced" and textual or to closely follow the manufacturers' advertising scheme.) To facilitate the agent's ability to market his products, their American or European manufacturers included generic advertising material with product shipments. At a minimum, this material included the manu-

Figure 1.5. A 1939 advertisement for Pilot radio. The simple text announces the arrival of a new shipment and remarks on "the contentment of all with the ease of their use and the reasonableness of their price." Source: *Falastin*, June 27, 1939, p. 6.

facturer and brand names in their signature fonts as well as brand logo and product image, suitable for reproduction with Arabic text promoting the product and the selling agent. Almost all agents produced some advertisements of this type, adding a relatively limited amount of text to announce the availability of particular models or promote particular

Figure 1.6. A 1935 Boutagy's HMV radio advertisement, with two different messages. The Arabic reads: "Listen to the Holy Qur'an every morning by means of the marvelous His Master's Voice radio." Source: *Falastin*, Feb. 23, 1935, p. 8.

product attributes. For some brands these simpler advertisements were the only ones produced.

In the case of His Master's Voice and, to a lesser extent, the Siera Super and Radio Midwest brands, the materials sent included more elaborate "boilerplate" ads designed for the brand's current domestic advertising campaign. The manufacturers' ads were generally larger in size and featured a product beauty shot coupled with text in English that promoted the brand and product by presenting particular technological innovations as selling points. As indicated by the "Dealer's Name" space in the advertisement shown in figure 1.6, manufacturers made little distinction between domestic and overseas vendors with regard to marketing. Both were expected to support the unified marketing plan designed by the manufacturer. However, this expectation ignored the cultural as well as literal translations required when selling overseas. In Palestine, the manufacturers' advertisements provided the foundation for the bilingual, hybrid creation that resulted. The selling agent added Arabic text to, as the manufacturer expected, identify himself as the product's authorized dealer. He also added advertising copy in Arabic promoting the radio set in some way to a Palestinian Arab audience. He then placed the advertisement directly with the periodical in which he wished to advertise. There is no historical evidence to suggest the mediation of an advertising agency, although several were operating in Palestine at the time. Relli Shechter notes that some manufacturer-agent agreements arranged for the two parties to share advertising costs. It is not clear whether HMV paid any portion of Boutagy's HMV advertisements, although evidence of this would aid in explaining their number and prominence.[57]

One of the consequences of this hybrid form of advertisement was the blurring of distinctions between the brand of the product being promoted and the "brand" of the selling agent. Figure 1.6 gives only a mild indication of the ways in which Boutagy's Stores' HMV radio advertisements promoted the stores as much as the HMV brand. In this case, the promotion of Boutagy's is incorporated into the narrative of the Arabic ad copy: the solution to the customer's problem is an HMV radio "from Boutagy." The Arabic text also closes with two common Boutagy's advertisement taglines: "who does not buy, looks" and "with every radio a gift." The effect of such hybridization was to link brand and agent, product and seller, in ways perhaps not envisioned and likely not appreciated by the manufacturer.

Advertising Themes: Radio on Radio

If the simpler radio set advertisements focused on the radio set itself, including technical improvements or increased availability, the more elaborate advertisements—and particularly those of Boutagy's Stores— covered a range of themes. What they shared was a certain narrative complexity—an attempt at creating a world for the consumer. As noted above, the narratives of these advertisements "placed" radio sets as gifts for new brides, offered them as means of keeping current with world affairs, suggested them as entertainment for the home, recommended them to increase business in shops and cafés, or identified them as accompaniments to the more fantastic lives of world explorers. With the exception of the last, most focused on the ways in which radio sets could enhance the lives of *consumers in Palestine*, providing a deep sense of contextual specificity.

This specificity was perhaps most apparent in the series of mid-1930s advertisements that linked radio sets to particular radio stations or radio station broadcasts. While communicating the potential for new experiences and new communities promised by radio's social aspect, the stations promoted the ways in which this sociality might be set within national or regional boundaries.

On Thursday, October 3, 1935, readers of *Falastin* found a bold-print, large-font headline at the top of page 8: "A New Station in Palestine for Broadcasting." The headline introduced not a news article but an advertisement for HMV radios placed by Boutagy's Stores. Beneath the headline was a photograph of men in white lab coats testing the workings of a roomful of HMV radio-gramophones and a block of Arabic text taking up roughly the same amount of space beneath the photograph. The text announced:

> To our gentle readers and our virtuous patrons we bring glad tidings and joy. As has been anticipated, the government has been pursuing diligently the completion of the preparations of the modern broadcasting station in Ramallah, which is expected to be ready this October for operations and for spreading the official news [al-akhbar al-rasmiyya] and for valuable lectures and talks by doctors and learned men and experts, and [for] music and all the matters that work to advance the country and to put it in line with the awakening [al-nahda] cities. It is a given that joining in listening to the station [is] for whomever a good thing, especially because [the station] will spread news of great use and will benefit every one of us in any situation equally, for no merchants can dispense with it, and no salaried employees [muwadhdhafeen], and no property owners, because it gathers from many types of news the many things of which every individual yearns to apprise himself, and concerns everyone who is in Palestine.[58]

The second paragraph of ad copy shifted the focus from the future Palestine broadcasting station to the benefits of listening to it on an HMV radio set purchased from Boutagy's: clear sound reception and a lifetime of guaranteed repairs from Boutagy's trained staff. The ad closed with a reminder that "in the experience [of testing an HMV radio at Boutagy's stores] lies the virtue of proofs [of its superiority]," as well as a tagline that closed most Boutagy's advertisements: "Visit Boutagy's Stores even if once a year / hurry to Boutagy's Stores in Haifa, and Jaffa in front of the Government Serail," and a list of other Boutagy's-affiliated HMV agents in Palestine.

Although this was the first Boutagy ad in *Falastin*'s pages to headline the nascent Palestine station, the station was mentioned in the copy of several earlier advertisements. For the previous few years Boutagy had been running advertisements whose narratives featured letters sent from customers throughout Palestine to Émile Boutagy, the stores' general director, asking for his advice or sharing their solutions to particular problems: boredom, disconnection from world events, poor business at the family's coffee shop, the need to find the perfect gift for one's fiancée. His response, printed below the text of the original letter, tailored itself to the individual writer's problem but always offered the same solution: buy an HMV radio set from Boutagy's. The ad printed in *Falastin* on July 23, 1935, was the first to link this solution to the pleasure of listening to the future Palestinian station. This ad was more morbid than most, featuring an orange tree farmer in Tul Karm so unhappy with the dullness of his life (with long evenings spent "killing time" [*wa aqtulu al-waqt*] smoking *argileh*, drinking araq, and playing the card game *shidda* after his labors in the groves) that he was contemplating hanging himself from a rope tied to the branch of one of his orange trees.

Émile responded jovially: "Your problem is simple, *ya sidi* [sir]." He proposed two solutions: either the morose farmer should hang a rope swing from the tree in his orchard and sit on it while dreaming nostalgically of his childhood happiness or he should buy a radio gramophone from Boutagy's. With this, his evenings would be filled with music and entertainment, in his house or out in the grove. As a side note, Émile's reply mentioned that "[with] preparations for the upcoming opening of the Palestine Broadcasting Station in the outskirts of Ramallah we have prepared ourselves by obtaining radio sets to begin to distribute them in monthly amounts to all classes of people."[59] While conveying information incidental to the ad's narrative theme, this statement suggests that at least on the supply side there was an expectation that the new radio station would drive consumers to increased radio set purchases—and that these consumers would be reassured to know that Boutagy's was preparing by increasing its inventory.

The July 23 and October 3 advertisements were two of a number of radio set advertisements appearing in 1935 and 1936 in the local press that mentioned the nascent PBS as a selling point. These ads drew on the earlier precedent of heralding the inauguration and subsequent broadcasts of the Egyptian State Broadcasting Service (ESB) in Cairo as a means to encourage radio set sales. The Boutagy's ad that ran on January 25, 1934, for example, alerted readers to a "Very Important Announcement! Issuing from Boutagy Stores Haifa—Jaffa—Jerusalem—Amman." The text below mixed news reportage–style writing with copy promoting both HMV radios and Boutagy's related service:

It has been as good as decided that the official government station in Egypt will begin wireless broadcasting in the middle of next March.

At that time it will become possible to hear the news and lectures and music night and day. We do not think a person or a family will be found [who is] able to manage without a guaranteed radio, because it is among the greatest producers of diversion and pleasure, cultivation and education for the young. In accordance with this we announce to the gentle public that he will find at our shops beautiful guaranteed radio machines of the authentic mark "His Master's Voice," with prices from 10 guineas and up, with facilities for payment. Our service and our guarantee have no equal even in Europe itself, since our specialists attend to the comfort and service of the clients at every time and place. In accordance with this we urge the gentle public to test our machines before buying from abroad.[60]

The Cairo station's inauguration at the end of May 1934 prompted I. Kumayko, the Jerusalem vendor of Zenith radio, to run a tie-in ad promoting Zenith radio sets as the means for hearing "music from all corners of the world" with "beauty and clarity such as you have never heard before."[61] Once the ESB was fully operational, Boutagy's and other radio set providers began to reference its programming in their ad copy, as in Boutagy's February 23, 1935, advertisement, shown in figure 1.6, which ran with the header, "Listen to the Holy Qur'an every morning / by means of the marvelous 'His Master's Voice' radio."[62] The logic driving these ads seems to have been that consumers were more likely to purchase radio sets if they knew that doing so would allow them to access regional Arabic-language broadcasting stations in addition to the European stations broadcasting in various languages on medium- and shortwave.

By highlighting these stations advertisers were also providing consumers with examples of their radio sets' utility: radio sets give you access to these stations, which have programming you will enjoy and/or benefit from; and our sets give you the clearest, most reliable access. These assumptions are supported by the name and location of the one European station whose programs Boutagy's advertisements mentioned: the BBC Empire station, which broadcast in English to British colonies and overseas dominions. Boutagy's March 2, 1935, ad stated, "His Majesty King George V / broadcasts the Silver Jubilee speech on the radio / it is possible to hear it in all clarity with a His Master's Voice radio."[63] In this and in other similar "special broadcast" cases, Boutagy's ad writers assumed consumer interest in listening to BBC Empire presumably because Great Britain, Palestine's mandate authority, was the nation-state with whose fortunes the territory was then intimately entwined.

This use of Palestine-relevant radio stations as a selling proposition in radio set advertisements continued through the PBS's opening at the end of March 1936. The Boutagy's ad that ran on February 4, 1936, took the form of a news announcement: "News [from] Boutagy's Stores / of Haifa, Jaffa, and Jerusalem / inauguration of broadcasting station in Ramallah," with supporting text celebrating the station.[64] Two weeks after the PBS began broadcasting, an ad for Emerson Radio exhorted *Falastin*'s readers, "Listen to the Palestine Broadcasting Station from an Emerson radio."[65] It is possible that advertisements like these would have continued for some time after the station's opening. However, the outbreak of the general strike in April 1936 engendered the voluntary suspension of press advertising, as even those Arab-owned shops that remained open preferred not to publicize their dissenting position so boldly, and the newspapers themselves published shorter editions on at times erratic publishing schedules. When the strike ended in October, press advertisements for radio sets and other goods reappeared—but with new advertisements that employed different narratives and targeted other selling points. The PBS was left to promote itself directly to Palestine's radio listeners, while the consumer desire that radio set agents had previously conceived as encompassing Palestine's local radio station was now understood to have turned in other directions.

Whether this shift reflected advertisers' belief that the "buy our radio to listen to the PBS" theme was no longer as effective as other sales pitches or a more general Arab disaffection with the PBS that reflected its position as a government station in a time of particularly cold relations between Palestine's Arab community and its British mandate government is unclear. Certainly the PBS was consistently subject to more stringent news censorship than the Palestinian newspapers, which intermittently throughout the station's history accused it of broadcasts that included only the news that the government permitted rather than freely selecting the news of immediate relevance and interest to Palestine's communities. As the situation in Palestine's rural areas worsened in early 1937, the *Palestine Post* described the PBS's news policy as "bear[ing] a remarkable resemblance to the alleged practice of the ostrich," due to its tight censorship on Palestine news.[66] In early 1938 this censorship engendered a brief standoff between the mandate government and the newly opened BBC Arabic service, which broadcast news of the trials and executions of some of the Arab participants in the 1936 revolt—news that the PBS had not been permitted to broadcast for fear of inciting further unrest.[67] The mandate government protested; the BBC replied that its credibility to Arab and all listeners rested on its dispassionate reportage of the news, free from the mandate or any other government's interference.

It may be that advertising radio sets via the PBS was more effective when the station was new, before the hopes that various listening communities had invested in it were compelled to give way before the mandate government's concerns, particularly in times of crisis like the strike and the widespread Arab revolt that followed. However, this must be balanced against other evidence that the Arab listening audience continued to grow, as well as government reports submitted to the League of Nations Mandates Commission. As noted above, they described the station as having attracted a broad-based audience precisely because it broadcast logistical updates, notifying listeners of curfews, road closures, and similar matters of day-to-day concern. [68]

Radio Selling during World War II

The dip in the number of radio set advertisements in the Arabic press during the general strike of 1936 and the unrest that followed was more than matched by the almost total disappearance of radio set advertisements during World War II and the disturbances that marked the end of the mandate. A tally of the number of radio set advertisements published each year in *Falastin* clearly indicates the precipitous nature of the decline during these latter periods.

In each of the latter two years of the 1936–1939 "disturbances," *Falastin* published fewer than ten radio set advertisements. The market was only beginning to recover when the war began and wartime sanctions were imposed on various commodities, including radio sets. Although merchants were allowed to sell the sets they had in stock, obtaining new sets for sale became almost impossible due to a trifecta of obstacles: limited set production in England and the United States, where manufacturers found it more profitable and more patriotic to switch from radio set to war materiel production; limited shipping opportunities as the European war made Mediterranean shipping dangerous and expensive; and severe import restrictions imposed by the British mandate government in Palestine.

Merchants like T. S. Boutagy & Sons were able to continue selling

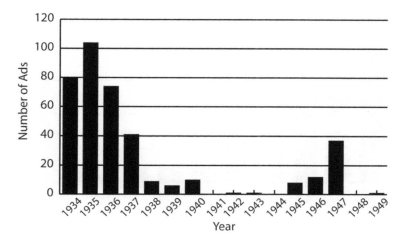

Chart 1.1. Total number of radio set advertisements (commercial and private sales) published annually in the newspaper *Falastin* from 1934 (two years before the PBS began broadcasting) to 1949 (a year after the mandate ended).

through 1940, when the end of the "false war" and the commencement of serious military engagement combined with low stocks put many under severe financial pressure. The *Statistical Handbook of Middle Eastern Countries* recorded the decline in the value of radio set and part imports from 1938, the last full year before the war began, through 1943.

Year	Value (Palestinian Pounds)
1938	233,068
1939	282,975
1940	243,513
1941	130,735
1942	158,207
1943	55,484[69]

The value of radio-related imports in 1941 was just over half that in 1940, with a slight recovery in 1942 and another dramatic fall in 1943. Statistics for 1944 and 1945 would likely show a further decline. The Post Office showed a similar dropoff in the number of radio licenses

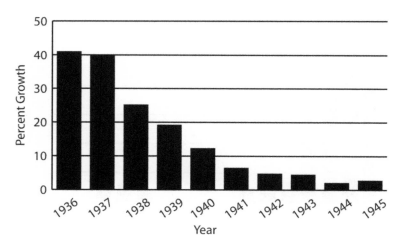

Chart 1.2. Annual percentage growth in Palestine radio licenses as recorded by the Palestine Post Office. Sources: ISA RG 2 16 361 15–16 Chief Secretary's Office—Avoidance of the Infringement of Copyright in Broadcasting [Vol. I, 1937–1943, and Vol. II, 1943–1946] and ISA RG 2 16 361 39 Chief Secretary's Office—Agreement with the Performing Rights Society in respect of items broadcast by the Palestine Broadcasting Service [1946–1948].

purchased. Although the number of radio licenses continued to grow, the double-digit percentage growth of the late 1930s was replaced by the war years' low or mid-single-digit increases.

The 40+ percent increases of 1936 and 1937 and the 25 percent and 19 percent increases of 1938 and 1939, respectively, were followed by the anemic growth rates of wartime, which ranged from 12.3 percent in 1941 to lows of 2.1 percent in 1944 and 2.8 percent in 1945. Even for those Palestinians with money to spend, the opportunities for radio set purchasing were few.

The change was equally evident on the pages of *Falastin*: from 1941 through 1944 the only radio set advertisements that appeared were one-time notices posted by individual sellers, such as the advertisement published on January 17, 1942, by Naʿim ʿAud of Jaffa, which stated that he had a Cadet radio and car radio to sell,[70] or a similar advertisement placed on January 23, 1943, by Hussein Minadila of Haifa, which listed a number of used goods for sale, including "radios of different types, electric and gas stoves, electric fans, electric teakettles and coffeepots, washing machines and other electric household fixtures [*lawazim al-manadil al-kahraba'iyya*]."[71] These advertisements were spare, functional, and—above all—rare.

Like other sellers, Boutagy's coped, renting radio sets and other goods by the month and continuing its layaway purchasing programs. At the same time, Émile Boutagy and other merchants complained directly to the mandate government's Office of the Economic Adviser, headed from 1938 until the end of the mandate by Geoffrey Walsh, a civil servant brought to Palestine from Kenya,[72] as well as to other government wartime bodies. In 1943 Boutagy wrote a six-page, single-spaced letter to the newly appointed head of the newly created War Economic Council, a body with jurisdiction over imports and trucking, among its other responsibilities. In it, he detailed the difficulties that he and other "luxury goods" retailers, as wartime regulations termed them, had faced in the previous four years: confiscation of store goods without recompense; prohibitions on imports, including the importation of goods available from Egypt and other neighboring states; confiscation of cars from private homes and businesses; preferential treatment for certain companies regarding licenses to sell particular goods; and high inflation due to the unnecessary restriction on sales of cooking stoves, sporting cartridges, and other goods Boutagy considered neither essential to the war effort nor egregiously luxurious.[73]

In addition to shortages of goods and restrictions on imports and sales, the fear with which European governments of all types viewed radio broadcasting created a hostile atmosphere for radio users. In the late 1930s, Britain was only one of many states whose governments considered radio an all-powerful medium, capable of influencing its listeners to a degree that newspaper editors could only dream of with regard to their readers. While this may have encouraged as many listeners as it discouraged, government policing of radio set usage and ownership was far-reaching, affecting both public (café and community) and private (home and business) listening practices. In Lebanon and Syria, French mandate territories, the fear of what people might hear on the radio was compounded by a fear of *where* they might hear it and how they might respond. In February 1940 the government banned the purchase of car radios and two-way communications systems similar to walkie-talkies. Car owners who already had radios or communication devices in their cars were required to obtain licenses for them, presentable on request by any government official, by registering with local public security centers. They were instructed to do so by February 15 or face fines and forcible removals.[74]

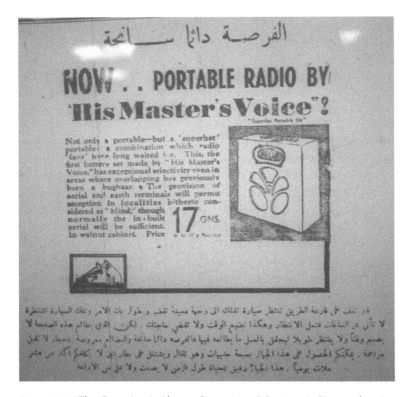

Figure 1.7. "The Occasion Is Always Opportune," Boutagy's Stores advertisement for His Master's Voice radio. Source: *Falastin*, June 9, 1940, p. 6.

In Palestine the problem of controlling where people listened to the radio was compounded by the recent introduction of radio sets whose internal aerials made them not only easier to use but movable from one location to another. A June 1940 Boutagy's advertisement promoted the new HMV "Portable Radio," a mid-priced battery-operated radio.

Although the Arabic text appears to suggest that this radio could be carried around in a car so that busy Palestinians stuck in blocked intersections did not waste their time, "portable" was a misnomer. The radio was more accurately transportable: capable of being moved to a new room or a new location without requiring its user to first reposition and reconnect an external aerial. The increased mobility of radio sets such as this one made them doubly difficult for the mandate government to manage. The lack of an external aerial meant that officials could no longer identify which buildings housed radios merely by looking at their roofs or exterior walls, and their transportability made it possible for owners to hide their sets in case of a search or to listen to them in secret.

Between limitations on supplies, difficulties in shipping, and government restrictions on sales, ownership, and usage, the war took its toll on Arab Palestine's radio set sellers. Advertising resumed after the war— but slowly, as radio set manufacturers in Britain and the United States required time to reconvert their factories to radio set production, relieve the backlog of domestic orders, and ship new radio sets to Palestine.

Radio Selling: 1945 and After

Even the *Palestine Post*, which ran more radio set advertisements during the war than did *Falastin* (largely due to the increased English-speaking market, as British and other Allied troops appeared in Palestine, which served as a staging ground for North African and Levantine operations), saw new radio set sales ads reappear only gradually. Through the spring and summer of 1945 the *Palestine Post* ran mostly radio repair advertisements, and those advertisements for new radio sets promised their arrival sometime in the future. T. S. Boutagy & Sons was the first to place a sales ad for a new radio set and other household appliances; it appeared on May 2 and May 4, 1945.

> Book now for post-war delivery [of] refrigerators, radios, domestic appliances, etc.
>
> In switching over from war-time to peace-time production our principals are anxious to determine the volume of orders that will follow victory and the elimination of [sales] controls. We therefore invite bookings for postwar delivery of refrigerators, gas cooking ranges, electric cookers, wireless receivers, pianos and domestic appliances. Those booked reservations will have delivery priority when the flow of consignments begins after the war. No deposits are required and no commitments are involved.[75]

Boutagy's prescience with respect to victory may have encouraged the firm to be overly optimistic regarding postwar delivery dates. An advertisement placed by Philco Radios agent Ampa Ltd. the following month was less confident of the speed with which its stocks would be replenished; the company stated merely, "We hope to offer you soon the most advanced designs of PHILCO RADIOS and of all other PHILCO PRODUCTS."[76]

After the declarations of victory in both Europe and Asia, other radio companies (and their agents) had begun making similar virtues of necessity, appealing to customers' patriotism and desire for the latest technologies in hope that they would continue to wait. A November 1945 RCA ad described its "laboratories in war and peace":

> The primary aim of RCA Laboratories is to increase the usefulness of radio to the public. Scientific investigations, continuously conducted, are directed toward constant improvement in every branch of radio. During the war, the efforts of RCA Laboratories were turned toward developments for the armed forces. Many outstanding discoveries in radio science have been put into practical use and made available to the Allied Forces on land, sea, and in the air. With the resumption of production for the civilian market, the knowledge, experience and skill accumulated by RCA Laboratories will result in new and finer RCA products. Finest radios and other appliances, bearing the world-famous RCA trademark, will contribute to the enjoyment of living.[77]

The advertisement said nothing about when the RCA radios whose production benefited from these "outstanding discoveries" might be available for purchase. Meanwhile, advertisements were appearing in *Falastin* promising small numbers of "the first English radio manufactured after the war"[78] and new postwar Pilot radios from the Aoun Brothers, the company's Palestine agents.[79]

By spring 1946 radio set shipments were appearing with some regularity in Palestine's ports, a fact highlighted in advertisements such as a June 22, 1946, Pye radio ad in *Falastin*, which announced that "a second load of radios" had arrived in Palestine.[80] As indicated in chart 1.1, radio set advertisements continued to grow throughout 1946 and 1947, although the number of advertisements placed in 1947 did not yet reach the number published a decade before. Moreover, the Arabic advertisements placed lacked the creativity Boutagy's 1930s advertisements had exhibited; postwar advertisements were uniformly short, with text describing the radio set's technical qualities and availability and the seller's location and payment plan options, if any. Many advertisements were published with no product image—and those that had an image included only the set itself rather than a photograph of the set in a listening context or a more fanciful rendering of attributes such as the "magic brain" or "magic eye."

Although the Post Office continued to record a dramatic rise in the number of radio licenses, these reflected radio set purchases driven by something other than advertising. The number of licensed radio sets jumped from 58,604 at the end of 1945 to 86,667 in 1946—a 47.9 percent increase in only one year. The following year's increase, to 115,334, was almost as sizable—a 33.1 percent increase from 1946. Palestinians were buying radio sets as quickly as they came available, the effect of five years of pent-up demand. Radio set sellers seemed to realize that consumer desires required no prompting and wisely chose to save money on advertising. Before the war holiday-related radio set advertisements were a staple of both papers, leading to a sizable uptick duirng the summer holdiday seasons. However, the number of advertisements placed in both *Falastin* and the *Palestine Post* during fall 1947 was lower than the number placed in summer. From November to December *Falastin* published no radio set advertisements; the *Palestine Post* published only four. Regardless, radio sets continued to sell.

The situation worsened as the chaos surrounding the end of the mandate set in. *Falastin*'s erratic publication schedule, with the paper appearing on a semiregular basis in January–April 1948 and February–August 1949 and the rest of the time not at all, hints at the turmoil in the country. The local Arab economy largely shut down, with almost no advertisements appearing in the paper during these final months. As mandate Palestine collapsed in the warfare that ended with the creation of the state of Israel, those who did continue operations found conducting business increasingly difficult. In July 1948 Émile Boutagy wrote to the *Palestine Post* in response to an editorial promising law-abiding Arabs the full protection of the Israeli government and, at some point in the future, full citizenship.[81] "For one whole month now I have been trying to get some sort of pass or permission to visit my numerous clients and friends at Tel Aviv, as well as to salvage what is left of my branch at Jaffa," Boutagy wrote, adding that despite having met with numerous government officials he remained unable to gain access to either city.[82] While his willingness to take his business problems to the *Palestine Post* suggests a continuing faith that the newspaper's influential readers would recognize if not intervene to end the injustice done to an Arab writer, the Boutagys' business frustrations were mounting.

The Boutagy family endured the situation in the newly formed Israel for another year, protesting new laws like a luxury tax on refrigerators and a ban on the import of records and radio sets with arguments that focused on Israeli tastes, reflecting their acceptance of the new political reality. "Music to Israelis is an integral part of their existence," Émile

Boutagy wrote in a March 1949 letter to the new minister of finance that was published in the *Palestine Post*. "Statistics reveal that Israel is a bigger consumer of records and radios per individual than any other country in the world."[83] If the Boutagys were bothered by the rhetorical switch they made in order to accommodate the new national identity of their consumers, they did not indicate so publicly. Their concern was for the success of their business—which after 1948 relied increasingly on Israeli patronage.

Ultimately, however, and like many Arab Palestinian families, the Boutagys left Israel. Unlike many Arab Palestinians, however, who fled with little more than their lives under the direct threat of Israeli attacks, the Boutagys were able to choose the time and conditions of their departure. Nearly six hundred thousand Palestinians were made refugees outside the land of their birth, and few of those displaced thought that their departure would be permanent. Without disparaging the Boutagys and the few other, often elite families who chose to leave only after unsuccessfully attempting to reconstitute their mandate-era lives in postmandate Israel, it is worth considering whether their displacement was of the same order.

Different branches of the family went in different directions: Émile's son Toy went first to Amman and then to Beirut, where he built a new trading goods establishment headquartered on Patriarch Hoyek Street in the city's downtown.[84] Émile followed his son to Amman and remained there for the rest of his life. His brother Charles, who in June 1948 had been kidnapped from his hotel and held for interrogation by a group of armed Jews and subsequently arrested by the Israeli authorities on suspicion of black market trading, sold his hotel interests and moved his family to Australia in August 1949.[85] Charles's departure highlights the primary difference between the Boutagys' departure and that of most other Arab Palestinians. When his family left he put a notice in the *Palestine Post*'s "Social and Personal" section in order to "say goodbye to all his friends whom he could not contact personally."[86] Other siblings moved to the United States and Canada. With the departure of the Boutagys, whose 1930s HMV radio set advertisements evinced the greatest creativity with regard to selling consumers on the experiential benefits of radio, the last lingering traces of the mandate era's large-scale Arab merchant involvement in radio set sales and radio set selling disappeared. The possibility of coexistence in a Palestine that permitted both Jews and Arabs meaningful—even if uneven—participation in commercial, civic, and political life was no longer something in which even the Boutagys could believe.

From Urban Consumption to Rural Intervention

The radio set advertisements that peppered the pages of Palestine's Arabic- and English-language newspapers in the 1930s and 1940s were among the most common and most innovative advertisements of their day. They not only threw radio's double nature—as a broadcasting medium and as a symbolically rich commodity—into sharper relief but also pointed to the new listening practices developing around radio. These in turn fostered the emergence of various listening communities, oriented around language, work, gender, time of day, and—perhaps most crucially—broadcasting language. Advertisements supported these communities, adding an aspirational, middle-class element to radio listening and radio ownership. Radio sets were presented as entry-level, affordable luxury goods that communicated "modern" and "cosmopolitan" to friends and neighbors—and as a crucial part of a middle-class, urban Palestinian existence.

Yet many Palestinians lived in rural areas and villages. While radio set advertisements targeted urbanites, the mandate government targeted rural Palestinians, seeing radio broadcasts and radio sets as a vehicle for modernizing what they considered a backward population. Intervention seemed to government officials especially urgent in the midst of the Arab revolt, the strength of which lay primarily in Palestine's rural areas. As the mandate government tightened censorship controls over PBS broadcasting, it also reached out to rural listeners, hoping to both attract and influence them. But were government officials' suspicions well founded? And were their views of "peasant" listeners—as backward and susceptible to anti-British propaganda—accurate? The next chapter takes up their experiences.

CHAPTER 2

Peasants into Palestinians:
Rural and School Broadcasting

In the wake of the 1936 general strike, some in the Arab community viewed the PBS with suspicion. Listeners of all communities criticized the station for its censored news broadcasts—a censorship more stringent than that enforced on Palestinian newspapers or on the BBC's Arabic broadcasts. Yet Palestinians continued to tune in, and by 1938 the station was building a local audience. The willingness of prominent Palestinians to join the station administration—including the well-known poet and nationalist Ibrahim Tuqan, who served as its first Arabic section subdirector—contributed to its credibility as a local institution. Listeners were also attracted to the station by the local musicians, scholars, and community figures who appeared on air as guest artists and speakers. Although the news broadcasts were censored, they did provide some information—unavailable on other stations—on local developments. Arab Palestinians also tuned in to the PBS for government communiqués and situation updates and for updates on citrus and other commodity prices. Although the size of the listenership should not be exaggerated—it was still a small percentage of Palestine's Arab population—the increasing number of radio licenses throughout the late 1930s indicated that radio listening was growing at a steady and sustained rate.

However, British mandate officials grew increasingly concerned that the largest segment of Palestinian society, rural Palestinians, was not tuning in. In 1922, mandate statistics indicated, nearly 493,000 people, or approximately 76 percent of the total population, lived in rural parts of Palestine. Of these people, 452,000, according to the same statistics, were Muslim, with an additional 18,000 rural Christians.[1] By 1931 the rural population had risen to nearly 650,000, with 572,000 Muslims and 22,000 Christians living in rural areas. While urban areas had grown even faster, rural Palestinians still accounted for 67 percent of the total population. The numbers suggest the importance of rural areas for British development schemes as well as for achieving harmony between Palestinian Arab and Jewish communities.

After the 1929 riots the British mandate and home government had begun paying increasingly close attention to the "desperate position" of Arab peasants,[2] which they considered a cause of the riots. They saw Arab peasants as starved of land, victims of moneylenders' punitively high interest rates, and increasingly alienated from the modernization taking place in Palestine's urban areas and feared that these three factors would lead to further Arab-Jewish confrontations. After the Simpson report of 1930 the British mandate government began several initiatives designed to anchor rural Arabs to the land and to improve the quality and security of their lives. While much of their effort went into land tenure and agricultural education, they also turned to radio. These officials saw radio as a vehicle for bringing rural Arabs into the modern age through special programming on the PBS—programming that would also communicate a positive view of the British and their efforts in Palestine.

On the other hand, British mandate officials also feared that some rural Arabs *were* listening to radio—but to the "wrong" frequencies. During the mid- and late 1930s, British mandate and home government officials worried that rural Arabs were tuning in to the Arabic-language stations established by Italy and Germany. Officials worried that these broadcasts would worsen a situation already made difficult by the ongoing unrest of the Arab revolt—a revolt that continued in rural areas long after it was suppressed in Palestine's cities. Instead of cutting rural Palestinians' access to radio, they hoped to channel it into the safe, pro-government broadcasts of the PBS. This chapter looks at mandate government efforts to bring rural Palestine into the radio fold in a controlled and didactic manner. As a counterpoint, it examines contemporaneous Arabic-language radio advertisements targeting rural consumers and uses them to consider what the British government missed about rural Palestine and radio broadcasting.

Farming on the Air

The first extant mention of a radio station for Palestine is in a report published in 1930 in the wake of the 1929 uprisings. The British mandate and home governments appear to have ascribed these uprisings to what they came to call the "plight of the fellahin":[3] the recent low crop yields and resulting severe indebtedness to moneylenders, coupled with reduced plot sizes thanks to a wave of land sales to Zionists in the mid- and late 1920s, of which the sale of the Sursock estates was perhaps the best known.[4] These hardships led increasing numbers of peasant farmers to seek employment and residence in Palestine's urban areas and caused desperation and discontent among those who remained on the land.

In response the British mandate government began enacting and revising a series of laws designed to protect Arab Palestinian farmers, for example, the Land Disputes Possession Ordinance of 1933 and the Protection of Cultivators Ordinances of 1929, 1931, 1933, and 1936. They also attempted to resettle Arab peasants made landless by the sale of the lands they had farmed, although this seems to have been an almost entirely unsuccessful project.[5] The British home government became involved as well, through its commissioning of two reports: the famous Simpson report of October 1930 and the less well known report issued earlier that fall by C. F. Strickland, a recently retired civil servant who had spent his working life in British India. Both addressed the situation of Arab peasants (whom they invariably called fellah), and both proved influential in guiding British mandate policy regarding rural Arabs in the 1930s.

John Hope Simpson's report was a broad survey that sought to explain Palestine's recent unrest by considering three areas: Jewish immigration, Arab land settlement, and the development of Palestine's rural and industrial sectors. Simpson devoted a full section to the "position of the fellah" and described them as being in dire straits. "Evidence from every possible source tends to support the conclusion that the Arab fellah cultivator is in a desperate position," Simpson concluded. "He has no capital for his farm. He is, on the contrary, heavily in debt. His rent is rising, he has to pay very heavy taxes, and the rate of interest on his loans is incredibly high."[6] These twin themes of desperation and debt continued through the report, with Simpson describing the farmer's life as "one of great struggle and privation."[7] Yet he also took pains to clarify that "the fellah is neither lazy nor unintelligent." The position of Arab farmers was desperate not because of their own shortcomings but because they were held back by three interconnected external forces: a lack of education that prevented them from learning about scientific farming methods, a taxation and moneylending system that kept them from accruing enough capital to invest in more modern farm equipment, and plot sizes shrunk through land sales intended to pay taxes or debts owed.[8]

To ameliorate the position of Palestine's Arab peasants, Simpson proposed an improved and expanded rural education system, a reduction in government taxes, resettlement of landless peasants, cooperation between the Jewish and Arab communities for development, and limitations on Jewish immigration. In one sentence that more than any other may have doomed his report to the controversy and rejection it (and the concurrently issued Passfield White Paper) ultimately faced, Simpson concluded that "there is at the present time and with the present methods of Arab cultivation no margin of land available for agricultural settlement by new immigrants, with the exception of such undeveloped land as the various Jewish Agencies hold in reserve."[9] The Simpson report was shelved and its view on immigration and the Palestine government's "duty to . . . look upon the country as one unit" rather than consider the welfare of the Yishuv in isolation was ignored. However, the Simpson report laid out a number of concerns about the straitened circumstances of rural Arab Palestinians that informed mandate officials' view of them—and influenced the mandate government's interventions in their lives.

Simpson's report, although broader in scope than Strickland's, overlapped with the latter's in several ways. The text of each report refers to the other, and the two reached similar conclusions regarding the crippling effects of indebtedness on the rural Arab population's capacity to withstand either government taxes or their shrinking plots. The heart of Strickland's report was a proposal to create a system of cooperative agricultural societies by which Arab farmers could obtain credit for investment purposes—new plows, larger plots—rather than to pay the interest on their existing debts. Strickland's report considered the financial, educational, and societal circumstances in which most Arab farmers lived. It included detailed suggestions regarding cooperative societies, debt relief initiatives, and marketing programs—all tightly focused on agricultural concerns.

Strickland's report also reflected his tendency to see Palestine through the lens of his experiences in the Punjab. "The Arab cultivator of Palestine is a man similar in temperament, standard of life and agricultural practices to many of the Muslim cultivators with whose conditions I have been familiar in the north-west of India," he wrote. Like Simpson, however, Strickland considered Arab farmers' handicap to be the debt they labored under: how could they focus on current events or education when their primary concern was their indebtedness? In other words, he attributed what he saw as their backwardness to their situation and not to any lack of intelligence or capability. Instead, as with the farmers of northern India, Strickland appeared to see in them a certain nobility.[10] His report described in almost anthropological detail the organization and functioning of societies like that of rural Palestine, but in his conclusion he turned to a new subject: Arab farmers' decision to leave their farms and migrate to urban areas, a decision born of desperation.

Yet Strickland's final proposal had nothing to do with cooperative societies and little to do with agricultural reform. Hoping to tap into what he described as the "very acute intelligence" of the Arab farmer,[11] he advocated using technology to connect rural Arabs to their urban brethren. In short, he suggested radio. A government-owned radio station, he argued, could provide education and entertainment to farmers and their families while they still remained in the village. In making this suggestion, he again drew on his experiences in India, where British colonial officials had been trying to use radio broadcasting as a rural development tool since the late 1920s. There, officials tried to implement village broadcasting or "community listening" schemes, first envisioned as separate broadcasting stations dedicated to rural programming and later reconfigured as daily or semiweekly "talks to farmers" programs on All-India Radio.[12]

Strickland argued that a radio station in Palestine could do similar work. Broadcasts would expose Palestine's farmers to the modern farming methods they needed to improve their lives while neutralizing whatever pull Palestine's cities were having on rural communities. "My final recommendation," he said,

> is that if possible a public utility company be formed under the partial control of Government . . . for the broadcasting of news in Arabic throughout the villages in Palestine. The Arab is an intelligent man but frequently illiterate. His ideas are subject to perversion by biased or inflammatory news. I should like to see a receiving set and loud speaker owned or leased by the village as a whole, installed in the village meeting house and kept in order by the touring staff of the broadcasting company.

Who would pay for this project? Strickland suggested that the villagers themselves would be willing to underwrite the cost if the programming were sufficiently appealing.

> I find it incredible, though I have been frequently assured, that an Arab village will not subscribe for the maintenance of such an installation at

a moderate figure. The news supplied should of course not merely be Government statements or instructive material. General news which at present reaches the village in a distorted form could thus be supplied in a true form; there should also be amusing matter, music and other entertainment. The idea may be novel, but I am convinced that the great lack of rural life throughout the world is the lack of novelty and variety in interests. The effect would not be immediate, but I do not doubt that in the end Government would be well repaid both financially and from many more important points of view.

While Strickland here appeared to offer a positive view of rural Arabs, he cautioned against giving them full control of the set that they might purchase, again drawing on his experience in India. "The receivers for communal use might be of the special kind contemplated . . . for Indian villages," he noted, "fixed to receive on a single wavelength only." Only by limiting rural Palestinians' access to radio broadcasting to a British government station could Strickland conceive of it as a public good.[13]

While Simpson's report had been heavily criticized by the Yishuv and by Zionist supporters in Britain, Strickland's proposal for a government-owned radio station aimed at rural Arabs received enthusiastic support from Palestine's English-language newspaper, the *Palestine Post*. The *Palestine Post* was Zionist in outlook; however, because of its language it was read by the British community in Palestine as well as English-speaking Arabs and hence might be considered the period's newspaper of record. The paper's support was constant and longlasting: it faithfully covered each of Strickland's many public appearances and reprinted many of his talks almost word for word, providing a platform for his views and endorsing them to Palestine's elite, English-speaking communities.[14] In March 1933, for example, the *Palestine Post* covered a speech that Strickland gave on the subject to the Jerusalem Rotary Club. He categorized the virtues of rural broadcasting as follows: it would be an efficacious ("Broadcasting would provide a means of access to illiterates, superior to any other"), humanitarian ("It would change the outlook of the cultivator, improve his condition, and would supplement the work of [Government] departments in the betterment of his health, his education, and his agricultural methods"), and politic ("[It] would be a most useful organ . . . whenever there was need to explain some cause of friction in the country") instrument for moral and effective governance of the rural Arab population.

In July the paper reprinted in full an article Strickland had written for the British radio aficionados' journal *World Radio*; the *Palestine Post* agreed with his characterization of the Holy Land as a site of increasingly sharp contrasts between modern and medieval, haves and have-nots. Calling village broadcasts a "much needed service to rural Arabs," Strickland argued that the visible disparities between the primarily urban Jewish population and the largely rural Arab population would lead to rural depopulation and urban proletarianization if steps were not taken to bridge the "widening" gap while also contenting young rural Arabs with country life. He explained to readers that "the population of the Holy Land exhibits to a visitor the widest differences of economic level and social outlook." Presenting Jews and Arab Palestinians as almost polar opposites, he described the first as urban and advanced, the second as rural and old-fashioned, and neither as much engaged with the other. "The busy Jew of Jerusalem and Tel Aviv," he wrote,

> brushes past the slower, but acutely conscious, Arab of the towns; the industrious and scientific cultivator of the Jewish settlements amazes and irritates the puzzled peasant of the Arab villages. The gap is widening, and tension is not growing less. . . . The great majority of the Arabs dwell in villages, engaged in a primitive cultivation, indebted to local Arab merchants, maintaining an Oriental standard of life and Oriental customs. Schoolmasters, health officers, agricultural experts strive to teach them, but the limited budget of the country cannot provide such men in sufficient number to overtake the distance between Arab backwardness and the rapid Jewish advances. Arab women in particular are inaccessible, and without the women it is useless to teach the men. The younger folk become discontented, wander away to the towns, and leave the villages to boredom and decay.[15]

The picture that Strickland painted was gloomy; the situation of Arabs sounded dire and almost impossible to alter. Yet Strickland's point was that the government must work to improve things for Palestinian Arabs. If the mandate government's previous initiatives had failed, it must try something different to ameliorate Arab "backwardness."

Although Strickland died the following year, his vision of paternalistic, rural-focused outreach lived on in British home and mandate government conceptions of radio broadcasting in Palestine as well as in the pages of the *Palestine Post*. By 1935 the station was under construction and various constituencies were laying claim to its operation. Criticizing the mandate government for keeping mum about the station's broadcasting program, the *Palestine Post* in early July 1935 noted that "[it] was the late Mr. Strickland's hope that village radios, tuned in [to] a Government broadcast, would enable the fellahin to shed many superstitions, prejudices, and false rumors. Who will take charge of this important aspect of the station?"[16] The British mandate government responded almost immediately, by issuing a communiqué published in the official gazette and reprinted in most local newspapers. After touching on a number of station and broadcasting issues, the communiqué closed with a paragraph on "loud speakers for villages":

> His Excellency the High Commissioner is particularly anxious that the benefits of broadcasting shall be enjoyed by the rural, as well as by the urban population and is therefore arranging for the experimental installation of loud speakers of special design at 100 villages and settlements. The programmes of the Jerusalem station will contain items (e.g., short talks on agriculture, education, health, etc.) intended to be of practical value to rural listeners. [17]

The communiqué followed both the spirit and the letter of Strickland's recommendations. The new Palestine Broadcasting Service would include regular programming aimed at rural Arab Palestinians; the mandate government would facilitate their access to the PBS by providing village radio sets. From the moment of its conception the urban institution of Palestine broadcasting had a heavy rural component.

The PBS and Its "Talks to Farmers"

The British mandate government's approach to rural broadcasting was heavily influenced by its view of rural Arab Palestinians as peasants whose lives followed a timeless traditional pattern. British officials understood these fellahin, a word they were quick to adopt and employ, as Palestine's oppressed underclass. They considered the fellahin peasants stuck in medieval times, politically exploited by traditional elites, set upon by greedy moneylenders, and falling ever more behind as the Yishuv's modern agricultural settlements brought cheaper and more abundant produce to market. The last was closest to the truth. As Ylana Miller notes, "By the early thirties . . . the internal pressure of population growth and land sales, combined with the attraction of a monetary income, had led some villagers to look for at least temporary work in the cities."[18] The combination of changes in farming practices and the shift to a monetized economy, coupled with ongoing political and social changes, had deeply disrupted the fabric of rural Palestine. With European politics growing increasingly heated, British home and mandate government officials worried that Palestine's Arab farmers, whether those still on the farm or those who had relocated to urban areas, could be mobilized by domestic or German/Italian propaganda into a destabilizing force. If so, they might escalate the situation in Palestine, at a time when local resources were stretched thin by the effort to control the Arab revolt. This would require the commitment of British troops and money at a time when both the British home government and its mandate government in Palestine felt less and less capable of providing either.

Whether the British were correct in their concerns about radio broadcasts' ability to spark peasant uprisings is debatable. However, the intensity of their fear is discernible in their commitment to initiatives intended to mitigate what British officials saw as a rural threat. The mandate government devised several programs, which might be broadly divided into two categories: social welfare and education. The government's rural broadcasting and radio set distribution initiatives fell within this second category, as did its investments in public schooling and training programs. The British mandate government viewed education as the necessary prerequisite to the social reform and transformation of Arab Palestinian society that it sought. Consequently, it promoted education and curricula that improved the lives of those in each social class while reinforcing the classes themselves. The operative notion of "appropriate" education reflected a paternalistic type of "don't fill their heads with nonsense" view, one that infantilized rural Palestinians by considering them either dangerous or ineducable. As Ellen Fleischmann explains:

> Although purportedly interested in "improving" the lives of peasants and the less affluent Palestinians, the British were alarmed about the prospect and inherent "danger" of class transformations and social mobility. As part of their strategy to stall that likelihood and process, they utilized educational policy. Its keynote was the development of a two-tiered approach to the educational system in which the rural population received a distinctly different kind of education than did the peoples of the cities or towns. The system was geared toward keeping the social classes in their place.[19]

Miller's study of rural Palestine's relations with the British mandate government reaches similar conclusions. In her view mandate government officials engaged in a quixotic quest to preserve "traditional values" and patterns of life—"quixotic," because by the 1930s both had already been irrevocably altered. [20]

Rather than provide broad training in machine and other advanced technology, British educational efforts for rural Palestinians focused on literacy and small-scale improvements to existing farming and animal husbandry practices. These efforts ignored the very real socioeconomic strains coming to the fore in rural Arab Palestine in the mid- and late 1930s—the product of land sales, population growth, and changing economic and political circumstances brought about by the 1936 revolt and longer term factors.[21] Mandate government involvement in rural Palestine increased throughout the decade, though scholars have concluded that its efforts did not meet with great success. It could neither "bring significant economic relief nor . . . effectively control the growth of industry, the expansion of the market in land, or the development of large-scale, intensive agriculture. Instead, local officials worked to protect villagers against the necessity, and perhaps the desire, to alter received patterns of existence,"[22] which they did through education intended as much to buffer rural Palestinians against societal change as to acclimate them to it. Such was the vision that informed the mandate government's rural broadcasting efforts.

Programming

The Palestine mandate government's broadcasting initiatives were based on five assumptions. First, the British home and mandate government officials defined rural Arab Palestinian radio listening as an activity done in a large group. They perceived the rural Arab Palestinian listener as a man—despite recurrent statements that the only way to reach the Arab family or to change Arab society was through "the Arab woman"—who listened to radio in public and in a crowd. This contrasted with British listening practices. In Britain listening was largely an individual or small-group activity; statistics put the average number of listeners per set at two or three, most of whom listened at home. While some people may have listened in pubs or restaurants, the standard of British radio listening was that it was a largely private, domestic activity, with people listening to radio sets at work or at home. (The situation was similar in the United States: Susan Douglas notes, "People certainly listened to radio by themselves in the 1930s and 40s, but especially during the early hours, radio listening was largely a family affair.")[23]

To British officials, this way of listening was normal, engaging with all the associations that normalcy implied: urban, modern, civilized. Consequently, consular officials, Colonial Office staff, and mandate government bureaucrats alike viewed "the Arab masses'" practice of listening to radios in cafés and other public gathering places with condescension. (They might have been surprised to learn that in France, Italy, and other European countries group listening practices were the norm, not the exception, with the average number of listeners per set numbering five or more.) They also viewed it with suspicion. Although the government's rural broadcasting initiatives relied on large-group listening (supplying individual families with free radio sets would have been too expensive), officials' views remained colored by the assumption that "proper" radio listening was an intimate, domestic affair. Communal village listening appeared at once backward and threatening; the group's capacity to become a crowd, or even a mob, meant that what was broadcast required careful government scrutiny.

Second, the British mandate government understood the PBS's rural programming as a discrete category: rural folk would listen to these programs; urban folk, to the rest of the station's broadcasts. No overlap was envisioned: urban Arab Palestinians would be bored by the simpler rural programming, while rural Palestinians listening to urban programs would be frightened or—worse—alienated by the modern music and sophisticated language.

This second assumption influenced the rest. Third, the hours for rural broadcasts were different because the government understood that rural Palestinians followed the circadian rhythms of a world without electricity. The news broadcasts for these "country Arabs"[24] were scheduled in the early evening, around 7 o'clock; those for urbanites were scheduled a few hours later. Fourth, government officials agonized over the appropriate level and quality of Arabic appropriate for these broadcasts. Their anxieties centered on the news broadcasts—the most critical programming because it offered the best chance of giving the British view. They wondered how well rural Palestinians could comprehend standard Arabic, if at all, and if not, how to "translate" the formal Arabic in which news broadcasts were written into the colloquial spoken form. A Colonial Office memo described the process, and the problems, as follows:

The bulletins are compiled and edited by the English news-editor, under the general supervision of the Director of Programs, and are then translated into Arabic. The translation into Arabic, and also the subsequent delivery at the microphone, have been a source of considerable difficulty because a) men who can translate accurately at high speed are rare, b) there is no calligraphy for colloquial Arabic, and therefore c) the translations have to be made in what may be described as good journalistic Arabic and have to be more or less paraphrased into colloquial Arabic during delivery by the announcer at the microphone. A special technique for this difficult operation is gradually being perfected, and the type of Arabic speech used is such as to be acceptable to, and clearly intelligible by, the majority of Arabic-speaking peoples in the Near and Middle East.[25]

How well this worked—and how much language engineering rural Palestinians required—was not clear. By mid-1938 High Commissioner Wauchope appeared satisfied with the broadcasts' linguistic progress: "by dint of continually emphasizing the need for a simpler speech in these programs and through the able assistance of the Chief Arabic Translator in the Chief Secretary's Office, the Director of Programs has now been able to make his news and his talks understood and popular." [26]

Anecdotal evidence suggests that this progress may not have been sufficient. An oral history interview conducted (for other purposes) in the late 1990s with a resident of a village called ʿArrarah described village listening in the 1940s. A community set had been installed in the house of one of the village's "educated people." "Men would come after work to his private *diwan* [parlor or formal living room for receiving guests] to listen. He would [turn it on] for the news and when the broadcasting was over he would turn off the radio and 'translate' the news into a more comprehensible language."[27] It could be that this audience was listening to the later evening news broadcast—the one with language and topics meant for urban listeners with a greater command of formal Arabic. Given that the village appears to have been the recipient of a community listening set, the "educated man" may have received government encouragement to host listening sessions during rural broadcasting hours. If this was so and villagers still requested "translations" of the broadcasts, the language register used for these broadcasts was still too abstruse for rural Arab Palestinians. (If on the other hand these villagers were listening to the later news broadcasts, government officials' assumptions about the hours villagers kept and their willingness to restrict their listening to "their" broadcasting programs were equally in error.)

Fifth, the PBS's rural broadcasts were programming with a purpose. Although the mandate government divided them into "three categories—a) entertainment, b) information and c) education,"[28] all were intended to serve a larger purpose: to educate and integrate rural Palestinians into the modern world—a world overseen by benevolent British mandatory officials. The news and talks to farmers broadcasts met these goals, in part by adding musical and other entertainment as buffers and enticers. The entertainment programming was intended to draw rural listeners to "their" programming, with music and talks designed to appeal to what British officials understood to be rural tastes. (By bookending these "core" programs with entertainment, they also protected listeners from the PBS's urban programming.)

An undated 1937 or 1938 mandate government memo outlined the officials' understanding of what should fill these three categories for the PBS's rural broadcasting program. Entertainment, it stated, "naturally occupies the greater proportion of time"—an interesting assertion given the minimal role it played in the rural broadcasts' "educate and elevate" objective. This memo took a rather positive view of rural listeners' ability to adapt to modern, urban culture. While current entertainment was composed of "oriental music of a type acceptable to rural listeners," the latter were understood to "gradually acquire fresh tastes as more . . . material is put before them." Rather than treat them as sui generis, the memo focused on the universality of their response: "In their own stage of development they react just as any other people do, liking best what they already know, but learning to appreciate what has hitherto never come their way." [29]

The memo continued with a list of "considerations" that had been taken into account when developing the rural broadcasts' entertainment programming:

> Short items are preferable to long ones.
>   Villagers are often sensitive in that they do not appreciate criticism of themselves, even if this is presented in a humorous way.
>   Most agriculturalists have a preference for religious items such as recitations from the Quran.
>   They dislike any literary dialect.
>   They are conservative in their tastes.

They prefer men rather than women artists.

They prefer soloists rather than concerted items.

They are very critical of the slightest mistake or inaccuracy either on the part of announcers or artists.

Most village artists are shy of applying for auditions, and so they have to be searched out. It is essential to choose them from many different villages, and therefore, so far as finance permits, the Broadcasting Service often has to select a totally untrained person from a village and train him. . . .

Story telling, accompanied by rural music, is popular.

Folk-songs are always appreciated, and so are unsophisticated variety programs.

Occasionally villagers like to hear well known singers and monologists of the more sophisticated type, although they would not like these as part of their daily program.[30]

From this matrix of likes and dislikes the mandate government oversaw the creation of an entire array of rural entertainment programs.

The memo also commented on the talks broadcast on the radio station, which covered "useful" topics ranging from community organization to personal care and stood in an equally didactic position vis-à-vis rural Arab Palestinian listeners. The level and quality of Arabic used in these talks were carefully considered: "In preparing talks for rural listeners the mentality and the way of life of villagers is borne in mind. Very simple language is used, and ideas are simplified as much as possible."[31] While the PBS's urban broadcasts covered a wide range of genres, from history to ethics, literature to politics, whose subjects had little immediate practical utility, talks given during the rural broadcasts were almost entirely practical. The memo noted:

Talks are given on the advantages of cooperation and cooperative societies, on elementary hygiene by qualified doctors, and stories are adapted from the Arabian Nights and similar books. One Children's Hour a week is usually of a type suited to rural listeners and is directed by an educated village lady who is experienced in children's work. Perhaps the most popular talk is that known as the "Madafa" [guest house] talk in which the character of an intelligent countryman has been created to conduct the village guest-house assembly each week. Every sort of constructive, practical, and useful subject is discussed both by the guests and the host.[32]

If a constant flow of talks on "every sort of constructive, practical, and useful subject" did not entice villagers to turn on and tune in, the talks to farmers—which covered such topics as manure fertilizer, particular citrus farming techniques, and crop rotation—might have done little more. The memo noted that the talks "have been subject to the defect that they have had to be written by specialists in the Department of Agriculture who know nothing of broadcasting technique." It further observed that "the talks often have to be delivered by people unknown to the farmers."

The assumption that farmers would neither be interested in hearing nor willing to follow the advice of strangers was indicative of government officials' views of rural Arab Palestinians as clannishly suspicious of outsiders and unknown new ways. Rather than dismiss their suspicions as backward or unsupportable, it appears that the director of agriculture recommended changing the department's style in favor of better (more listenable) broadcasts and greater audience participation. He suggested that "the men [from the Department of Agriculture] giving the talks could follow them up by visiting the villages and establishing contact with the listeners." The director requested that the department's agricultural experts work closely with the PBS's director of programs to ensure that their talks were satisfying as broadcasts, as well as vehicles for conveying valuable information. He also proposed developing a "farmer's corner" broadcasting program, in which farmers would read their questions on air and department representatives would answer in colloquial Arabic.

The goal of such a program would have been to create a dialogue between the two communities, bringing rural Arab Palestinians to the table as partners in an ongoing conversation in which both sides were understood to have valid questions and contributions.[33] However, it does not appear that this proposal was ever realized; at least, no record of such a program exists in the PBS program schedules. The reason may have lain more in late 1930s' radio broadcasting's technical restraints, as what were then called "outside broadcasts" were relatively cumbersome to orchestrate and markedly more expensive than studio broadcasts. In any case, its absence meant that the Department of Agriculture's broadcasts on the PBS remained more didactic than collegial, resembling formal lectures more than radio talks.

The PBS's educational programs for rural listeners fit in the broader context of the station's general educational programming. Its school broadcasts varied considerably over the life of the station; at times no broadcasts were offered, although the Children's Hours, which aired consistently, did target school-aged children. The director of education for Palestine, Humphrey Bowman, was deeply sympathetic to Arab Palestinians and particularly concerned to improve the educational life of the rural populations. While he appears to have doubted the capacity of radio broadcasts to serve as educational vehicles for schoolchildren, he supported the PBS's rural broadcasts unreservedly, for the practical instruction and entertainment they provided. His hesitation stemmed from the passivity of radio listening: "it is a principle of all effective instruction that it should require practical activity and response on the part of the pupil." In his view radio broadcasting would only become an effective educator if a trained professional were overseeing the broadcasts and equally trained teachers oversaw the reception and related activities by students in Palestine's classrooms.

Yet in a 1939 article, "Rural Education in the Near and Middle East," Bowman praised the mandate government's rural-oriented radio broadcasting and its radio set distribution scheme. Describing radio as "of great value" for both rural Arabs and Jews in Palestine, he explained that the government sets were housed in village schools (rather than the guest houses or mukhtar's home, as government documents indicated), where they were "available both for school use and for all who care to listen." Again, though, he praised the rural broadcasts generally rather than any specifically educational program put on by the station: "The Arabic programme, lasting an hour or so daily, given at a suitable time soon after sunset, contains a variety of items—news, songs, music, talks—and is widely popular."[34] Bowman also wrote not as someone involved in producing these broadcasts but as an educator working to achieve similar goals by different means. Although the PBS's rural broadcasts were intended to be educational, their target audience was composed of adult male farmers. Agricultural experts, not educators, were those whose advice the mandate government sought.

Bowman might have recognized that a different type of education was taking place via the aspects of the PBS's rural programming he found worthy of praise. The talks to farmers and other broadcasts provided practical training, but they also did—or at least could have done—something more. Radio educates, but like education itself, its "curriculum" is broader than the precise subjects it covers. Much as Foucault's investigations into disciplinary power demonstrated how schooling children educates them into patterns of civic behavior and norms of sociality, the PBS's rural radio programs were also vehicles

for teaching citizenship. By providing rural Arab Palestinians with mediated access to the modern world, these broadcasts could have served
to knit them more firmly into the national body of mandate Palestine.
That they did not reflected the ways in which the mandate government
officials involved in the PBS's rural broadcasts misunderstood the rural
Arab Palestinian listening audience.

The sensibilities that the "Rural Programs for Arab Listeners" memo
identified as those that the PBS rural broadcasts had taken into account, as well as its listing of subjects deemed appropriate for rural audiences, indicate that rural Palestinians showed little interest in the talks
to farmers and other "rural" programming. In his work on mandate
Palestine's rural economy, Amos Nadan cites a 1939 Gaza Subdistrict
officer's report that in the three villages with government radio sets,
an average of only thirty-seven people attended each week's talk.[35] This
was a minimal return on the costly and time-consuming investment
that was the village radio set program—especially given the difficult
political context of the late 1930s. The PBS's rural Arabic broadcasting became caught up in a larger issue—that of British home government fears of anti-British Arabic broadcasting from Italy and Germany.
These fears led the British home government to increase the PBS's Arabic news broadcasts and to begin broadcasting Arabic news on short-
wave via the BBC—developments that in turn affected the PBS and its
rural Arabic broadcasts.

Radio Bari and the Formation of the BBC Arabic Service

By the end of 1936 the British government in London was beginning to
express an interest in exercising more direct control over the PBS—an
interest sparked by shifts in the political winds of Europe. The British
home government's concern about European politics' impact on Britain's role in Palestine, which would fully intersect with PBS broadcasts
in 1938, was first evident in 1935, when the House of Commons began discussing Italian radio broadcasts to Arabs in Palestine and Trans-
Jordan.

On Friday, October 25, 1935, the *Times of London* published its
usual report on Thursday's House of Commons discussion, which had
reflected members' increasing distress at Britain's tense relations with Italy. The consequence of the new antagonism between them was an Ital-

ian campaign to attack Britain in its most vulnerable spots: its mandate territories. Captain MacDonald, MP from the Isle of Wight, inquired whether the Colonial Office was aware that the Italian government was broadcasting anti-British propaganda in Arabic to Palestine and Trans-Jordan. He requested copies of these broadcasts and assurance that the Colonial Office was responding "appropriately," suggesting that his fellow MPs recognized what a nightmare a propaganda-fueled insurrection in Palestine would be, given Britain's then-limited military presence in the Levant. In response, Southby at the Treasury assured MacDonald that the colonial secretary had taken steps to address the problem through diplomatic channels: "[His] attention has been called to certain statements broadcast in Arabic by the Italian station 'Radio Bari,' and copies of the reported text . . . have been communicated to him. He understands that the matter has been brought to the notice of his Excellency the Italian Ambassador." In conclusion Southby noted that "[it] may be added that the arrangements for the Government of Palestine's own broadcast service are now almost complete, and that this will be operating in the near future."[36]

In other words, the government was responding on two levels: by raising the matter with Italy's ambassador to Britain and by readying a counterforce in the form of a Britain-friendly Palestine broadcasting station. This response marked the beginning of several years of active and often anxious collaboration among the Colonial Office, the Foreign Office, the Palestine government, and the BBC to address the anti-British hostilities of Palestine's various communities, which—for Arabic speakers at least—they considered likely to be heightened by Radio Bari's vitriolic broadcasts. Their concerns were reflected in government memos and in parliamentary discussions back in London: the specter of Italian propaganda loomed large in the British imperial mind.

Alarm at Bari's potential for inciting Arab Palestinians to rebellion reflected 1930s understandings of the power of radio. Government bureaucrats around the world feared radio propaganda as a threat that they could not see, could not censor, and could not block: in short, a force that they could not control. While concrete examples of successful radio propaganda were few, the fears remained. For British officials in London, those fears coalesced around the broadcasts of Radio Bari and the idea that Bari's broadcasts could further alienate Arab Palestinians, worsening the dangers of the Arab revolt. (Despite its concerns, the British government appeared to have no concrete evidence of Bari inspiring or intensifying the revolt.) The British government's capacity to respond to these broadcasts via the PBS, however, was complicated by its limited powers as a mandatory authority. Any action that appeared to serve Britain's interest, rather than Palestine's, might raise the ire of the Permanent Mandates Commission, which could lead to fines. Countering Radio Bari's propaganda with PBS broadcasting was not a simple matter.

British relations with Italy had begun deteriorating in the early 1930s, when the Italian government began attempting to extend its influence beyond Italy's borders. In March 1934 the Italian government inaugurated Arabic-language news and entertainment programming on its medium-wave station at Bari. These broadcasts aired throughout the region, from North Africa to the Gulf—reaching not only Italian Libya but the various British and French colonies and mandate territories as well. Callum MacDonald has suggested that these broadcasts were

> not at first directly anti-British. They consisted of cultural propaganda which attempted to increase Italian influence in the Middle East by praising Italy and the Fascist system. . . . This cultivation of Arab opinion had two main aims. The first was to restore Italian prestige in the Arab world which had been damaged by the Senussi massacres during the recent reconquest of Cyrenaica. The second was to register Italian interest in an area [the Levant] from which Italy felt unfairly excluded by Britain and France.[37]

However, Britain responded to Italy's invasion of Abyssinia in October 1935 with sanctions and harsh criticism, and Bari's tone soon changed. Arabic-language broadcasts now attacked Britain as an imperialist power, encouraging local populations to rebel, and lauded Italy as a champion of Arab self-determination. "The aim of such violent assaults was to whip up Arab nationalism and create problems for Britain in the Middle East on the assumption that if British troops were tied down in security duties they would be unavailable for use against Italy."[38] Palestine, Trans-Jordan, and Egypt, whose populations already chafed under the British yoke, were an ideal audience.

Despite awareness of these broadcasts, the British government was slow to formulate an effective response. Concern over anti-British broadcasting continued throughout 1937, as reports of Bari's broadcasts attracted ongoing parliamentary—and thus media—attention. On March 9, 1937, the *Times* reported that House of Commons debates included one MP's query regarding anti-British broadcasting aimed at

Palestine that was rumored to be emanating from Egypt. In response, the undersecretary said that "no broadcasting in Arabic for Palestine of an undesirable nature is known to have taken place from any station in Egypt."[39] Broadcasts of "an undesirable nature" were regularly appearing on Radio Bari, though, with nothing more than Britain's weak diplomatic protests to deter them.

Additional discussions in Parliament appeared throughout the spring and early summer, with MPs continually requesting that appropriate measures be taken to silence or counter Radio Bari and the Foreign Office continually assuring them of its diplomatic successes in obtaining the Italian government's promises to moderate Bari's tone. In addition, readers' letters and editorials published in the *Times* indicate that the paper and its influential readership had taken up the issue. Although a November 4, 1937, report in the *Times* quoted a Foreign Office representative as stating that since June "it has not been considered necessary to make any representations to the Italian government on press or broadcast questions,"[40] the issue was still being raised in Parliament and in *Times* editorials in December. By then, however, the British government had abandoned diplomacy in favor of counter-broadcasting. Its plan was twofold: medium-wave Arabic news broadcasts on the PBS and short-wave Arabic broadcasts on the BBC's new World Service.

BBC Arabic

The BBC Arabic program had been jointly developed by BBC staff and Foreign Office officials, a decision made after much debate within the BBC regarding the value and appropriateness of its expansion into foreign-language broadcasting.[41] BBC administrators worried that such broadcasts would be seen as propaganda, damaging its credibility with British and overseas listeners. It worried that Foreign Office interest in the content of BBC foreign-language news broadcasts would compromise its independence and render it a less than impartial news source. Numerous meetings, memoranda, and agreements (written and verbal) addressing broadcasting independence, personnel, and financing were required before the BBC agreed to introduce what would ultimately become its World Service.

BBC concerns were not unfounded: the service was intended to counter anti-British propaganda by providing fair, if British-friendly, news to audiences around the world. Consequently, the service was not inaugurated for all languages—just those of the "hot" regions, the

Middle East and North Africa. To allay Italian suspicions (which, while justified, would have led to unpleasant diplomatic confrontations) that the new service was primarily aimed at Arabic-speaking audiences already receiving Bari's broadcasts, a BBC Spanish program, directed at Latin America, was begun at the same time. Dispelling BBC fears that the new service would be castigated as propaganda, it instead received a warm reception in Britain. The *Times* issued a glowing editorial, declaring that "[the British] public will give the same warm welcome as was given in the House of Commons" to BBC foreign-language broadcasts and emphasizing that these would laudably provide "straight news" to regions of the world beset by propaganda.[42] The warm welcome was partly due to increased public awareness of Bari's broadcasts, which continued their daily attacks on British presence in the Middle East. Until the BBC service could begin operations in early 1938, Foreign Office officials, apprehensive that Italian propaganda might further inflame tensions in Palestine, sought an interim solution. They found it in Jerusalem.

On August 6, 1937, the Colonial Office's undersecretary of state wrote to the Palestine High Commissioner, proposing to use PBS Arabic news broadcasts to attract listeners around the region. The PBS and Bari both broadcast on medium wave, so listeners with medium-wave sets would be able to easily switch from Bari to Jerusalem. (Medium-wave sets were less expensive and generally considered more popular than short-wave sets.) The PBS had been on the air for just over a year; Egyptian State Broadcasting was older and had a larger audience. However, the situation had changed in Egypt since 1934, and the Colonial Office felt that its efforts to influence the Cairo station would anger Egyptian authorities already sensitive to British government influence. To provide the PBS with Arab world news to fill its extended news broadcasts, the undersecretary proposed attaching an Arabist to the Foreign Office's news division. He would follow the anti-British wireless broadcasts from Bari and other hostile stations, collect relevant news items, and draft bulletins for translation and broadcast in Palestine. However, the undersecretary noted that use of the Jerusalem station was a temporary solution and that for the Colonial Office the ultimate goal remained Arabic-language news broadcasts from British territory.[43] Broadcasting from Britain would allow the Colonial Office greater latitude in terms of the topics covered and the degree of "British view" expressed than broadcasting from Palestine.

Several additional British memoranda followed, laying out three key elements of the planned news broadcasts: two reflecting ongoing government debates and one a relatively short-term issue. First, they focused on news broadcasting, rather than entertainment, as the way to win listeners. An August 28, 1937, memo, headed "Special Arabic Broadcast News Service," argued that the service needed to attract an audience beyond Palestine. "The idea . . . is to attract the Arab listening world to the Jerusalem program [by] virtue of its outstanding Arab news service and of its general and political interest." The memo envisioned two primary audiences among Arab listeners: an educated, urban intelligentsia and the less sophisticated "fellahin and village folk." It believed that these listeners were not interested in the Europe-oriented bulletins provided by Reuters and other international news agencies but hungered for detailed reportage on events occurring in the region. Listeners *would* tune in to the PBS if it offered fast, accurate, and comprehensive news broadcasts covering news that mattered to them. This, the memo suggested, would be a double victory for the British government. It would keep listeners from being exposed to Bari's anti-British propaganda, and it would allow listeners to develop a positive view of Britain and its role in the Middle East.[44]

Second, these memoranda revisited the older debate over medium- versus short-wave broadcasting. Since the early 1930s consular staff and other semiofficial observers of Palestinian life had noted that Arab receiver set owners tended to purchase the less expensive medium-wave receivers rather than the more powerful short-wave receivers preferred by European Jews and British subjects. Hence the PBS broadcast on medium wave: a less expensive but more effective means of reaching the widest Palestinian audience. Yet the BBC Arabic programming was scheduled to broadcast on shortwave, after research suggested that Arabs did have access to short-wave receivers. In his history of the BBC Arabic service, Peter Partner noted that in 1937 the Foreign Office had consulted with the mandatory government in Palestine, as well as PBS officials. Partner wrote, "The answers from Palestine emphasized the good reception there of the Bari program on the short wave [from the Rome station, which rebroadcast Bari's program]. They also asserted that 90 percent of Arab license-holders in Palestine had short-wave sets."[45]

Gerard Mansell, historian of the BBC World Service, stated that a medium-wave station was not the solution because Radio Bari was not the problem: "What most Arabs were listening to was Rome on short wave, not Bari on medium wave. The case for a Foreign Office–run medium wave transmitter was thereby much weakened."[46] This information regarding Arab listening habits is curious, as it ran counter to all previous reports on Arab listeners. However, it proved influential in the Foreign Office's decision to broadcast the new BBC service on shortwave. Others in Palestine and the British government criticized this decision on the same grounds: Arabs were more likely to own medium- than short-wave receivers. On December 29, 1937, one week before BBC Arabic went on the air, the *Palestine Post* commented:

> [The BBC] Arabic broadcast service is meeting with a bad snag insofar as Arabs in Palestine are concerned. To hear Daventry you must have an instrument equipped with short wave receptivity. But the sets which the Government has distributed to one hundred or so villages are only of medium wave. Most of the individual Arab possessors of radios are also unable to tune in to London. Consequently, though the station of Bari can be obtained on a medium wave, the majority of Arab listeners in this country will not be able to hear the British programme especially arranged in Arabic.[47]

The *Post*'s solution: increase the PBS's Arabic programming to reach a regional audience, making a "temporary" solution into a permanent one.

The third key element of the undersecretary's memo was the issue of using the PBS for the planned news service. Although it proved a shorter-lived issue, the question of station and location caused numerous headaches for British officials. Under the terms of the League of Nations mandate for Palestine, the British government was required to encourage the development of Palestine as a Jewish national home and to prepare it for independence.[48] As a result, Britain was not supposed to utilize its Palestine or Palestinian assets to further its own interests. The creation of the PBS had caused no concern—since establishing a radio station was a sign of statehood and hence a sign that Britain was moving Palestine toward independence. However, using the PBS to broadcast pro-British news broadcasts, some feared, might raise the League's ire. A Foreign Office memo cited a British official stationed in Palestine, who cautioned, "Any items that were definitely counter-propaganda in the sense of being obviously designed to give the lie to Italy could not in any case be broadcast from a mandated territory and should come from London on the short wave."[49]

Later that summer a Foreign Office official raised the same issue, suggesting that it had not yet been resolved. "It has been suggested that the use of the wireless station at Jerusalem for this purpose, if maintained for any length of time, may be open to objection," he stated, "on the grounds that it was at variance with the spirit of the Mandate." To avoid criticism from the League of Nations, he noted, "His Majesty's Government are therefore considering the advisability of building a new wireless station in Cyprus."[50] The Cyprus station was intended as a temporary measure, to be used until the BBC's Arabic service was ready to broadcast on shortwave from Daventry. (Cyprus's status as a crown colony made British activity there less subject to international oversight and opprobrium.) But building a new station would have been expensive. After much debate, the Cyprus plan was discarded: the station's short life would not justify the cost.

In any case, the Permanent Mandates Commission seems not to have minded—and complaints from Italy were minimal. The PBS broadcasts, overseen by the new Jerusalem Liaison Office, began operations in September 1937.[51] The PBS offered two additional news broadcasts each day: a "village and coffee shop bulletin on unsophisticated lines," broadcast at 7:00 P.M., and a "less local and more international bulletin," broadcast at 9:45 P.M. and intended "essentially for the Arab intelligentsia."[52]

The new BBC Arabic broadcasting service went on the air on January 4, 1938. After all the preparation, the service had a rough start. Few listened, and those who did criticized its broadcasts. Arab listeners complained that station broadcasters spoke with unattractive accents, while the Foreign Office detested the BBC's candor in reporting British reprisals for the 1936 uprisings in Palestine, which officials considered likely to inflame the situation further. Mandate government officials agreed while also complaining that the BBC programming was too "Western" to appeal to local audiences. In any case, reception was often poor and the quality of programming equally disappointing.

Reactions

In Palestine, Arab listeners took issue with their portrayal as easily swayed by Italian propaganda. *Falastin* reacted angrily to accusations that the Arab population was vulnerable to Bari's propaganda—and to the hope that it would prove equally so to that of the BBC. On January 7, 1938, its front-page editorial stated:

England through its Arabic broadcasting has undertaken a war with Radio Bari, which England claims has a great influence on breaking the Arabs away from them, and on the energy of the movement in Palestine. We do not hate that the Arabic language seduces London, and Paris, and Berlin, and Bari, just as we do not hate that countries vie in allegations.

In other words, the editorial suggested, it welcomed Arabic-language broadcasting from European countries and did not mind the internecine quality of European politics. "We are content with the Arabs and the quality of their affection," the editorial continued,

> but we hate greatly that we are accused of stupidity, and that it is said of us that we are influenced by what Bari broadcasts, or by what London broadcasts. The reality is that the Arabs understand Europe . . . and they know that all of what its nations pretend with their flirting is nothing except hypocrisy on the one side and a clash between colonial agencies on the other. The worst of what we hate of this propaganda is the allegation that Radio Bari [has] all that influence over the movement in Palestine.[53]

The editorial argued that Arab listeners could see through European propaganda and that listeners could enjoy Italian programming without adopting a pro-Italian stance on British governance. John Heyworth-Dunne, a professor at the School of Oriental Studies in London, noted after fieldwork among elite Palestinians that Bari "received very little attention until we ourselves were kind enough to give it publicity in our own press at home." He added that "[interviewees] told me that Bari was absolutely harmless, and that very few people were even curious about that station. . . . [I]t is thanks to the British press that Palestinian Arabs have become curious about it." In any case, he suggested, those who believed Bari's message "are already so poisoned against the British that a little extra poison really does not matter."[54]

In the end, Bari does not appear to have played a decisive role in turning Palestinian public opinion against the British. As Heyworth-Dunne noted, those hostile to the British mandate did not need a radio announcer to provide reasons for them to dislike British rule. And those who supported British rule were not likely to be swayed by Italian propaganda. Bari did appear to have commanded a certain audience once the war broke out—at least for its news broadcasts. One Palestinian recalled being "constantly next to our radios" during the war, eager for any news. "Particularly the older generation listened every night to the news bulletins transmitted by different stations, friendly ones as well as enemy ones." Although enemy stations were banned, "in secret many liked to listen to the Arabic news coming from Berlin and Bari."[55] For Arabic speakers, there would have been few other European broadcasting options outside Bari, Zeesen, and the BBC.

Yet much of the evidence for Arab Palestinian listening to Bari came from urban elites—those eminent families with whom British officials like Heyworth-Dunne socialized or interacted. When it came to rural listeners, what could mandate officials do to ensure that their access to radio broadcasts reflected a pro-British stance? The question was an urgent one, since by 1937 the main energy of the Arab revolt had moved to rural areas, many of which seemed barely under British control. What, British officials wondered, could be done with such an inscrutable, and potentially dangerous, population?

Village Radio Sets

The village broadcasting scheme—a two-part invention requiring both the distribution of government-subsidized village sets in rural Palestine and the development of programs aimed at rural listeners—had begun in tandem with the PBS's launch. The distribution program began with a significant government investment: one hundred sets had been purchased for distribution, at a cost of LP35 each. Each set would be placed in the village guesthouse or school to facilitate collective listening.[56] By June Palestine's representative to the League of Nations Permanent Mandates Commission stated that forty-one villages with a thousand or more inhabitants had been supplied with sets;[57] by May there were seventy-three, and that fall an additional twelve sets were distributed. The remaining fifteen were held in reserve as spares and replacements.[58] To qualify for a radio set, villages had to meet certain requirements. One was size: a May 1939 Chief Secretary's Office file comment noted that the provision of sets was "limited to villages of not less than 1,000 inhabitants."[59] This number changed over time: by June the following year, the minimum appears to have been reduced to six hundred, where it remained for the rest of the mandate.[60]

Initially, the cost of the sets was to be considered a long-term, interest-free loan taken out by the government on the recipient villages' behalf. However, this idea was discarded almost immediately. In February 1937 the Post Office proposed to the Chief Secretary's Office that leaders of the villages receiving government radio sets sign a contract specifying agreed terms of use. A final version of the proposed contract form was approved in March; its introduction signaled an attempt to instill a type of accountability for the usage, housing, and general care of the set. No suggestion was made that the village owned the set or that the government had considered the amount of its purchase cost a loan.

The contract included fairly standard provisions regarding the government's and the community representative's responsibilities and a few points giving Post Office officials what might be described as surveillance rights over recipient communities. The contract was fairly detailed in assigning responsibilities; for example, regarding the radio set batteries, it stated:

> Government shall maintain the Battery in good working condition and the Representatives of the Community shall arrange that whenever recharging is necessary the Battery shall be delivered to the Post Office of [space for town or district name] and there exchanged for a charged battery in good working condition.[61]

The contract further specified how communities could be reimbursed for the costs of traveling to and from a particular post office for a battery change. The level of detail regarding battery recharging and travel costs illustrates the highly legalistic and somewhat forbidding tone of this contract. While the terms suggest that the mandate government was willing to shoulder a considerable bureaucratic and financial burden with regard to these sets, the contract's specificity and formality may have sent a different message to the community representatives who reviewed and signed it.

The contract's other provisions may have reinforced the cool message—such as the broad oversight privileges that the mandate government reserved for itself regarding where and how the set could be placed and used. Recipients were required to provide a "room or building free of all expense to Government" in which the radio set would be housed and used; selection of the room was subject to the approval of the district commissioner or his representative. Similarly, any officer "empowered by the Postmaster General" was to have access "at all reasonable times" to the room, the radio receiver, its battery, and its aerial and loudspeaker (the latter was intended to make the radio broadcasts audible to all members of the village who gathered to hear them)—with no advance notice required.[62]

During the late 1930s the government made much of pretuned radio sets, which prevented recipients from tuning in to any other broadcasting station—especially Italy's Bari or Germany's Zeesen. Reflecting the government's concern, the contract enumerated the recipient community representative's responsibilities regarding the sanctity of the pretuned set. The representative was contractually obligated to "ensure that the Receiver is not interfered with in any way by any person whatsoever." Community members were allowed only to turn the radio on and off and to remove or insert a battery "for the purpose of forwarding it to the Post Office of [town or district name] aforementioned." The mandate government was even suspicious regarding the community's use of the radio set batteries: would they use them to power some other appliance and allow the government to pick up the expense? Would they use them to power a nonapproved radio set?[63]

Were these pretuned radio sets as firmly under the government's control as its officials believed? In November 1938, a few years into the set distribution scheme, Chief Secretary W. D. Battershill explained that the sets distributed were pretuned so that they broadcast only the station (and the programming) that the mandate government wished, the Palestine Broadcasting Service; recipients were thereby prevented from tuning in to other stations.[64] (As medium-wave sets they would in any case have been incapable of receiving most European stations.) Referring to a conversation on the subject the previous weekend, Battershill reassured an unnamed general:

> These village sets can only be altered so as to take in broadcasts from Bari, Berlin etc. by expert wireless mechanics who would have to use additional apparatus[es] to effect the change. In the Postmaster General's opinion there are very few Arabs in the country capable of doing this. Further if such an alteration was made it would be spotted during the periodic inspections of village sets which are carried out by the Posts and Telegraphs Department.[65]

Battershill was likely correct; at least none of the existing records document such "abuses" of the government sets. Those whose only access to radio came through government sets likely listened only to the PBS.

The Post Office's draft version of the contract specifying donor's and recipient's rights and responsibilities put greater emphasis on the literal costs of poor stewardship: "Should the Community Receiver be in any way interfered with or damaged, except in unforeseen, or unavoidable circumstances, the said [representative's name] shall be held responsible for the payment of the cost of making good such damage."[66] This provision was removed from the final version, revealing the tension between the contractual obligations that the Post Office thought villages receiving radio sets should incur and the reality, reflected in the government's abandonment of the loan scheme, that the government's position was more that of marketer to a somewhat skeptical audience. Some of the officials involved also appear to have viewed the set distribution program doubtfully. In May 1939 a member of the Chief Secretary's Office described it as "the experiment of community listening" and declined to recommend further concessions, such as free radio licenses, to recipient villages.[67] (Other documents do suggest that license fees were waived; distributing free sets while requiring villages to pay the annual license fee would seem counterintuitive.) The chief secretary himself was more positive, stating in a letter written the previous year that while "it cannot be said that the life of the villagers has as yet been materially altered . . . or that they take every advantage of the facilities provided," the program would bear fruit in the long run: "four or five years may well justify hope of the ultimate success of the service."[68]

Over time, the mandate government's set distribution scheme seems to have taken on a life of its own, as awareness of the program spread through rural Palestine. Surviving documents from the Chief Secretary's Office include a few requests for village radio sets sent by village mukhtars. Interpreting the presence of these documents is difficult. Were they saved as samples of a larger collection, or because they were rare? Interpreting their words is equally challenging—particularly when the requests so neatly match the mandate government's expectations for village broadcasting. For example, in October 1941 Sheikh Amin Muhammad Hamzeh wrote to the High Commissioner to request a set for Shaʿab, a village near Acre. Both the Arabic original and the English-language summary have been preserved in the Chief Secretary's Office files. Hamzeh presented his request in terms almost ideally suited to British officials' expectations. He

> prays God to grant Great Britain victory over its enemies in this war, and requests that Government may be moved to assign a wireless (radio) set to their village, so that the secluded inhabitants may follow up the news of the dreadful war, and listen to the agricultural talks which are being broadcast by the Palestine Broadcasting Service and act according to the instructions of the agricultural experts.[69]

The reasons that Hamzeh gave to support his request dovetailed perfectly with the mandate government's expectations of why rural Arab Palestinians would desire a radio set: to ameliorate their "secluded" state and learn from the "agricultural experts" who spoke during the Palestine Broadcasting Service's talks to farmers. They also wished to keep up with the war news—a request framed by a statement of support for British war efforts. Government officials may have read this request as an indication that the village set distribution program and talks to farmers broadcasts were having precisely the desired impact. Without suggesting that Hamzeh's reasons were disingenuous, his rhetoric is read here as an indication of the creative flexibility with which rural Palestinians employed the mandate government's rhetoric to meet their own needs. For the residents of Sha'ab, the advantages of receiving a free radio set, complete with servicing and battery replacement, might have outweighed the disadvantages of the set's restricted tuning capabilities.

The British mandate government envisioned the village radio set distribution program as one involving Palestine's rural Arab population: "The [rural broadcasting programs] are designed for the Arab rather than the Jewish community, because most of the communal sets are in Arab villages and because the line of demarcation between the outlook of town and country Jews is not clearly so well marked as that between town and country Arabs." [70] The first reason was a tautology; the second reflected British and Yishuv (and probably some Arab Palestinians') views about the relative advancement of Palestine's Jewish population. However, some newly created Jewish villages and kibbutzim did request free radio sets. Jehoash Hirshberg credited the creation of the PBS and the mandate government's set distribution scheme with increasing both the number of radios on the kibbutzim and residents' interest in local (rather than short-wave European) broadcasting. He described their impact as follows:

When the PBS was founded in March 1936 the British government distributed radio sets in rural settlements. Kibbutz Givat Brenner first placed the set in the common dining hall where the constant noise prevented any proper listening to music. Information about music broadcasts was not readily available, and one of the members complained that members sit at the radio and "aimlessly turn the knob in search of something worthy of listening to." Yet broadcasts of important events were treated with special attention. In preparation for the transmission of Toscanini's inaugural concert of the Palestine Orchestra the kibbutz rescheduled its weekly General Assembly; dinner was served earlier than usual and the dining-hall doors were locked at 8:30 P.M. for the entire length of the broadcast concert in order to allow for attentive listening. Soon Givat Brenner acquired two additional radio sets which were placed in small "radio cabins" where music lovers crowded to listen to concerts "despite the rain in winter and the mosquitoes in summer."[71]

This may be a generous assessment of the mandate government's contribution to the cultural life of kibbutzim; the few requests from Jewish settlements extant in the Chief Secretary's Office files were rejected. Some, however, refused to accept the government's rejection. In March 1939 Ha-Kotzer, the labor organization for agricultural settlement (Irgun Poalim le-Hityashvut) that had founded Kfar Hittin, wrote the Chief Secretary's Office, which in September 1937 had rejected Ha-Kotzer's request for a free radio set on the grounds that the 120-person settlement was too small, with the news that it had purchased a battery-operated set. Having done so, the labor organization expressed its hope that the government would waive the required annual license fee; the government declined to do so.[72]

While the success of the village set distribution program is debatable, the government's commitment was not. The generally parsimonious mandate government dedicated a significant amount of money to the purchase and maintenance of radio sets. The LP3,500 spent in 1936 on the first hundred battery-operated sets represented the equivalent of seven times the annual salary of the PBS's top administrators. Maintenance costs added another LP19 per set in the first year alone.[73] Ten years later, in November 1947, Postmaster General D. H. Mackay listed the labor, materials, and transportation costs of maintaining the 195 battery-operated village sets (maintenance for the 217 electricity-operated sets installed in schools and other communal listening spaces added only minimally to these costs) at LP8,000 per year, or just over LP41 per set in annual maintenance costs.[74] These numbers represented the high end of the government's financial outlay. Both the chief secretary and the public information officer protested these expenses (which nearly doubled early 1947 estimates of LP28 for the year) even while acknowledging that the Post Office's maintenance activities were neither unnecessary nor extravagant. However, they were inescapable. Radio sets—particularly battery-operated ones—appear to have required frequent maintenance, perhaps even more when used frequently and/or in rural areas.

Radio Set Distribution as a Business Opportunity

That the government's radio set distribution scheme relied largely on battery-operated radio sets made it an appealing business prospect for many of Palestine's selling agents. For them, the distribution scheme offered a way to increase sales of a product they were already selling—to urban as well as rural consumers. It would be misleading to assume that the battery set market was exclusively composed of rural or lower-middle-class consumers. Palestine's low and slow electrification rate, coupled with the high cost of electricity even in urban areas where it was available,[75] discouraged many Palestinians (Arab and Jewish) from using electricity at all or for anything more than nighttime electric lighting. Although plug-in radio sets used small amounts of electric current,[76] urban consumers appear to have been no less likely to purchase battery-operated sets. While electric sets might have appeared more "modern," battery-operated ones offered the advantage of fixed operating costs and the ability to operate independent of any variations (or cuts) in the electricity supply.

As a result, little stigma or automatic linking of "battery-operated radio" to "rural (or poorer) consumer" is evident in 1930s and 1940s radio set advertisements. On the contrary, advertisements for radio batteries and battery sets appeared in the *Palestine Post*, a paper whose ads targeted Palestine's relatively elite community of English speakers (a group likely to have more substantial discretionary funds), throughout the mandate period. While ads for batteries of all types appeared on a regular basis, radio set battery ads were particularly in evidence during the late 1930s. Some battery manufacturers linked particular models to certain radio set brands. A 1938 Eveready Air Cell Battery ad asked, "Why bother recharging radio batteries when an Air Cell Receiver gives you these advantages?" and in answer listed its thousand-hour operation with no need for recharging and no variation in power strength. The advertisement advised consumers to "see the new Air Cell Radios at your dealer's today," drawing an association between the battery brand and the radio set brand.[77] Batteries and battery-operated radio sets were each part of the array of "modern" commodities circulating in Palestine in this period; advertisements give no indication that their disconnection from the electrical grid made them any less "modern," any less convenient, or any less desirable than plug-in sets. Consequently, when the government went looking for radio sets to loan out to Palestine's Arab villages, it had many options.

The mandate government's financial investment in the village set-distribution scheme brought financial benefits to those radio set sellers lucky enough to obtain the government's business. Sellers had to be able to provide not only battery-operated sets at a good price but also the technical expertise to reconfigure them as pretuned, single-station sets. During the 1930s a number of brands and dealers were involved; by the 1940s the government's business went to Pye Radio and its Tel Aviv–based agents, the Matalon Brothers.[78]

In 1939 and 1940 Boutagy's Stores made several attempts to acquire this business. Sensing an opportunity to expand its government dealings at a time when private sector sales were declining, Émile Boutagy suggested that an agreement with Boutagy's would allow the mandate government to capitalize on the firm's experience with supplying the British armed forces and with for-hire radio set agreements generally. In letters sent both to the chief secretary and the High Commissioner, Boutagy proposed that the mandate government hire two hundred radio set receivers, electric or battery operated, at a monthly rate of LP1 for electric sets and LP2 for battery sets, its standard hire rate. (He expressed the firm's willingness to negotiate terms and rates if the government placed a large order.) In return, Boutagy's would take care of "delivery, service, battery consumption, repairs, replacements and every conceivable service connected therewith."[79] The annual rent of LP24 for a hire set was slightly lower than the early 1947 estimates of LP28 in annual maintenance costs, but it was probably higher than the 1940 costs and left the government with no equity in radio sets. The Chief Secretary's Office acknowledged Boutagy's letter but declined to do business with the firm.

Had the mandate government enjoyed a more generous budget, it is possible that more radio sellers would have benefited from its patronage. From the first years of the set distribution program, mandate government officials noted that "a larger supply of receivers is necessary if the broadcasting service to rural communities in Palestine is to become really satisfactory from the administrative, social, and educational points of view." They wistfully commented on the desirability of encouraging "dealers to introduce onto the Palestine market really cheap sets for listening to the local program, as there are many thousands of people in Palestine who cannot even dream of buying a radio set at anything like ruling market prices."[80] However, the government's budgetary and logistical restrictions meant that the number of battery-operated village sets never exceeded two hundred. At almost all moments demand exceeded supply, and at times there were no sets to be had.[81] Assuming that each set served 1,000 people, the government's set distribution scheme reached 200,000 people—a significant number, if all were listening. If Nadan's 37:1 ratio is more accurate, the scheme reached only 7,400 or 8,000 people—a much smaller percentage of the population.

The Radio Set Distribution Program: World War II and After

The distribution scheme continued through World War II, although in abbreviated form. For one thing, the mandate government's fear that Palestine's Arab population would listen to and be "infected" by Bari and Zeesen had lessened. Stories on Radio Bari had almost entirely disappeared from the local newspapers by mid-1938, and by June 1940 the High Commissioner was noting, "Italian broadcasts are frequently listened to but less out of sympathy than from curiosity as to news they contain."[82] For another, the mandate government during the war was concerned with controlling Palestinians' access to radio sets, not with distributing more sets. Shipping restrictions and wartime budgets likely made the distribution project more difficult to support.

After the war, when shipments of radio sets resumed, the program appears to have been ready to ramp up again. British mandate government officials expressed their continued belief in the program's effectiveness, although the situation in Palestine had changed in several key ways from the late 1930s. Nonetheless, a member of the Chief Secretary's Office wrote in December 1945:

> It is accepted that the provision of wireless sets to Arab villages is one
> of the most efficacious means of Government publicity and propaganda,
> particularly at times when feeling is inclined to run high, as at present.
> I therefore recommend that extra provision should be made in the es-
> timates of the P.I.O. [Public Information Office] 1946/47 for as many
> additional sets as possible. 100 new sets does not represent a great net
> increase in proportion to the large numbers of Arab villages which we
> have to reach.[83]

It is difficult to imagine that by 1946 farming techniques were uppermost on most Palestinians' minds. Rural Palestinians more likely tuned in to the PBS for local news updates on an increasingly tense situation than for anything else. Although budgets for the final mandate years offer little concrete proof that the distribution project continued, the official's comment above suggests that some, at least, hoped to use the old village broadcasting program to ameliorate new tensions.

Rural Broadcasting Initiatives around the World: The Palestinian Case in Context

The British mandate government's rural broadcasting initiatives on the Palestine Broadcasting Service were not unique to Palestine. They participated in a much larger global phenomenon, one that stretched throughout the British Empire and around the world. The development of government sponsored rural broadcasting programs was the product both of the troubled economic times of the early 1930s and of the related intensification in European and U.S. governments' fears of dangerous rural "others," whether such others were located in the colonies or at home. Concerned about the destabilizing, proletarianizing effect of out-of-work rural populations migrating to urban areas in a fruitless search for employment, these governments turned to rural broadcasting initiatives as a means of defusing the rural-to-urban threat. Rural radio programs were designed to bring rural populations "in from the cold," introducing them to modern, urban culture and making them informed, engaged citizens while at the same time convincing them to be content with their lives on the farm.

The closest parallels with rural broadcasting efforts in Palestine could be drawn from similar initiatives in India. The resemblance was not accidental. It came via the original proponent of rural broadcasting for Palestine, C. F. Strickland. Strickland's support of rural broadcasting and village set-distribution programs developed during his time as a civil service officer in India; his work promoting rural broadcasting in Palestine was an extension of his ongoing interest in Indian broadcasting. Strickland remained an advocate of Indian village broadcasting even while working to promote radio broadcasting in Palestine.[84] For India, Strickland shared the view of the conservative Guardian movement. The Guardian movement, like the Palestine government, supported broadcasting as a means of keeping villagers from succumbing to the lure of the cities and abandoning the land. However, it also considered rural broadcasting a way to maintain the cultural "purity" of Indian villagers. The Guardian movement promoted radio as a modern tool for shielding rural Indians *from* modernity rather than as a tool for bringing them, in however mediated a fashion, into its fold.[85]

Moving beyond the bounds of the British Empire, the U.S. Midwest was also the site of numerous rural broadcasting initiatives. The context in which the American initiatives developed was in many aspects quite different from that in Palestine, and a comparison of the two must be carefully mapped to avoid facile conclusions. However, the limited parallels are themselves useful. The United States used a market model, whereby radio broadcasting developed into a dual system of private commercial and public nonprofit stations; Palestine, in contrast, inherited Great Britain's noncommercial, single-station, government-regulated broadcasting model. However, the U.S. model, with its reliance on consumer interest, private enterprise radio set purchasing, and audience-driven programming, can be employed comparatively to identify where rural Arab Palestinian radio listening interest lay—since the evidence indicates that the Palestine mandate government's broadcasting initiatives were doing little to help it develop.

American interest in radio's penetration of rural communities was heavily influenced by early-twentieth-century constructions of rural life as isolated and of rural migration to urban areas as "flight." The first was conceived as a social problem and the second as a national danger, presenting the twin threats of a depleted food supply and increased crowding and social unrest in America's cities. As Randall Patnode has argued, the farmer was transformed from an icon of American productivity and steadfastness into an other whose backwardness served as a foil for the new American ideal: an urban, modern life signaled by the purchase and adoption of modern technologies. Patnode's study of 1920s American periodicals finds frequent connections drawn between farmers and radio for precisely this purpose: "In 'othering' the farmer (or potentially any consumer group), the press made the embrace of technology by everyone else appear more natural and inevitable."[86]

For these new "problems" a modern solution emerged: radio broadcasting. Radio's new identity as the technology of particular benefit to rural Americans, with the corollary understanding that rural Americans had the most to gain because they were the most behind, was quickly absorbed, naturalized, and reproduced. Today's scholarly studies and period reports alike have adopted the term *benefit* without question. It is used almost without exception when describing 1920s and 1930s radio. As the agricultural historian Reynold Wik wrote twenty-five years ago in a synthetic piece for the journal *Agricultural History*, "Rural Americans may have benefited the most from radio because they were the most isolated and had the most to gain from an improved communication system."[87]

The same rhetoric of practicality that drove the Palestine mandate government's rural programming choices influenced rural broadcasting in the United States as well: "The farmer's main interests were practical. He wanted the daily weather forecasts to help protect his property and help in the management of his affairs." The broadcasting of weather reports was begun in 1921 and by 1923 had spread to 117 stations whose daily reports could be heard around the country. Farmers began expressing a similar interest in broadcasts of livestock and commodity prices; radio stations responded. This interplay of broadcaster initiative and audience response, or audience request and broadcaster response, was not found in Palestine. U.S. broadcasting initiatives differed from Palestine's mandate government initiatives because they were largely audience driven. As a result, rural Americans became a steady and growing radio audience.[88] They demonstrated their interest by buying battery-operated radio sets, so that by 1926 approximately one million farm families owned radios.[89]

In addition to the practical benefits of weather reports, commodity prices, and other farm programs, radio was expected to fill a cultural and social need, particularly among youth and farm wives. Wik writes, "People thought that the radio would keep young people on the farm. It would reduce the boredom of those isolated in lonely places and thus preserve the family farm." Researchers believed that farm wives in particular would benefit from the pleasant "diversion" of daytime radio broadcasting, which would counteract the isolation of their daily lives. However, the postwar depression of the early 1920s meant that "radio did not reverse the trek to the city"; entertainment could not compensate for poor harvests and insufficient incomes.[90]

Government and social science interest in the rural benefits of radio broadcasting picked up again in the 1930s. In 1935 Edmund Brunner, an education professor at Teachers' College in New York whose research focused on radio's social benefits, chaired a symposium titled "Radio and the Farmer." Its panels discussed the ways in which radio was improving the cultural lives of rural Americans right where they lived and reiterated social scientists' foundational beliefs about the role of radio in rural America. First and foremost, the symposium supported the belief that radio broadcasting had greater value for rural than for urban Americans. Along with telephones, automobiles, and regular postal mail and package delivery service, radio was "rapidly banishing the physical and cultural isolation" that previously plagued rural America. Radio both entertained and informed, whether individuals (women's programs educated housewives about housekeeping and kept them company during the day), families (news broadcasts at mealtimes fostered discussion of agricultural and national news), or communities (plays and dance tunes encouraged evening gatherings).[91]

Results of a survey of rural community leaders reinforced the researchers' hypothesis that "because they are largely dependent upon radio for the entertainment, cultural and educational features which urban dwellers may find in part elsewhere, the radio has greater value for farmers as a group than for other radio listeners." They repeated the truisms that radio made the younger generation more likely to remain on the farm and ameliorated the lonely silence of the farm wife's days.[92] Of course, since many of these "community leaders" were local university professors and civic figures with an urban education, their opinions might have been less representative of America's farm communities than the symposium's researchers recognized. [93] Whether farmers themselves had internalized a sense of their own isolation, whether rural youth considered radio broadcasts an adequate substitute for urban life, and whether farm wives enjoyed daytime broadcasts to the extent and in the manner that researchers assumed is unclear. Certainly, however, the audience-driven model of American radio broadcasting ensured that their voices were heard and their interests taken into account to a far greater degree than were rural Arab voices in Palestine.

Beyond these benefits, community leaders stressed the role radio played in bringing the farmer into the national body of citizens. First, radio integrated the farmer culturally, making him more like urban Americans, so "that the farmer is no longer a person apart." Second, radio had a strong "citizenship value" for the farmer:

In acquainting farmers with national and international developments and problems; in acquainting the farmer with the relation of agriculture to other industries; and in making the farmer understand his important place in our national economic and social structure, the radio tends to make him a better informed and more cooperative citizen, and, consequently, from the national viewpoint, a more effective farmer.[94]

The benefits radio brought rural America thus rebounded on urban America as well, by producing farmers with urbanized tastes and views who nevertheless understood why they should remain on the farm. While the system in Palestine was quite different—a government-controlled radio station and government-distributed sets—the goals were rather similar. There is nothing unusual or inherently Middle Eastern or even especially colonial about the British mandate government's rural broadcasting efforts—other than, of course, officials' persistent blindness to what rural Arab Palestinians really wanted.

Selling the Rural: Private Enterprise and the Rural Market

The greatest problem that the Palestine mandate government's rural broadcasting program faced may have been the discrepancy between British government perceptions of rural Arab listeners and the reality of their lives. The PBS talks-to-farmers broadcasts and the village set-distribution programs reflected the British government view of rural Palestinians: poor, uneducated, oppressed peasants whose discontent, if mobilized, could cause deep social unrest. However, the broadcasts' combination of didactic technical talks and patronizing cultural programs did little to encourage anyone, rural or urban, to tune in. Moreover, the village set-distribution scheme reached only a limited percentage of the rural population.

This does not mean that rural Arab Palestinians rejected radio or remained outside its orbit. Rural folk tuned in to other programs on the PBS and other stations that were more responsive to their interests and desires. They were able to do so because they had begun purchasing radio sets of their own. Radio set sellers learned quickly that the rural radio market not only existed but was active and savvy, and they targeted rural buyers with offers of installment plan payments and home servicing. Rural Arab Palestinians were not necessarily unsophisticated or uniformly poor. Many were well aware of both the pleasures of radio listening and the statement made by the presence of a radio set in one's home. Although their homes may have been less electrified, they were a market with enough purchasing power for Arab Palestine's largest trading goods store to develop a marketing and servicing program aimed solely at them. While the British mandate government busied itself with broadcasts on the "rotation of crops, agricultural pests, manures, horticulture, [and] vegetable growing,"⁹⁵ merchants like Boutagy's Stores helped rural Palestinians connect with urban Palestine in other ways.

Like other Arab Palestinian firms, Boutagy's ceased advertising during the general strike of 1936, which began in April. After the strike ended in October, Boutagy's resumed its advertising, with ads similar in layout and feel to its early 1936 advertisements. While most of its advertising reflected the urban perspective common to radio set advertisements of the period, one campaign in particular targeted rural and urban consumers alike. Starting in 1934, Boutagy's radio set advertisements had featured letters sent from customers to Émile Boutagy, the stores' general director. These letters asked his advice regarding particular life problems: boredom, a sense of disconnection from world events, desire for religious instruction, poor business at the family coffee shop, the need to find a gift for one's fiancée, and so on. The tone was friendly and personal: a heart-to-heart talk with a trusted friend. Émile's reply was printed below the original letter, a layout similar to that of an advice column. While some ads featured customers in urban settings, others—like the sad Tulkarm farmer mentioned in chapter 1—were clearly rural. From an urbanite's perspective, these narratives might have had a slight comic edge, although it is difficult to retrospectively determine how 1930s readers would have responded to mentions of suicide in an advertisement. However, a more careful reading might reveal that Boutagy's was presenting rural Palestinians as customers—and not as backward peasants in need of government intervention.

In November 1936 Boutagy's Stores began running a new series of HMV radio advertisements that featured a photograph of a fellah family posing proudly with their new radio set. While Boutagy's other radio advertisements generally did not include an image of the radio set, these new ones emphasized it. Advertisement after advertisement showed rural Palestinians—men, children, and sometimes young women—posing with their HMV radio purchase.

In addition to the photographs, the text of these advertisements marked them as different from previous Boutagy's HMV ads in key ways. Although following the same letter-and-response structure, the villagers' letters were addressed not to "'Azizi Émile" (Dear Émile) but to "*hadrat al-fadl*" (Distinguished Sir). The intimacy of the former was replaced by the formality of the latter. The letters themselves were also different—business-like rather than emotive. They were written not for advice on personal problems but to orchestrate a radio set purchase from a company whose products and servicing were known to the writers. The advertisements' headlines reinforced this new focus on rural purchasing by blending village names with their inhabitants' purchase orders, as, for example, the December 1, 1936, ad, which stated, "[Even] from Qaysariyya they want a radio from Boutagy."[96] Together, the ad copy and headline suggested that radios were now so popular that even desert nomads and rural villagers were buying them. They also suggested that these were discerning customers, buying according to product quality and service rather than as naive country bumpkins seduced by the novelty of radios.

These consumers were discerning but responded to different selling points from Boutagy's early 1930s HMV target market. On November 25, 1936, a man named 'Ali wrote from Dabouriyya to order an HMV radio.[97] The headline, which called HMV "the most innovative radio in the world," noted further that "they [the people from Dabouriyya] are not content with a traditional machine [*jihaz taqleedi*]." However, the radio set 'Ali sought was one specially suited for rural life. He asked for a battery-operated set capable of a thousand hours of lis-

Figure 2.1. "In Yajour They Are Blessed with a His Master's Voice Radio," Boutagy's Stores HMV radio advertisement. Source: *Falastin*, Dec. 3, 1936, p. 7.

Figure 2.2. "The Most Innovative Radio in the World," Boutagy's Stores HMV radio advertisement. Source: *Falastin*, Nov. 26, 1936, p. 7.

tening. Moreover, he stated his intent to use Boutagy's easy payment plan, paying five guineas on receipt and one guinea each month until the radio's purchase price was paid in full. (Radio sets ranged in price. The models advertised in this period ranged from 11 to 38 guineas, or L11.5 to L40, with the Palestinian pound being equivalent to the British.)[98] When installation payment options were mentioned in earlier Boutagy's advertisements, they appeared at the bottom of the ad, next to store location information and the Boutagy's tagline, "Visit Boutagy even if only once a month," rather than integrated into the ad copy. The new advertisements do not indicate whether in fact more consumers began paying in installments, but they do suggest that this option had become more acceptable and that Boutagy's consumer base was broadening to include consumers who if not less wealthy had less ready access to cash.

The rural consumers portrayed in Boutagy's HMV ads might have had less cash wealth, but they were clearly informed about both the pleasures of radio listening and the practical advantages of purchasing from Boutagy's. Nor did the store give any indication that its battery-set radio purchasing *fellahi* (farmer) or *bedawi* (rural) customers were in any way second rate. Instead, advertisements like that of

February 4, 1937, welcomed them, saying, "Boutagy's radio brand His Master's Voice gives life to, educates, and entertains all classes of people."[99] The November 26, 1936, advertisement described Émile Boutagy's reaction on receiving a radio order from a small area outside Haifa as follows: "Boutagy took the letter and after five minutes chose the radio desired by the patron." Rather than hand the letter off to subordinates or disparage a man whose expressed desire for a radio both "easy to move and light for carrying" did little to suggest a sophisticated city dweller,[100] Émile himself is shown filling the order, restoring the personal relationship between seller and buyer suggested by the original "'Azizi Émile" ads.

This display of direct customer service reinforced what appears to have been a larger project by Boutagy's Stores to capture the rural market not merely by offering battery-operated radios but by providing free delivery and servicing as well. The letters of numerous advertisements referred to Boutagy's "special cars," which made delivery and service calls even to the mountain and desert areas. Boutagy's made this a selling point, as in the February 24, 1937, advertisement's headline, which noted that "His Master's Voice radio is dispatched to Haneen despite the difficulty of the roads" (*wu'urat al-tareeq*).[101] Their ads also referenced a longtime Boutagy's promise of free repair for the life of the radio—a promise made more real by the company's decision to bring its mechanics to its customers rather than require customers to bring their defective merchandise to a Boutagy's store. To offer such servicing throughout Palestine indicated a substantive commitment by Boutagy's to its rural patrons.

Boutagy's Stores' treatment of rural Arab Palestinians as valued and discerning patrons contrasted sharply with the British government, in Palestine's view, especially in connection with radio. The British government, mandate and home alike, saw radio in rural Palestine from what Richard Bulliet might call the "view from the center."[102] The British government was interested in radio's capacity to influence rural Arabs but also frightened of it. They feared its power over unworldly villagers around the region, whom they regarded as a homogeneous group with no prior exposure to the medium and hence no inoculation against its ability to seduce them.

As noted above, the British Foreign and Colonial Offices in early 1937 began collaborating on a "special Arabic broadcast news-service"—an extension of the PBS's regular Arabic news service. British officials believed that additional news broadcasts would give Arab listeners in Palestine and the region more opportunities to hear the British—rather

Figure 2.3. Palestine Broadcasting Service musical ensemble. Source: Public Information Office PBS Arabic Section photographs, ISA/RG15/M/2242/31.

than the Italian or German—point of view on current events. In August 1937 the Colonial Office in London advised the service to address itself to two discrete publics:

> [the] intelligentsia and the fellahin and village folk generally, who are largely unsophisticated and inclined to emotion and affected by religious influences which tend to color their outlook. Arab politics in simple language would interest them and as much simple and vivid information on current Arab affairs as could be collected. They are interested in the more important political personalities of the Arab and to a lesser extent of the general world—kings, prime ministers, etc. but are not capable of absorbing much general political news on international lines, though they are quickly impressed by striking facts particularly on martial topics—i.e. the launching of the 1000th airplane by Great Britain; the trials of a gun that shoots 150 miles.[103]

The Boutagy's HMV advertisements offer a "view from the edge." They indicate that something else was taking place with respect to radio and rural Arab Palestinians. These ads focused not on bringing the wonder of radio, or the clarity of the British perspective, to naive fellahin but on engaging them as sophisticated consumers with a clear understanding of both the pleasures of radio listening and the importance of buying a good radio set from a service-oriented sales agent. The sharply topical, Palestine-focused copy found in earlier Boutagy's ads addressed not the urban, upper-middle-class Arab Palestinians presumed to have purchased most radio sets but rural consumers with sufficient disposable income to buy similarly priced, location-appropriate battery-operated sets. These consumers were aware that they were at some remove from the rest of the world and that radio was a tool to bring them closer.

As the February 17, 1937, advertisement's headline noted humorously, "New Geographic Information: Irbid is not so far from London thanks to His Master's Voice radio." Nor was this focus short-lived: Boutagy's continued advertising to rural Palestinians through the early 1940s. For example, a May 1940 advertisement that in English promoted HMV's latest battery-operated "town and country" radio set proclaimed in Arabic: "A His Master's Voice Radio on Every Orange Tree in Palestine." Addressing itself to the "fellah," the Arabic copy managed to promote radio listening as a means of relaxation and also to comment on government policy—emphasizing local concerns and focusing inward. These statements contrasted dramatically with the English copy's outward-focused promise that with this radio set "the gay cities of the world are yours in your home,"[104] emphasizing the topicality of Boutagy's ad copy.

If the urban focus of most early Boutagy's HMV advertisements provided evidence for the emergence of an urban, consuming middle and upper middle class in mandate Palestine, the rural focus of these ads seems to indicate that the same process was occurring outside urban areas. (It also indicates *Falastin*'s commitment to delivering its newspapers to rural subscribers—a commitment that justified Boutagy's placing its rural-focused advertisements with the paper.) Advertisements showing village men posed proudly with their new radio might have amused *Falastin*'s urban readers, but the target market seems to have responded seriously—and receptively.

Conclusion

The PBS talks-to-farmers broadcasts and the village set-distribution programs give the British government view of rural Palestinians: poor, uneducated, oppressed peasants whose discontent, if mobilized, could cause deep social unrest in Palestine. This view emerged in the context of mandate government reports on the hardships faced by rural Arab Palestinians, which became a government concern starting in 1929. It grew more acute as the Arab revolt shifted from an urban to a rural phenomenon in late 1936, following the end of the general strike. On the one hand, this concern spurred mandate officials to put their concern for rural Palestinians into action, propelling the radio set distribution project and the development of broadcasts specifically intended for rural listeners. On the other hand, the Arab revolt intersected with British home government concerns about Arabic-language broadcasting from Italy (and, later, Germany), resulting in tighter censorship of radio broadcasts. Together, these events produced lasting changes in the PBS's news broadcasts, reinforcing station administrators' view of Palestine as populated by multiple, discrete populations whose access to news about the country must be tightly controlled.

While the government focused on at once introducing benighted rural Arab Palestinians to the urban and protecting them from it, Boutagy's focused on selling that same population on its latest purchase. Those consumers bought radio sets and tuned in to whatever station—and whatever programs—they chose. In most cases, they seem to have chosen not to tune in to the programs that the mandate government considered "theirs": the talks to farmers and other agricultural programming held as little interest for rural Arab radio listeners as they did for their urban counterparts. While the British mandate government busied itself with broadcasts on manure, merchants like Boutagy's Stores helped rural Palestinians connect with urban Palestine directly.

The discrepancy between the government's views of rural Palestinians as backward and potentially dangerous and Boutagy's views of them as geographically dispersed but important customers was sometimes evident within the PBS administration itself. In part, this issue arose from a tension inherent in a mandate radio station: it worked both as a sign of Palestinian statehood and as a vehicle for government projects of modernization, pacification, and control. While the mandate government understood the PBS as a state institution serving the public good as understood by its British administrators, Palestinians—Arab and Zionist—understood the station as fulfilling one of the key interwar requirements of state sovereignty, a state-owned broadcasting station. While the mandate government sought to use PBS programming to foster a peaceful, pro-British population, Palestinians working for the station sought to harness its programming to foster and reinforce a Palestinian national identity. The next chapter examines how PBS employees, working under Arabic section controller 'Ajaj Nuwayhid, employed PBS programming to promote a self-consciously modern Arab Palestinian nationalism. Focusing on women, they maneuvered through the strictures of wartime broadcasting to build and strengthen listeners' sense of themselves as Palestinians. In doing so, PBS employees—rather than British station administrators—became the primary actors.

CHAPTER 3

Broadcasting a Nationalist Modernity: The PBS Arabic Section

This chapter examines the changes that World War II brought to the Palestine Broadcasting Service: tightening of home and mandate government controls over the station, including closer censor scrutiny over what was broadcast on air and the requisitioning of broadcasting hours for Allied programming. Despite the reassertion of government prerogative over the station and its broadcasts, the PBS Arabic section conveyed the message of Arab Palestinian progress most strongly during this period. These messages of progress centered on the educated, "modern" women who were guest broadcasters, reflecting the nationalist modern vision of 'Ajaj Nuwayhid, who led the Arabic section during the central war years.

The PBS on the Eve of War

By August 1939 the PBS had been on the air for over three years, broadcasting in Arabic, Hebrew, and English to listening communities whom station administrators perceived as discretely divided by language, taste, and identity.[1] Although the Hebrew and Arabic sections had the same programming categories—children's hours, theatrical productions, light entertainment, serious musical performances, and educational and ethical talks—their content differed. The addition of the Colonial Office–funded "special" Arabic news service introduced in 1937 as well as the talks-to-farmers programs meant that Arabic dominated the station's on-air time. Hebrew listeners discomfited by the inequity of the broadcasting allotment were reminded that it served the public good by targeting the segment of the Palestinian population most likely to be influenced by Italian and German propaganda and most in need of the station's "educate and elevate" influence. As members of Palestine's wealthier and more educated stratum, Palestine's Jewish community was also reminded that its members could more easily afford the short-wave receivers that would enable them to tune in to European stations for music, entertainment, and news in languages they understood.

Although some in the Arab community viewed the PBS with suspicion because of its status as a government institution, the relevance of PBS programming (coupled with the relative lack of alternatives) helped the station build a local audience. The popular skepticism about the government's intentions that existed was as likely to be manifested in critical listening as in a tuned-out radio set. Moreover, the willingness of prominent local figures to join the station administration—starting with the famous poet and nationalist Ibrahim Tuqan, who served as its first Arabic section subdirector—also helped build the PBS's credibility as a local institution.[2]

As noted above, Tuqan's willingness to work at the PBS highlights the more nuanced position that elite Palestinians often took with respect to the mandate government—and that British officials took with respect to men like Tuqan. Both groups demonstrated a willingness to work together in particular instances or on particular issues, provided that they could do so without compromising their public reputations. In this, both sides demonstrated a striking pragmatism—much like what Philip Khoury identified as the "honorable cooperation" policy of the National Bloc in mandate Syria.[3] What distinguished Palestine from Syria was the frequency with which members of elite Palestinian families cycled between positions in (or proximity to) government offices and time in exile or prison. In the case of Tuqan and the PBS, Tuqan received the professional validation of a prominent leadership position at a major new cultural institution while the station gained credibility from being associated with such a highly regarded figure. The station would enjoy a similar boost in its credibility when 'Ajaj Nuwayhid was hired—helping it attract listeners during the slump of the war years.

Listeners were also attracted to the station by the Palestinian musicians, scholars, and prominent community figures it employed, as well as the regionally known figures brought to the station as guest performers or speakers. While the news broadcasts were censored in advance by the Public Information Office, they did provide information on local developments. Although the size of the listenership should not be exaggerated—it was still a small percentage of Palestine's Arab population—statistical reports on the increasing number of radio licenses (required of every radio set owner and renewable on an annual basis) obtained from the Post Office throughout the late 1930s indicated that it was growing at a steady and sustained rate.

The PBS Arabic Section in Wartime

The outbreak of hostilities among the European powers in September 1939 ushered in a host of changes in the Palestine government's relations with radio sets and radio broadcasting. Since the mid-1930s the British government in London and the mandate government in Palestine had been concerned about radio's power to transmit anti-British propaganda. The shift to wartime meant that what the government had previously considered propaganda it now considered part of active warfare—and began acting accordingly. In addition to tightening restrictions on what British and Palestinian stations could broadcast, the government began attempting to prohibit citizens from listening to certain stations. After a delay brought on by procedural concerns and bureaucratic slowness, it also began confiscating so-called enemy sets.

Enemy Sets and Hostile Listeners

In November 1939 the United Kingdom's postmaster general issued a set of defense regulations covering the possession and use of wireless transmitting devices. By the following year, the governments of Palestine and Trans-Jordan had begun enforcing those regulations.[4] While the Public Information Office (Palestine's ministry of information) assumed direct control of the PBS, the Chief Secretary's Office, in conjunction with the postmaster general, the inspector of police, and the custodian of enemy property and others, set about registering and confiscating "enemy radio sets." "Enemy sets" belonged to those Palestinian residents or subjects who, though remaining free to go about their daily lives in the country, the Palestine mandate government considered enemies of Britain and the Allied war effort—starting with German citizens but extending in principle to known (or assumed) German and Italian sympathizers.

Palestine's radio licensing system made it easier for the mandate government to identify which of Palestine's resident enemies owned a radio set. But what the mandate government was expected to do with these radio sets once the "enemy" status of their owners had been determined was a gray area. Staff at the Chief Secretary's Office deliberated over the appropriate course of action in minutes like this:

> A.G. "I would be glad if you would advise under which regulation or law the wireless sets of enemy aliens who are at liberty can be held in safe keeping? They can be refused licenses but does this enable the wireless sets to be held by the PMG?" (Minute dated May 16, 1941)

> C.S. "It will, I think, suffice if the Assistant Inspector General (CID) refuse the applications and state that the sets are being retained by the PMG in safe custody until they can be returned to them. If the applicants, or any of them, contest this decision orders under regulation 17 (1) (a) of the Defense Regulations can be made prohibiting the possession of wireless sets by such persons." (Minute signed "Solicitor General" and dated June 2, 1941)[5]

This discussion followed one assessing jurisdictional issues concerning which government office had the right to confiscate enemy sets. Although they initially were assigned to the new Custodian of Enemy Property Office, in March 1941 the Postmaster General's Office had persuaded the Chief Secretary's Office that wireless receivers were a special case. Then acting deputy postmaster general G. D. Kennedy argued that possessing a radio set was equivalent to possessing a radio set license, which meant sets fell within his domain; the Chief Secretary's Office agreed.[6]

The two offices also dealt with the question of whether Palestine's postmaster general could legitimately assign the confiscated sets to government and other agencies in need of wireless receivers rather than have them sit out the war in storage. The Chief Secretary's Office staff seems to have reached the consensus that doing so was acceptable, since set owners were being financially compensated for the loss of their sets.[7] The postmaster general agreed and sent a letter to the chief secretary in late July 1942 outlining the rationale for requisitioning enemy sets for government use and the process for doing so. The number of radio sets available on the market had dwindled since the war began, a product of increased demand and an effectively unreplenishable supply, the letter argued. Meanwhile, the Post Office, the British armed forces, and the inspector of police were in need of radio sets and could make use of the enemy sets otherwise sitting idle in the postmaster general's care.[8]

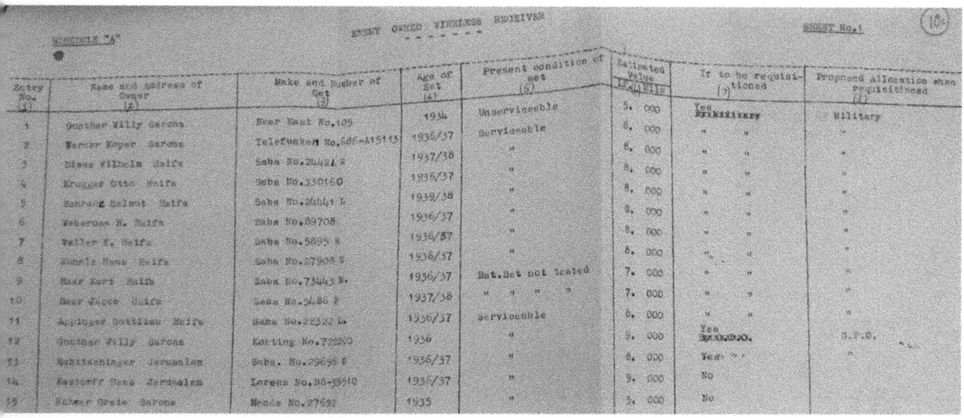

Figure 3.1. Partial listing of "Schedule A" enemy receiving sets cataloged on July 27, 1942, for possible requisition. Note the relatively advanced age of these sets, which reflected contemporary consumption practices. Radios were purchased, used, and repaired when they malfunctioned. Relatively few Palestinians could afford multiple sets or to replace their set when a more technically advanced model was introduced. Source: ISA RG 2 109 1 Chief Secretary's Office: Postmaster General on Enemy Sets.

Attached to the postmaster general's letter were two registers, one for "enemy owned sets" and one for "sets owned by enemy subjects," which listed the owner's name and address, the set's brand and model number, year of production, current condition (serviceable or unserviceable), estimated value, whether the government sought it for requisitioning, and if so, to which government branch. For example, Koper Werner of Sarona appeared as an "enemy" who owned a "serviceable" 1936/7 Telefunken No. 686–A15113, which the government estimated to be worth 8 Palestinian pounds and assigned to the military for requisitioning. Yet Herman Lauer of Haifa, another "enemy," owned a "serviceable" 1936/7 Lorenz No. 18857 also valued at 8 Palestinian pounds that the government chose not to requisition.[9]

The issue of payment inspired the sole comment written on the letter. The postmaster general had noted that "payment for requisitioned sets will presumably have to be effected either now or later to the [Custodian of Enemy Property Office, for enemy subjects] or the enemy subject or his representative," but suggested delaying payment unless the requisitionee or his agent agreed to a price that reflected the Post Office's valuation of the set. A note penciled in next to this paragraph asked, presumably referring to Axis-controlled lands: "Will this be used as a precedent for reprisals against British peoples?" It is unclear whether it was only the delayed payment that aroused the writer's concern or the idea of requisitioning radio sets (and other property) itself.

Wartime Listening Restrictions

If the confiscation and requisitioning of enemy sets was a short-term solution, controlling listening opportunities and reissuing radio set licenses under more restrictive terms were longer-term responses. Owners of sets that transmitted radio broadcasts to a large listening audience, like café and restaurant owners, faced particular scrutiny. In a June 5, 1940, story on blackout practice in Bir Sab'a, *Falastin* noted that the mandate government had "forbidden the use of radio in public shops," although radio set owners were asking that it reconsider and "permit them to use radio receivers in accordance with their desires."[10] On June 9, 1940, *Falastin* reported that the Lydda province's new radio license was ready for retrieval by "the owners of cafes, restaurants, public places and cars who have requested the licenses." Licensees were to "place these licenses in frames above the radio apparatus for their inspection by the police or government officials."[11]

The mandate government's scrutiny continued as the war effort intensified. Although the archives show little evidence that any Palestinians were arrested, tried, or convicted for violating the initial license restrictions, the mandate government continued to insist that users of radio sets in public venues obtain and display special licenses. In October 1941 *Falastin* printed an article titled "From the Official Gazette" that included an amendment to the "Emergency Law in the Matter of Radio Licenses":

> It is not permitted for anyone to obtain or use a radio apparatus in a café or restaurant or any licensed place [*makan murakhkhas*] or shop or any other public place that the public enters, or in any car unless with a license issued from the competent provincial authority [*hakim al-liwa' al-mukhtass*]. The provincial authority has complete freedom to permit this license or to prohibit it as he sees fit, or to permit it with stipulated conditions.[12]

This amendment continued the restriction on public broadcasting and allowed individual authorities great discretionary powers to license radios for public listening. That the mandate government treated public radios as forbidden unless specifically licensed and approved for public use said little about actual violations or hostile listening practices. However, it illustrates officials' great anxiety about the power of radio broadcasting during wartime.

What was on the radio was legislated as carefully as where radio broadcasts might be heard. The mandate government forbade listening to Axis and other unfriendly countries' radio stations. Here again the evidence suggests that few Palestinians were punished for violating this restriction, and those who were all appear to have been listening in public venues; at-home listening was far more difficult to regulate. In late July 1940 *Falastin* reported on one of the first Palestinians punished for violating the wartime listening restrictions. Abd al-Rahman Hassan Mar'a had "turned on his radio receiver in his café in Salma village at 8:10 pm July 13, 1940, [and tuned in] to one of the foreign stations not licensed for general listening, in contradiction of Article 22 (a) 2 of the Defense of Palestine laws. He was fined 10 guineas [and will be] jailed for one month if he does not pay the fine."[13] While the fining and the newspaper coverage may not have been a happy occasion for Mr. Mar'a, a 10-guinea fine was equivalent to roughly one-fourth, the cost of a new radio set. In other words, the fine was relatively small and far less taxing than imprisonment or a trial.

Wartime Changes at the PBS

World War II also brought changes in the direction and structure of the PBS. Control over all programming was given to the Public Information Office, which had previously exercised oversight only over the news broadcasts.[14] With the start of the war, the purpose of all radio broadcasting changed. It no longer sufficed for the station to produce broadcasts designed to realize Palestine mandate government goals; all broadcasts were subject to the higher priority of supporting the war effort. Post- and prebroadcasting censorship continued and intensified during the war, including news but also other genres such as live speeches. Later in the war the PBS's controller of English and Hebrew programs, R. D. Smith, described the procedure for live speeches broadcast on the station as a

delicate problem . . . of censorship. [Britain's] Imperial Censor requires that no speech shall go out over the air unless a previously censored copy of it is in the hands of a switch-monitor, whose duty it is to cut off the transmission if there is any deviation from the exact text. No person has, to my knowledge, ever been exempted from this regulation except His Excellency, the High Commissioner.[15]

As a broadcasting medium under the control of the Post Office, the PBS was in some ways doubly responsible for its wartime communication.

This shift in programming rationale was evident to all listeners, since two aspects of the Allies' war effort soon necessitated the introduction of new programs and new broadcasting languages. First, Britain used the station to bolster the morale of the Allied troops stationed in the region by providing music, entertainment, and news broadcasts in languages ranging from Polish to Turkish. Second, Britain used the station to counter the Vichy regime by broadcasting pro–Free French news broadcasts aimed at the populations of Lebanon and Syria. By taking up airtime previously used for Arabic or Hebrew programming, these broadcasts curtailed the station's ability to serve Palestine's Arab and Jewish audiences. In addition, the wartime conversion of British radio set manufacturers' factories (see chap. 2), coupled with government restrictions on radio set importation, sales, and ownership, limited listenership growth. During the first year of the war, the station probably lost as many Arab listeners as it gained. While war developments increased interest in the PBS's news broadcasts, the changes in entertainment and musical programming made to accommodate Allied forces and anti-Vichy broadcasts were audible reminders that the station existed first and foremost to serve British interests, whether those of the mandate government in Palestine or the home government in Britain.

In early 1940 the British government began to recognize the negative impact that such a total (and largely ad hoc) rearrangement of the PBS was having on the listening habits of what it considered the station's most important constituency. As tensions soured the working relationship between the radio station and the Public Information Office, numerous government officials in Palestine and Britain expressed their concern that the PBS was not living up to its potential in terms of mobilizing popular support for the war. General dissatisfaction with the station's wartime performance led to an extensive reorganization program, which was effected during the spring and summer of 1940. To resolve the tension that had developed between the Public Information Office (PIO) and the PBS, a special committee was appointed. It confirmed the PIO's control over the news and publicity broadcasts of the English and Hebrew sections, as well as the additional languages. However, "on account of the importance of the Arabic broadcasts," the committee recommended transferring control of all Arabic programming to a "Controller of Arabic Programs."[16] This new position had broader responsibilities and greater control than that of the subdirector of programming that Ibrahim Tuqan had pioneered. In the summer of 1940 it was taken up by ʿAjaj Nuwayhid.

ʿAjaj Nuwayhid and the PBS

ʿAjaj Nuwayhid, who was born in Lebanon and held Lebanese citizenship, had lived and worked in Palestine since 1920.[17] A well-known pan-Arabist, he worked as a journalist and was known locally as an intellectual figure who opposed the British presence in Palestine. In the early 1930s he served as an adviser to Grand Mufti Hajj Amin al-Husseini and worked as assistant inspector of Palestine's shariʿa courts. Husseini may have appointed him to this position—as a Druze he otherwise would have been an unusual choice for this Sunni post.[18] Yet Nuwayhid's involvement with Palestine's Islamic institutions reflects the more nuanced and complex positions that men of his era often took toward religion. Weldon Matthews argues that Nuwayhid "saw in nationalism no threat to Islam, but instead feared that the Arab nation and Arab culture could not endure without Islam."[19] Matthews notes that Nuwayhid gave a series of lectures to the Young Muslim Men's Associations in 1928 and 1929, in which he criticized Afghanistan, Iran, and Turkey for their governments' secularizing measures while praising the Muslim reformer Jamal al-Din al-Afghani for his "defense of Islamic culture against Western cultural encroachment."[20]

Nuwayhid's lectures served as preparation for the founding of a new party, Hizb al-Istiqlal (Independence Party). The Istiqlal Party was Arab nationalist in orientation and was formed by Nuwayhid and others in the early 1930s to push for independence. Often described as a revival of the Istiqlal Party operating in Damascus in the early postwar period, it encouraged close relationships with the states of the former Ottoman Arab provinces. By the mid-1930s its members included several prominent Palestinians, as well as a number of "Syrians" like Nuwayhid.[21] (Nuwayhid's relationship with Husseini appears to have cooled as the Istiqlal Party became more active: party activists and Husseini both recognized that he could either retain his position in the mandate government or support Istiqlal but not both.) While Nuwayhid's political role seems to have provided some professional opportunities, he continued his work in journalism. In 1932 Istiqlalists underwrote a project for him to found a magazine—titled *al-'Arab* (The Arabs)—to promote pan-Arabism.[22] Although the magazine appears to have been short-lived, Nuwayhid's career continued. In the mid-1930s he worked simultaneously as a correspondent for Cairo's *al-Ahram* and as publisher of his own paper, *al-Shabab*.

In May 1936, one month into the Arab general strike, Nuwayhid was arrested for his political activities and sent to Jericho, where the mandate government often sent political prisoners. He also spent time in the government's prison at Sarafand.[23] After his release Nuwayhid resumed his work as a journalist. According to Matthews, Nuwayhid softened his anti-British stance after the publication of the 1939 White Paper on Palestine, which substantially curtailed British commitments to the Zionist cause in Palestine. In particular, it stated that Palestine was neither a Jewish nor an Arab state but "one in which Arabs and Jews share government" and would achieve independence within a decade. It limited Jewish immigration to 75,000 over the following five years, subject to what the White Paper termed Palestine's "economic absorptive capacity." Finally, it provided the High Commissioner's Office with "general powers to prohibit and regulate transfers of land," noting that in some areas land transfers should be "restricted" while in others there was "no room for further transfers of Arab land."[24] The White Paper was received with disappointment and hostility by Palestine's Zionist community and with optimism by Palestinian Arabs and supporters of an independent Palestine like Nuwayhid. At this point, Matthews suggests, Nuwayhid shifted from opposing to cooperating with the mandate government.[25]

Despite his record of opposition politics, arrest, and exile, Nuwayhid was at times intimately involved with the mandate government's activities. In 1935 he had been involved in the selection of the three final-round candidates considered for the position of subdirector of the Arabic section of the PBS. However, he had not been involved with the station since. Nor, given his record, would the British government in Palestine have seemed likely to want him there. Yet Ibrahim Tuqan, who was still working as the artistic director of the Arabic section, had a record equally marked by oppositional activities. The poems he wrote were deeply nationalist, and thanks to his words and his political activities, he too had faced the British mandate government's wrath.

Figure 3.2. ʾAjaj Nuwayhid (standing) at the Palestine Broadcasting Service offices with a Lebanese "zajjaleen" trio, which sang popular poetry in colloquial Arabic. Source: G. Eric and Edith Matson Photograph Collection, Prints and Photographs Division, Library of Congress, LC-DIG-matpc-14771.

Throughout the mandate period the British government attempted to domesticate such figures, hoping that by hiring them the government would benefit both from their talents and from a softening of the impact of their opposition to it. In the case of Nuwayhid, as well as that of Tuqan, the government enjoyed at best a partial success. Each man continued to work to realize his vision of an independent Arab Palestine during his tenure as subdirector/section controller, which vision influenced their professional actions as much as their personal ones.

The negotiations that took place between ʿAjaj Nuwayhid and the British mandate government began immediately. Nuwayhid was in fact offered the position of section controller twice—the first time in 1939. According to his memoirs, he accepted only after the government representatives consented to his conditions: total independence for the Arabic section, including its relocation to a building separate from the others; complete freedom to hire and fire employees without government advice or interference; and a generous budget to support improved musical and cultural programming.[26] While Tuqan remained with the station, Nuwayhid's jurisdiction extended to political and intellectual programming, while responsibility for the artistic programming remained with Tuqan. However, Tuqan resigned in late 1940,[27] after which Nuwayhid assumed responsibility for all non-news Arabic programming. His title itself signaled a difference from the station's other directors and from past Arabic section heads: *murāqib al-barāmij al-ʿarabiya wa al-nashr*, controller of Arabic programs and publication.

In June 1941 High Commissioner MacMichael described the situation in a telegram to the secretary of state for the colonies as follows: "in view of the importance of Arabic broadcasts from the point of view of propaganda the whole of the Arabic program was last year placed under an Arab controller Ajaj [Nuwayhid,] who works in collaboration with the Director of Programs as regards entertainment and instructional sides and under the Public Information Officer as regards [the] publicity aspect."[28] Nuwayhid had been hired on a temporary, renewable contract carrying an annual salary of 600 Palestinian pounds,[29] a respectable salary for the position and the time.[30]

Broadcasting a Nationalist Modernity on a Mandate Station

For the government, Nuwayhid's appointment had the great advantage of placing a strong and capable leader at the helm of the Arabic section, whose success at drawing and keeping an Arab listening public from Palestine and around the region British officials deemed crucial to achieving Britain's wartime objectives. Nuwayhid described the advantages of his appointment somewhat differently: it offered an opportunity to improve the cultural life of Arab Palestine and to place the radio station at its heart, thus helping it realize its potential to be a force for political and societal development. In his memoirs he listed ten roles for the PBS. The first item on his list attested to the deep interconnections that he as a pan-Arabist saw linking Palestine and the rest of the Arab world. First, Nuwayhid noted the PBS's multiple audiences, in Palestine and beyond: the station's transmitter was strong enough that the signal was heard clearly throughout the region. Consequently, the station was capable of—and in his view had the responsibility for—"strengthening the national link between the Palestinian interior nearby and the Arab expanses far away."[31] This dual sense of possibility and duty informed Nuwayhid's outlook, providing a foundation for the high standards to which he held himself and the other Arabic section staff during his time at the PBS.

The remaining nine aspects of the station's broadcasting with which Nuwayhid engaged himself in many ways surpassed the BBC's "educate and elevate" broadcasting model. He was deeply concerned about building a strong community, whether Palestinian or extended to encompass the Arab world generally, through high-quality musical, theatrical, and literary programming. For him, strengthening the bonds between Christian and Muslim Palestinians, between Palestinians and Trans-Jordanians, and among all Arabs meant not merely *more* programming, but *better* programming. He was not alone on this issue: listeners had complained about the recorded music played on the PBS for years. While Hebrew section listeners tended to complain about the station's reliance on less expensive recorded music rather than live orchestral and other performances, the Palestinian community focused primarily on the frequency with which certain records were broadcast.

In March 1940, for example, *Falastin* devoted several "Broadcasting Corners" to criticizing the station for taking the title of its "What the (Arabic-speaking) Listeners Want" program too seriously. The column complained about seeing "in one daily program three different times for broadcasting the selected records," and elsewhere described it as an "eccentricity" to see "one musical piece by one artist [broadcast] three or four times in one week when there are good musical pieces broadcast once in a month—or only once." The articles criticized the station for excessively playing two pieces in particular—one by Mary ʿAkkawi and one by Farid al-Atrash[32]—the first in part because "this record is very old and has musical and vocal errors."[33] These complaints shed light on contemporary ideas about radio broadcasting norms. The intimation of what constituted excessive airtime to these listeners—three or four times a week, let alone three or four times a day—suggests very different notions of aural pleasure than the globalized "Top 40" station model of the late twentieth century.

While the newspapers limited themselves to complaints about overplaying certain records, Nuwayhid in his memoirs described his frustration with the quality of the records the station had collected. He especially disliked the collection used for religious and national holidays, whose hymns and anthems he considered vulgar and ordinary. He first expressed his dissatisfaction with the selection to the other Arabic section broadcasters, assuming that they would share his tastes. When they continued to play these records despite his disapproval, he simply removed the offending records from the Broadcasting House studios, explaining later that he did so "in order to lift the level of Arab artistic taste to a better level."[34] Nuwayhid was similarly concerned that the station should work to bring listeners the highest-quality Arabic language—not only by using clear, error-free Arabic in their own broadcasts but also by fostering the language through poetry competitions, special Ramadan broadcasts, and other programming.

Nationalism and Religious Identity on the PBS

Nuwayhid concerned himself with these issues not so much for the current generation of Palestinian adults as for the next generation—the Arab youth of Palestine and their fellows beyond Palestine's borders. While the PBS had presented children's programming in discrete "Children's Hour" segments since its inception, Nuwayhid envisioned a program with something more than stories to teach its listeners. He wanted the children's programs, and the station's programming generally, to reinforce to children and adult listeners alike that they were part of the Arab nation (*al-watan al-ʿarabi*) and teach them the meaning of Arabism. Like other pan-Arabists of his era, Nuwayhid considered Islam an important common element for people around the region—regardless of whether they were Muslim, Druze, or Christian. According to Abu Shanab, the children's program had a signature song, broadcast during every session, whose lyrics included the following:

> O youth [*fata*], oh hero
> You are the torch of hope for tomorrow
> Your great feast day [*ʿeidak al-kabir*], oh youth
> Your great feast day is coming—when?
> As soon as the shepherd of the country [*al-watan*] comes
> Give us a tomorrow, redeem the country.[35]

While not sectarian, the song mixed national language and imagery with religious terms like "eid" and "redeem," illustrating the connections being drawn between region, country, and religion. Beyond the children's programming per se, the anthems and poems broadcast on the air, the religious and national holiday programming, and the level of language itself all worked to reinforce this broader lesson.[36] Did all this escape mandate officials at the station or at the Public Information Office? No extant documents suggest that Nuwayhid's programming was more heavily censored than other PBS programs, or that he was censured at all. Although numerous mandate officials spoke Arabic, his programming choices may have been subtle enough to avoid criticism.

Nuwayhid had expressed his desire to use the radio station for strengthening the bonds between Muslim and Christian Palestinians—a view stemming from his pan-Arabist position that Islam could serve as a unifying force for all people in the region, Muslim and non-Muslim alike. While the PBS had historically included some religious programming, under Nuwayhid the station's Arabic broadcasts subtly increased their Islamic content. In fall 1940, he organized a series of *adhaan* broadcasts, which aired with Qur'anic recitations at the times of the *maghrib* and 'asha prayers.[37] These broadcasts were praised by members of various religious communities. For example, the *Palestine Post*'s "Listener's Corner" applauded them: "Nothing could be more impressive than the voice of the muezzin through the silence of the night. . . . [T]he PBS has made it possible for all Moslem listeners with a radio set to listen to the call to prayers from a Sheikh whose clear diction and voice leave nothing to be desired."[38] *Falastin* also applauded the fruits of Nuwayhid's labors with editorials such as "At the Margin of Memory," which in April 1941 waxed grateful about the Arabic section's three days of programming in honor of the Prophet's birthday.[39]

In addition to Qur'anic broadcasts, Nuwayhid encouraged Islamically inflected programming of other sorts, for example, the broadcasting of "religious songs" such as "My umma returns to you, oh Prophet" during religious holy days.[40] (The station broadcast special programs on Christian holidays as well, but there is no record of the same type of talks on specifically Christian themes, for example, or of children's programs devoted to identifiably Christian narratives.) During the Hajj season, he successfully persuaded both the Chief Secretary's Office and the Saudi government to approve the broadcasting of messages sent from Palestinian pilgrims traveling on Hajj to friends and relatives at home. The public information officer supported his initiative, seeing in it an opportunity to present the station in a positive light not only in Palestine but throughout the "Moslem world."[41] Yet for Nuwayhid the appeal of the Hajj broadcasts appears to have lain more in their ability to connect Arab Palestinians with the rest of the Arab and Muslim world than to promote the PBS to a regional audience.

In addition to religious references and explicitly religious broadcasts, Nuwayhid encouraged well-known scholars to appear on the station, speaking on topics within their field of interest, personal or professional. Many spoke on subjects relating to Islam and the Muslim world. The well-known historian Abd al-Latif Tibawi, for example, spoke on January 3, 1941, on the topic "The Army in Islam," a timely one during wartime but also, again, a vehicle for connecting Islamic heritage and the national present.[42] The children's programming also worked to build a Muslim identity, as indicated by such "Talks for Children" topics as "The Story of Muʿawiya ibn Abu Sufyan," broadcast on March 1, 1941. Muʿawiya, governor of Damascus during the early caliphate, fought and killed ʿAli, Muhammad's son-in-law and cousin, after disputing ʿAli's legitimacy as caliph. He subsequently founded the Umayyad dynasty by designating his son, Yazid, as his successor—transforming the caliphate from an elected to an inherited position.[43] It is important not to over-interpret stories like these—the "Children's Hour" broadcasts covered a variety of topics, with "Oscar Wilde" scheduled for later that same week. However, Muʿawiya has historically been a figure more revered by Sunni Muslims than Shiʿi Muslims; and the Umayyad dynasty repre-sented one of the high-water marks of Syrian history. In this story, reli-gious identity and regional pride could conjoin.

Nuwayhid brought listeners to the PBS with other programming as well. The January 4, 1941, schedule listed a program of marches, tan-gos, waltzes, and foxtrots performed live on air by the studio orchestra, followed by the weekly sports roundup.[44] In March talks like Dr. Salim Hamdan's "The Free Man and Freedom"[45] addressed topics made more current by the war—and, perhaps, by the mandate itself. In the spring of 1941 the radio station organized a series of "special broadcasts" in which winning poems from the station's most recent poetry competi-tion were read on air. On May 1 the poems "The Air War," "Shake-speare," and "al-Andalus" were read, suggesting the breadth of topics covered.[46] The summer saw a series of "methodological talks" on the poetry of Palestinian and Trans-Jordanian poets, who were invited to read selections from their own work and to discuss their influences and inspirations.[47] In October the Arabic section broadcast a series titled "Reflections on Arabic Literature," which included a talk by Dr. Khalil Taqi al-Din, director of Lebanon's Government Printing Office, titled "The Night of Decline and the Dawn of the Rebirth."[48]

Among music lovers, Nuwayhid's tenure as controller of the Ara-bic section might best be remembered as the era of Jullnar. "Jullnar" was the stage name taken by Fatima al-Bizra, a young Syrian singer. Al-Bizra, who had come to Jerusalem to audition for the radio station ac-companied by her mother, wanted to sing but feared the stigma that often attached to female performers. Nuwayhid agreed to preserve her anonymity, and the studio christened her Jullnar.[49] She became the stu-dio's featured female soloist, and many PBS broadcasts included *qasi-das* and other musical pieces sung by "Miss Jullnar." Jullnar's renown

Figure 3.3. Undated publicity photograph of Jullnar and violinist Jalil Rukab.
Source: ISA/RG15/M/2242/28 Palestine Public Information Office.

should serve as a reminder that she was not the only female singer on
the PBS: a June 1940 *Falastin* feature by Daoud al-ʿIsa on "an hour at
the Broadcasting House" listed two women as members of the Broadcasting Group: Rajaʾ Filastiniyya (likely a stage name) and "Miss Mary
ʿAkkawi, Nightingale of the Broadcasting Station."[50] While al-ʿIsa
teased ʿAkkawi about her youth, noting "you, the tender sex, hate this
question" even at fifteen, he described Rajaʾ as hoping for "light movement although her weight exceeds 120 kilos." "God's protection to her
for health and strength," he concluded.[51] In general, however, women
on the PBS received less attention than their male counterparts and
were limited to entertainment or educational broadcasts.

In addition to Nuwayhid's concern with broadcasting to instill national and religious identities in Palestinian and Arab children around
the region, his vision for the PBS defined it as responsible for promoting the interests of another group that could be considered vulnera-

ble: Arab women. In his memoirs he described this simply as "the matter of the Arab woman in Palestine, and the Arab woman in the Arab world."[52] Nuwayhid could have meant, as many of his British colleagues would have assumed, the backwardness of Arab women. Instead, the programming he fostered made it clear that this was not the case. Nuwayhid's interest as section controller lay strictly in publicizing the advancement of Arab women and promoting their contributions to society. "The New Arab House" series was the first of several broadcasting initiatives designed to help the station realize its role in this regard.

Broadcasting Women: "The New Arab House"

On January 22, 1941, a combined British and Australian force completed its capture of Tobruk from the Italian army. Control of Tobruk, a seaport located in a strategic position on the eastern Libyan coast, was critical for securing the new British-created North African supply line. The Italian forces considered the city equally critical to their war effort, and to securing their perch in Egypt, which they had invaded in November 1940. With the help of German reinforcements, Italian forces under Erwin Rommel kept the city under siege until August 1941, when they retreated for the last time. The winter and spring of 1941 were filled with war news of immediate relevance for Libya's Levantine neighbors, whose British and French mandatory authorities were deeply involved in the war. In Palestine as elsewhere across the region, the daily newspapers' headlines and news articles were devoted to war developments, which took up the top half to two-thirds of the front page of each edition. An Italian-German victory in Libya would have prevented Britain and Allied forces from maintaining the supply lines that would have allowed them to wage serious warfare in the North African desert and would have threatened Britain with the loss of Egypt.

Yet in the midst of these developments, *Falastin* began devoting a large section of its front page to an entirely unrelated topic: household management. On Sunday, January 26, 1941, four days after Tobruk fell to the British, *Falastin* printed the transcript of the first in a series of PBS talks by Mrs. Salwa Sa'id that had been airing weekly since mid-December. The sixth talk in the series aired Thursday, January 23, three days before *Falastin* published the transcript of the first talk. The series included nine broadcasts of fifteen minutes each, airing every Thursday evening through February 13, 1941.[53] Mrs. Sa'id began with a talk titled "Household Management" or "Household Planning"

Figure 3.4. "Talks of 'The New Arab House,'" headline for transcript of second talk. Source: *Falastin*, Feb. 2, 1941, p. 1.

and continued with "The Natural Position of the House," "Household Furnishings," "Household Organization," "Cleanliness and Tidiness," "Household Economy," "The Kitchen," "The Dining Room," and "The Maid and Manservant." All these were reproduced in full in *Falastin*'s pages.

To have made the front page of *Falastin* in any form was no small achievement, as it was generally considered one of the most influential Arabic-language paper then published in Palestine. Like all newspapers in this period, its relatively high costs coupled with Arab Palestine's relatively low literacy rates meant that it was not regularly read by the majority of Arab Palestinians. However, multiple copy sharing and group reading practices made it accessible to a larger number of people than these circulation statistics suggest, and its high proportion of elite, bourgeois, and upper-class readers gave it political and societal influence.[54]

Wartime paper and ink restrictions had reduced *Falastin* to two pages printed front and back, about one-half or two-thirds its prewar size. Even with a corresponding reduction in advertising due to the shrunken wartime economy and much-tightened censorship laws regulating news and commentary, there still remained plenty of news to print—so these page limitations left little room for fluff or filler.[55] The editors' decision to publish transcripts of "The New Arab House" broadcasts on *Falastin*'s front page must have been carefully and consciously made, as the space required to publish each transcript required them to cut out much of the day's news coverage, which they did eleven times between January and March 1941. Each time, the transcript ran on the front page, taking roughly one-sixth its space, and continued on the third page, taking one-third to one-half its space.

In the thirteen years that the PBS was on the air, 1936–1949, this was the only time *Falastin* published full transcripts of the station's serials, though it frequently commented on the station's programming. *Falastin*'s printing of the "New Arab House" transcripts is a historical puzzle whose resolution offers a new perspective on the PBS's wartime programming. Why *Falastin* reprinted any PBS talks, let alone this series, and why the paper chose to reprint them on the front page during a sensitive moment during the war can be answered by understanding that *Falastin*'s interest in these talks reflected its editors' support for ʿAjaj Nuwayhid, the broadcasting station's newly appointed Arabic programming controller, and his vision for the station, which in some ways reflected their vision for the newspaper. (ʿIsa al-ʿIsa and Nuwayhid were personal friends.)[56]

Nuwayhid had come to the position with a conscious plan to make the station an influential, progressive voice speaking to and for Arab Palestine—a program that included a heavy focus on women broadcasters and women's broadcasting. An examination of the content and tone of this serial, as well as *Falastin*'s laudatory coverage of it, reveals the extent to which Nuwayhid and *Falastin* saw the PBS as a means of actualizing their shared vision of a nationalist Palestinian modernity. The harmony between the radio station's Arabic section controller and the newspaper's editors bears witness to a moment in which the two united in support of radio broadcasts that promoted a modern, progressive, urban, and bourgeois identity for Arab Palestine.

"The New Arab House" series was certainly not the first time a woman's voice, Arab or otherwise, had been heard on the air from Jerusalem: the PBS had employed women in broadcasting and in supporting administrative positions since the late 1930s. However, the status accorded Salwa Saʿid as a female broadcaster was different from those of the women who appeared as singers, book reviewers, musicians, and actors in station productions. Unlike many of the women in these categories, the station's programming schedule identified her by name every time she appeared on the air. She was a solo act, not part of an ensemble or in a supporting role. Like the (male) professors, doctors, and literary figures who were guest speakers with a particular area of specialized knowledge, Mrs. Salwa Saʿid was brought in to deliver the "New Arab House" series of talks as an expert in her field.

Saʿid was a graduate of the American University of Beirut (AUB) and daughter of a former mayor of Beirut, who had moved to Palestine after her marriage to a Palestinian-Lebanese man. In the *Falastin* reprints of her talks, neither the editors' introduction nor the transcripts themselves specified what made Saʿid an authority on household management, though presumably she had completed a related major at AUB. Yet she was quite clearly understood to be speaking with a scholarly knowledge of the subject rather than as an ordinary housewife speaking from personal experience. Just as the *Palestine Post* had identified her as "Madame" in its "Listener's Corner" coverage of her talks,[57] *Falastin* referred to her with professional deference as "al-adība al-faḍila," which might be translated as "the eminent woman of letters" or "the distinguished writer."

What did this expert have to say about household management? For scholars conversant with the style and content of the articles produced in the turn-of-the-century Arab and Ottoman women's press, a review of the content of Saʿid's talks reveals that they contain some familiar elements. First, Saʿid's intermittent use of "my Arab sister" invoked a culture of sisterhood common to the articles and editorials that appeared in early-twentieth-century women's magazines.[58] Whether this terminology was meant to draw community boundaries that excluded Jews or that stretched to include all Arab women is difficult to discern from the text, but the appeal to a shared familial bond was unambiguous. Second, Saʿid introduced a distinction between a mythic past characterized by oppression and a present marked by women's progress. She praised contemporary attitudes of respect for Arab women and their work in the home, saying that her sisters "thank[ed] God that today no longer [anyone] rejects us, we women, from those things that we have made for his sake; or attempts to wrest from us unlimited power in administering this little kingdom (the house)."[59] On the contrary: household administration [*idarat al-manzil*] was now recognized as "the highest sphere" and one requiring careful study, including the "path of reading in books" for knowledge.[60]

What distinguished Saʿid's talks was her definition of the household as a professional field. While she did refer to household planning and organization as an "art" (*fann al-tadbīr al-manzali*), most of the words she used were, like "household administration [*idarat al-manzil*]," more commonly found in business or politics. She compared this type of household improvement (*hadhihi al-daʿwa li-tahsīn manazilna*) to a more superficial kind focused on pretty appliances or elaborate meals that demonstrated selfish disregard for the privations of wartime conditions. "What we strive toward," she said, "is the administrative organization that makes our houses be in accord with our income and our capacity for [organization], and [in accord with] our inclination for development by degrees with modern taste and correct knowledge." Both organization (*tandhīm*) and administration (*idara*) suggested a rational, considered approach to household management borrowed from the professional worlds of business and politics.

The professionalization of household management was made possible in part by its development as an educational subject. The household emerged as a subject for formal, theoretical study in educational institutions around the world in the early twentieth century. Scholars such as Afsaneh Najmabadi, Timothy Burke, and Jacques Donzelot, among others, have described this process with regard to motherhood, hygiene, and the family, respectively.[61] Broadly (and crudely) put, these developments transformed domestic spaces, behaviors, and relationships into matters requiring professional training. Saʿid's attitudes toward her subject in 1941 can be seen as demonstrating the maturation of that transformation. This maturation was most evident in Saʿid's confident tone, which differed dramatically from the apologetic one of columnists of the period's Middle Eastern women's press and periodicals. Rather than ask listeners to pardon her lack of knowledge, Saʿid suggested that for her the problem was an embarrassment of riches. As she told her listeners, her challenge in drafting her talks was condensing her wealth of knowledge on "household matters" into a limited number of broadcasts.[62] Her expertise was vast, and she was eager, rather than hesitant, to share.

But with whom was she sharing? Who were the managers and administrators of the new Arab house to whom she addressed her talks? It is clear from the reprinted transcripts that Saʿid's new Arab house was one that only a narrow spectrum of Arab Palestinian women could realistically call home. The text of Saʿid's talks indicated that the women she was addressing were involved in such domestic enterprises as management and not as labor. As suggested by the title of one talk, "The Maid and Manservant," her imagined audience was composed of bourgeois and upper-class women able to afford servants. Her talks addressed their problems, not those of women working as servants.[63] Nor was she concerned with the particular problems of household management in rural areas, although the majority of the Arab population in Palestine in the 1940s was rural. The women who comprised Saʿid's imagined audience were city dwellers, living in and able to afford electricity, imported appliances, and running water. After all, they were able to tune in to her talks on the radio from their own homes, an appliance and a listening practice more common among relatively affluent urbanites.

Women's Advancement as the Sign of Modernity

For those bourgeois women listening to the PBS, "The New Arab House" broadcasts must have been a godsend. But why were they on the air at this moment—and what, ultimately, was *Falastin*'s interest in them? That the serial was broadcast in late 1940 and early 1941 was not coincidental. It was part of larger moment, one marked by an elite Palestinian Arab focus on both demonstrating and encouraging women's advancement as "proof" of the degree of Palestinian advancement. ʿAjaj Nuwayhid brought this focus to the PBS.

Nuwayhid's taking over the direction of the Arabic section of the Palestine Broadcasting Service was a crucial factor in getting more female broadcasters on the air during the winter of 1940–1941. Most were like Saʿid: well-to-do, well-educated women brought in as guest broadcasters to speak on a particular field of expertise. Some appeared as part of a larger "night of women" broadcast, as did the well-known women's movement activist and writer Matiel Mughannam and fellow feminists Shahina Duzdar, Asma Touba, Karima Nasr, and Shahra al-Masri on January 25, 1941—the night before the transcript of Saʿid's first talk was published in *Falastin*. That transcript ran next to an equally lengthy, laudatory editorial praising this "night of women" and summarizing each woman's talk—some covering "women's issues" and some covering more general issues, like Duzdar's talk on the wartime economy. Other women gave serialized or one-off talks on particular topics, as Saʿid did—most notably, the women's movement pioneer and writer Qudsiyya Khurshīd, who covered religious topics, for example, "The Muslim Woman during Ramadan" and a series on the history of Islam.[64] Women broadcasting on women remained a PBS programming theme in 1942, as with the series of talks given that summer by Mary Shehadeh, a journalist and the wife of Boulos Shehadeh, who published the paper *Mira't al-Sharq*, an early supporter of women's advancement, from Jerusalem.[65] Mary Shehadeh spoke under her maiden name, 'Aqila, on such topics as "The Society of Women" (*al-mujtama'a al-nisa'i*) and, with her husband, "Aphorisms of Arab Women."[66]

Women's broadcasts were included in the collected volume *Broadcast Talks*, which the PBS under Nuwayhid's direction published in December 1942. The *Palestine Post*'s review welcomed the collection:

> This is the first volume of a series to be published by the [PBS], containing a number of talks of permanent value. The second volume (in press) will bring poetical contributions, both classical and vernacular. It is an achievement to present the Arabic public in Palestine and the adjacent countries with such a gift. The book contains a mass of information which an Arab reader would look for in vain in other works.
>
> Finally, a few talks "pro domo": Sheikh Suleiman al-Ja'bari's exhortation on "Moslem morals and character building," Madame Asma Tuba's "To the Arab Mother," and Mrs. Mary Sarrouf-Shehade's scholarly resumé, "Education in the Arab Family." These are followed by Qudsiyya Khurshid's disquisition titled "Personality of Woman." The volume, edited by Khalil Beidas, was introduced by Ajaj Nuweihid, in charge of the Arabic section of the PBS. One reviewer commented, "The volume merits unqualified praise."[67]

The review did qualify the women's and other private sphere or personal talks by describing them as "pro domo," literally "for the house" and used in Latin to refer to speeches delivered in defense or promotion of one's own interests, which separated them from the political and historical talks mentioned at the start of the review. Morals, mothering, education, and women were evidently topics on a different order from Abdullatif al-Tibawi's "Moslem Armies," which the reviewer praised as "a scholarly piece of work," and current events talks by "prominent personalities" such as Muhammad Kurd 'Ali. While the *Palestine Post* might have taken a somewhat dismissive view of these talks, the radio station's decision to include them demonstrated that it did not. Publishing talks broadcast on the radio in book form demonstrated the station administrators' conviction that they had lasting value and that through them the PBS was making substantial contributions to Arab Palestine's political, social, and arts fields. Although future volumes were planned, this was the only book the PBS Broadcasting Service would publish, and the fact of it as well as the inclusion of female broadcasters points to Nuwayhid's innovation and drive during his time as the Arabic section controller.

As with Sa'id's talks and the "night of women" broadcasts, female broadcasters received lavish and complimentary coverage in *Falastin*—coverage quite different from the often harshly critical editorials published about the station both before and after the war. These were congruent with the numerous editorial and feature pieces that the paper printed in 1940 and 1941 praising Nuwayhid and his efforts to improve the Arabic section's broadcasting programs. However, of all his initiatives, only the women's broadcasts were singled out for praise. An editorial published on February 7, 1941, described the station as having done "a good turn" by hiring Salwa Sa'id to "pave the way" for the female broadcasters who followed in her wake and gave "the credit for this blessed awakening" to Nuwayhid. The paper described the women's speeches as "a display of their knowledge and genius" and thanked Nuwayhid for opening the door "for them to participate in service of their culture and society."[68] Such unqualified praise, of the actors as well as the station itself, was rarely seen in *Falastin*'s pages.

Falastin's treatment of Sa'id's broadcasts was perhaps the greatest statement of its support for women's broadcasting and the station changes under Nuwayhid. As to why her series was chosen over the others to be reprinted in its pages, the lack of extant sources makes the answer merely speculative. Perhaps the rationale was chronological: as *Falastin*'s February 7 editorial noted, Sa'id's was the first major talk given by a woman. Yet the paper described all the women's talks as "valuable." Did its editors worry that readers might disagree? Perhaps household management was considered a less inflammatory subject than the life of Muhammad as interpreted by a woman scholar (Khurshid), or of greater general interest than a chronology of women's progress (Shahra).

Perhaps it was also a better fit with political developments in Palestine. The subtitle that *Falastin* chose for the transcript of Sa'id's first talk used a phrase taken from it: "The unlimited power of women in the administration of 'their little kingdom.'" She explained this metaphor by adding "the home" in parentheses, evidently suspecting that either the phrase or the concept might not be familiar to all listeners. It would have been a familiar concept for another group, however. As scholars from Partha Chatterjee to Omnia Shakry have demonstrated,[69] twentieth-century nationalist theoreticians and leaders around the world shared the belief that nation building began not merely at but in the home. Each well-managed household served by its rational organization, its hygienic atmosphere, healthful cooking, and its educated and patriotic children as "proof" of society's advancement against colonial state claims to the contrary. For Palestine and the Class A mandate states proper, this proof had material consequences, for theirs were the only colonial structures established with a determinate if indefinite end point: political and societal maturity. At least theoretically, independence would come once each mandate state "proved" its readiness for independence to the League of Nations Mandates Commission. This connection between societal advancement and political self-determination was what made women's broadcasts and women's broadcasters so laudable. It also made "The New Arab House" worthy of inclusion in *Falastin* as a front-page item with the other political news of the day.

Nuwayhid's Legacy

'Ajaj Nuwayhid found few friends among British officials in Palestine. Their discomfort seems to have come partly from the incongruity of a colonial government hiring an avowed Arab nationalist to oversee Arabic programming at the government's radio station. Tensions arose between the British mandate government and Nuwayhid whenever their respective objectives—a well-managed mandate colony and an independent Arab Palestine—clashed. Ralph Poston, the English and Hebrew sections controller in 1941–1942, harshly criticized Nuwayhid in a July 1942 memo titled "British Propaganda in Palestine." (Although he resigned as controller, citing frustration with the station's administration, Poston had a long history of service to both the Palestine government and British broadcasting efforts. He had served as private secretary to the High Commissioner in the mid-1930s, and in 1938 conducted a survey of various government officials regarding Arab Palestinians' interest in the new BBC Arabic broadcasts.)[70] Poston described the medium-wave PBS as "undoubtedly the most important means of propaganda in British hands in the Near East" but added, "I do not think it is being properly used." He characterized the situation prevailing in the Arabic section as follows:

> Soon after [Nuwayhid's] arrival in the PBS steps were taken by the PIO on his behalf to secure the dismissal of the two Arabs who had been

trained as broadcasters and had run the Arabic programs since the inception of the station in 1936. He was thus in command of an important service of which he had not the least technical knowledge, and for which he received no training, with no support but comparatively junior announcers. He is a difficult personality who must be absolute master, and this led to the dismissal of the old staff at his instigation. Since that time he has had frequent changes of program staff (announcers etc.) and has lost the services of several of the outstanding musicians, including Mohammed Abdel Karim, one of the outstanding musicians of the Near East.

Describing Nuwayhid as "a good journalist, [who] has undoubtedly improved the news services and talks," Poston did not suggest firing him but rather limiting him to what he considered Nuwayhid's strengths: journalistic reportage and news broadcasting. "The Arabic Section of the PBS should be a) reinforced by more capable and less youthful staff under 'Ajaj eff[endi] and b) placed once more under the technical control and supervision of a trained broadcaster, who can help Ajaj eff to get the best out of the machinery at his disposal."[71] Criticisms like Poston's blended personal and professional attacks, suggesting that Nuwayhid was insufficiently mature or lacked the experience necessary for his post. By focusing on these aspects, they avoided the real issues: Nuwayhid enjoyed administrative independence, and his goals for Arabic programming did not match those of the British mandate government.

British officials' criticism could not hide the fact that Nuwayhid was an effective controller whose administration of the PBS Arabic section made an impact that lasted long after his resignation in December 1943.[72] His impact is apparent in the intensity with which mandate government officials criticized him. For example, a 1945 chief secretary's minute described him as "an individual personality who was the center of intrigues and jealousy until his retirement."[73] Perhaps they would have preferred someone more docile. In any case, they may have denigrated his character, but they were apparently unable to do much else. Nuwayhid left the Arabic section in greater control of the content it broadcast and free from direct daily oversight by the Public Information Office:

The final result of the solution of the war-time "set-up" was that the Public Information Officer had more direct control over the preparation of the English and Hebrew bulletins than over the Arabic, though he was responsible for the provision of the material for all three. The Arabic news staff works in the PBS building. The others work in the Public Information Office. [74]

During his time at the radio station, Nuwayhid had insisted on the Arabic staff's physical as well as organizational independence from the Public Information Office and, by extension, from the British mandate government. He argued that this independence would result not only in better programming but also in the greater confidence of the Arab Palestinian audience. The Arabic section's relative independence, which continued into the postwar period, certainly irked PBS Hebrew section listeners, which in turn pleased the editors of *Falastin*. An April 1943 editorial noted with some pleasure that the Hebrew-language newspaper *Haboker* had recently complained "about the lack of 'independence' of the Hebrew section" when compared to the "complete 'independence' which the Arabic section enjoys."[75]

The agreement may have galled British mandate officials, but it continued to hold. In May 1945 the Palestine Broadcasting Service was restructured. It was separated from the Public Information Office, and its programming and administration returned to a peacetime footing. The Arabic section was still treated as a distinct unit under the direction of a controller of Arabic programs—retaining much of the administrative independence it had enjoyed under Nuwayhid. While the Arabic section was no longer housed in a separate building, it enjoyed much greater autonomy than it had before the war began. 'Azmi Nashashibi, who served as controller until the end of the mandate period, continued in much the same vein as Nuwayhid. Like Nuwayhid and especially Tuqan before him, Nashashibi was a well-educated member of a local elite family with a history of oppositional collaboration with the British mandate government and an early career in journalism, including a stint as editor of *Falastin*'s weekly English-language publication.

Thanks to the administrative framework that Nuwayhid established, Nashashibi was able to navigate through the constraints of the colonial modernity that the PBS was created to support, instead using the Arabic section as a platform for promoting a nationalist vision of an Arab Palestinian modernity. He did so by continuing the modern focus of Arabic section programming, by, for example, requesting recordings of "songs from the latest Arabic cinema films" as well as "Koran, music, talks, etc.," from the BBC's Cairo office[76] when none were available in postwar Palestine. And he did so by traveling to Britain in 1946 for training at the BBC Arabic headquarters.[77] His stay at the BBC left him hungry to modernize the PBS further, and with it Palestine generally—starting with the introduction of street addresses. He noted disparagingly that "as for the Jerusalem station, the geographic address of its [broadcasting] building is 'between the central prison and the school for the deaf.'"[78]

The PBS Arabic section that Nuwayhid shaped and Nashashibi continued was one whose programming communicated a vision of nationalist modernity for Arab Palestine. Programs emphasizing the musical, poetic, and oratorical talents of Arab Palestinians—especially women—conveyed to listeners an image of Arab Palestinian culture as progressive and urbane. The Arabic section began communicating this message more clearly and more strongly during World War II, when the mandate government was reasserting its control over the station with respect to news censorship and broadcasting hours.

This parallel development suggests the weakness of the mandate government's colonial-style practice of hiring well-known oppositional figures in the hope of co-opting them or at least capitalizing on their reputation to make government policies and practices more palatable to the local population. What Ibrahim Tuqan may have wished to do with the Arabic section Nuwayhid was able to achieve: programming that communicated a self-consciously modern, sophisticated Arab Palestine in the face of Yishuv and British colonial assertions of Arab Palestinian backwardness. As part of this project, Nuwayhid included programming that highlighted religion, especially Islam. While Druze himself and while cognizant of Palestine's religious diversity, he seems to have focused almost entirely on Muslim religious programming, perhaps seeing in it a spiritual base for Palestinian national identity. The next chapter examines the station's religious programming more broadly, noting that the government's original decision to allow religious programming set in motion the PBS's longest-lasting legacy: government management of on-air religious expression.

CHAPTER 4

Putting Religion on the Radio

Much of the PBS's programming focused on cultural programs, which largely meant music and talks. Yet religion also played a crucial role—in entertainment programming and as its own broadcasting category. For the mandate government, a British Protestant institution attempting to govern Palestine's internally diverse Muslim, Jewish, and Christian populations, the state's relationship with religious institutions and practices required careful negotiation. To legitimize its presence, both within Palestine and before the League of Nations Mandate Commission, the mandate government followed Ottoman legal precedents on many issues, including religious ones.[1] But there were some areas of governance for which no Ottoman laws existed. There had been no Ottoman-era radio broadcasting, so when it came to creating a radio station for Palestine, British mandate administrators drew on British laws and administrative practices, including those related to religion. Perhaps as a result British officials—at the PBS and in other mandate departments—were the primary actors in religious broadcasting.

This chapter examines the PBS's attempts to regulate religious expression in a manner that maintained the government's claim to respect all faith communities. At the same time, PBS administrators were concerned—as was the government overall—not to risk the station administration appearing to or actually ceding control of the PBS to locals, whether lay or religious, of any faith. It considers three historical moments critical to the experience of putting religion on the radio in mandate Palestine: the PBS's initial decision to commit to religious broadcasting and its conceptual debt to the BBC, its inclusion of readings and sermons rather than full services in the station's weekly schedule, and its incorporation of exceptional broadcasts for holiday services and other major religious events. It analyzes the importance of each moment, seeing in the first a largely unrecognized choice that placed the government—as the manager of broadcast media—in the role of managing religion, in the second an attempt to maintain administrative control and keep the peace by proscribing the broadcasting of actual religious services and particularly sermons, and in the third a recognition of the central role that Palestine—and particularly Jerusalem—played in the three Abrahamic faiths celebrated around the world.

These moments fit in the broader context of a government taking on the responsibility to manage public expressions of religious identity in national media. This was especially true in Palestine, whose public sphere had been shaped by the framing of religious difference as a source of zero-sum competition between two groups, each claiming to be the national community. It also fit within British officials' view of Palestine. As Khalidi notes with respect to the mandate government's creation of the Supreme Muslim Council, "the British vision" was "of a Palestine composed of three religious communities."[2] British officials understood these communities in terms of political rights, but the government primarily conceptualized them in terms of religion—as wholly and permanently divided by religious identity. Hence British officials working at the PBS and in other mandate departments viewed religious programming through a sectarian lens. They developed religious broadcasts that had a divisive effect, promoting religious and sectarian differences among Palestinian communities rather than using religion, as Nuwayhid had, to connect Palestinians of different faiths. In this process, it was British administrators, rather than Jewish or Arab Palestinians working at the PBS, whose views and perceptions governed these broadcasts.

What were the immediate and midrange consequences of a divisive, sect-reinforcing approach? This chapter examines how Mandate Palestine's early history of managing rather than excluding religion from state-controlled mass media transferred British notions of radio as a "public good" to Palestine. It further investigates how the PBS's religious broadcasts helped British mandate officials cement notions of religious identity as central to Palestinian identities. It considers how British views of Palestinians as divided into three internally coherent religious groups contrasted with Palestinians' understanding of their own religious identity as more fluid and internally nuanced. At the same time, religious programming as a broadcasting issue highlights the growing importance of the PBS as a national institution.

Putting Religion on Palestine's Radio

The mandate government's decision to create space for religious broad-casts on Palestine's radio station made all subsequent developments possible. It appeared an obvious decision at the time, since govern-ment archives in the United Kingdom and in Israel give no indication that putting religious broadcasts on the radio was considered a conten-tious issue. The PBS's approach to religious services and other religious broadcasts stemmed from British ideas about the responsibility that a national radio station had to promote morality and to support the na-tional faith—ideas that had first found expression in the British Broad-casting Corporation. The BBC had incorporated religious broadcasts into its programming from its earliest days on the air and in 1926 es-tablished the Central Religious Advisory Committee (CRAC) to ensure a more systematic approach.[3] These broadcasts were not forced on the BBC; instead, the station embraced them, considering religious broad-casts a means to fulfill its "educate and elevate" mandate.

As Michael Bailey notes in his study of the BBC's early development, which argues that the station acted as an "extension of Christian pasto-ral guidance," official BBC materials themselves discussed religious pro-gramming in positive terms. These discussions started with the 1928 BBC Handbook and this statement: "When those who were responsible for Broadcasting set before themselves the object of raising the national standard of values and of a constructive idealism, it was obvious that the religious service should be one of the regular program features."[4]

The "obvious" harmony suggested here between the station's objec-tives and a Christian mission was aided by the fact that Great Britain had a state religion: the Church of England. Applying this approach to Palestine, with its multiple official faiths and denominations, compli-cated the BBC approach. This complication was exacerbated by Brit-ish perceptions of Palestine as a place populated by peoples whose pri-mary identity was religious. British officials envisioned Palestinians as first and foremost Jews, Christians, and Muslims, with deep chasms di-viding each community. As a result, rather than use religious broadcasts to bind the nation British administrators at the PBS used religious pro-gramming to reinforce the religious divisions that they believed were so important to people in Palestine.

Ideas of religious programming as encouraging morality and foster-ing community identity appeared "obvious" to British administrators at the time. Yet from a historical perspective, it is important to recognize that there was a choice made, even if an unconscious one. This choice reflected the mandate government's willingness to take on the responsibility for managing religious expression in this part of the public sphere, as well as an assumption that taking on such responsibility was a normal thing to do. This assumption was made explicit at the very start of the PBS's life. The station had opened in March 1936 with great ceremony and with a broadcast by the High Commissioner, Arthur Wauchope. While noting that the station would steer clear of politics, he promised, "Its main object will be the spread of knowledge and culture. Nor, I can assure you, will the claims of religion be neglected." By taking the view that religious faiths had "claims" on public broadcasting, the mandate government shifted its focus from explaining why, for example, no religious broadcasts would be allowed or would be limited to those of only one faith. Instead, it set itself up for a different challenge: the unending labor of managing these claims and translating them into broadcast airtime.

How did the station, its administrators, and the mandate government address the actual management issues involved in putting religious services on the radio? There were two key moments: first, the regularly scheduled broadcasts—those used for readings of holy texts and, later, weekly services—and second, the exceptional broadcasts for holiday services and programs. Respecting the claims of religion may have sounded simple in the abstract, but in a multifaith, multidenominational environment such as mandate Palestine's, translating this into actual practice was a complicated process. It required the government to first identify which government officials and offices had the authority to allocate broadcasting hours and adjudicate any disputes and then to decide what kinds of religious services would be broadcast, how frequently, how many hours per week or day, and how these hours would be divided not only between the state's three religions—Christianity, Islam, and Judaism—but also between the various denominations or sects of each.

General principles regarding what would be broadcast on the station and who would have authority to decide seem to have been established fairly easily, with ultimate decision-making power firmly in the hands of the PBS's British administrators. (Most of the discussion within the government and in the local press during the PBS's early days focused on the degree of news coverage the station would be allowed to provide. Both expressed much less concern about cultural or other programming.) The PBS's commitment to religion was not realized through broadcasting the various faiths' weekly religious services. Instead, the

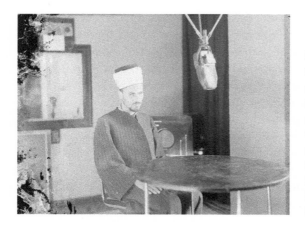

Figure 4.1. Unnamed Qur'an reciter or adhaan caller at the PBS studios, no date. Source: G. Eric and Edith Matson Photograph Collection, Prints and Photographs Division, Library of Congress, LC-DIG-matpc-14322.

PBS broadcast weekly readings of religious texts that broadly represented each faith community on its holy day. For example, a typical Friday program in early April 1936 included a reading from the Qur'an (in Arabic) by a Sheikh Sobhi and a *siddur* (a Hebrew-language prayer book) reading given by a Dr. Epstein.[5] Such broadcasts seem to have fulfilled the "claims of religion" without adding further controversy to Palestine's contentious climate.

The only hint of controversy came in a few small pieces published in the Arabic press relating to the quality of the Qur'an reciters or, in the case of Amin al-Husseini, their identity. In June 1936, barely two months after the PBS had begun broadcasts, *Falastin* published a letter from al-Husseini complaining about an article recently published in "one of the papers" of Palestine. In his letter he noted that the article had stated that Yahya Lababidi, subdirector for Arabic music, had told him that he was no longer welcome to recite the Qur'an for the PBS. "This news is a lie and a disgrace without validity," al-Husseini wrote. "I am still connected to the station mentioned and diligent in reading the Holy Qur'an."[6] This exchange suggests the subtle tensions that religious readings could provoke. It also suggests the stature of the PBS, as well as its close connections with the mandate government. Al-Husseini was not merely one of the hundreds of sheikhs in Palestine who could have recited the Qur'an for the PBS. He was the Grand Mufti, head of the British-created Supreme Muslim Council and the official representative of Muslim interests in mandate Palestine.

Surprisingly, broadcasting readings on their faith's weekly holy day proved an issue for some groups who protested the station for targeting them with religious broadcasts during their communities' days of rest. While most Jews in Palestine seem to have accepted Saturday broadcasts, Agudath Yisrael, an anti-Zionist political party with a deep commitment to Orthodox Judaism, lobbied for nearly a decade to convince the PBS to stop broadcasting during the Sabbath—the day Orthodox Jews refrain from work, including running electrical or battery-operated appliances like the radio. As a result, Agudath Yisrael's members had boycotted the station entirely. Nine years after the PBS began broadcasting in Palestine, the situation had not changed. "Agudath Yisrael makes almost no use of the PBS," a June 1945 item in the *Palestine Press Review* stated. "[Its] leaders and rabbis . . . do not broadcast because the radio is used also on the Sabbath." Yet the group did note that the PBS had recently righted what the group called "the wrong so far done to Orthodox Jewry," by ending programs broadcast during the Jewish Sabbath that it considered "annoy[ing]" to Orthodox Jews. Religion was not the only issue, however: Agudath Yisrael complained, "The radio in Palestine is being used by non-Orthodox Zionists for the spreading of their influence," and argued that as a government station, the PBS should not "discriminate."

Although Agudath Yisrael was a minority group, its complaint is a reminder that Palestine's religious communities were internally and externally diverse and that Palestinian residents quickly came to see the PBS as a space that should, as a public good, serve all.[7] They in turn were quick to protest when the station appeared to favor other communities or ignore theirs. Linking the idea of radio as a public good to the High Commissioner's promise that the PBS would respect the "claims of religion" increasingly made PBS religious broadcasts a management project. It required constant negotiation to ensure that each denomination received adequate airtime, without allowing one faith (or sect) to dominate. The religious broadcasting issues that arose also led to ongoing negotiations with other government departments, as well as challenges to the station's autonomy. These challenges intensified after World War II.

New Challenges after World War II

Arab-Zionist hostilities had quieted during the war, but its end brought heightened tensions and new conflicts. For the PBS the end of the war brought changes in upper management and an administrative reorganization that ended direct government control and stringent wartime censorship. With respect to religious broadcasts, the changes also included relaxed restrictions on broadcasting weekly services. The expansion of religious broadcasting into actual services engendered new management challenges, whose resolutions indicate both the degree to which the PBS remained connected to the mandate government and the central role it played in mediating between religious communities and helping shape a normative on-air presence for each faith.

The first challenge involved the PBS's existing practice of broadcasting weekly readings from various communities' religious texts, a practice that was also being modified. (One postwar change involved changes in the station's on-air time. In the 1930s the PBS broadcast in the afternoon and evening. Only after the war ended did it begin regular morning broadcasts, which made airing some religious services more feasible.) In April 1946 the PBS planned to host a group reading of the Bible, an ecumenical gathering that included representatives from the Roman Catholic Church, the Anglican Church, and the Church of Scotland. However, when the group gathered to prepare for the reading, each wished to read from his own sect's translation. Station director Edwin Samuel (who was not Christian) insisted that they all read from the same Bible—the version authorized by the Church of England. The Latin patriarch protested to the High Commissioner, stating, "We naturally will not agree to the use of a version which we do not have and consider it a very high-handed action on the part of the Director. The Churches agree that this imposition . . . is incorrect."[8]

For the period this was direct criticism. It resulted in a flurry of anxious discussions among the chief secretary's staff, who seem to have been horrified by the station director's decision and the possible political fallout. "It must be . . . out of the question for any form of control to be exercised over the version of the Bible used in these broadcasts," one official wrote in file comments. "It is fortunate that the Latin Patriarch appealed to Your Excellency instead of, for example, telegraphing to the Pope," commented another.[9] Others underlined and added exclamation points as commentary in file documents, including a statement that Director Samuel had "ruled" on the acceptable Bible—the marks suggesting that these officials considered "ruling" something beyond the director's authority. The following month, the chief secretary sent a detailed letter of apology to the patriarchate that included an explanation of what had been done to ensure that the issue would not arise in future broadcasts. The letter stated, "The Director of Broadcasting has been instructed that . . . the Christian communities must have liberty to use that version of the Bible approved by their respective ecclesiastical authorities." With that, the issue seems to have been resolved. However, it remains notable for two reasons: it allowed the Chief Secretary's Office to reassert its primacy over the PBS, and its resolution required considerable expenditure of time and effort on the part of PBS and other governmental officials.[10]

The second management issue came from the postwar introduction of full religious services on air. Unlike the weekly readings, the station did not commit to broadcasting each sect's or faith's service each week. The PBS had drawn up an annual schedule, allocating to each sect a certain amount of broadcasting time from the overall pool of time allocated for religious broadcasts. Allocations were made according to a "proportionally representative scale" that had been determined by Samuel in collaboration with the District Commissioner's Office.[11] The total time allocated was fixed, but the amount of time allocated to each sect proved negotiable. In late 1946 the Greek Coptic church requested more hours for its 1947 Sunday masses. The church's representative bolstered its request by noting that "there are over 10,000 Coptic inhabitants in Palestine, who have churches, convents, and property." As a result of their numbers and their physical presence, he added, "they feel that they are entitled to an increase in numbers of broadcasts of the Coptic Mass"—illustrating one of the ways in which Palestinian communities laid claim to the PBS, using its status as a public good for all to meet their own particular group's needs. But the Greek Coptic community's argument for more airtime extended beyond the number of Copts in Palestine. The request also invoked the two million Copts in Egypt, describing them as a PBS listening community (one perhaps not incidentally located in a former British protectorate) that "anxiously and impatiently await to hear their mass broadcast from the Church of the Holy Sepulcher." [12]

The Greek Coptic patriarchate had made its request to three authorities in three locations: the Chief Secretary's Office, PBS station director Samuel, and Jerusalem's district commissioner—a sign of just how confusing mandate Palestine's overlapping jurisdictions could be. Samuel and the district commissioner took up the request but rather than expand the overall number of hours allotted they examined the records for 1946 to see which communities had not used their allotted time that year. Assuming that these communities might do the same in 1947, Samuel and the district commissioner turned to them—of which there were evidently several—asking, as Samuel reported to the chief secretary, "whether they would be willing to give up some of their [1947] broadcasts in favor of the Coptic community."[13] The process took several months, but by March 1947 Samuel reported that Palestine's Greek Catholic community had agreed to give one of its broadcasts to the Greek Coptic community,[14] another example of the PBS and other government offices mediating between religious communities.

While suggesting the capacity of broader ethnolinguistic affiliations (Greek) to trump narrower sectarian ones (Coptic vs. Catholic), this episode also highlighted the way in which the PBS and its administrators, as well as other government officials, themselves not only became involved, but actually managed both the original allocation and the intercommunal negotiation of religious broadcast hours. Further, these religious communities made little complaint about the station's right to do so. The Greek Coptic leadership had accepted the PBS's authority to allocate time for religious broadcasts, and to do so based on population. Buying in to this system, it justified the request for additional hours by citing the number of Copts in Palestine and in Egypt and indicating the social weight of the numbers by pointing to the community's properties. The community did not attempt to challenge the PBS's authority by arguing for additional hours overall, for a different means of allocating hours, or for the right of faith communities to determine the allocations themselves.

It was PBS personnel, in conjunction with government officials, who determined the "proportional" weight of each of Palestine's religious communities and confirmed their status with airtime. This gave the PBS a highly active role in assessing and working with Palestine's faith communities: it acted not only as their arbiter but also as their broker, which in turn suggested that these communities had the final say over the distribution of their allocated hours. Finally, this episode highlighted the degree to which the PBS was both a distinct entity and a subsidiary of the much larger mandate government—not only due to its position as part of the Post Office but also through its close dealings with the Chief Secretary's and other offices. To say that the PBS was putting religion on the radio and managing religious communities' claims to airtime was also, and more fundamentally, to say that the mandate government was doing these things—that managing religious expression on the air was a government project. Yet as suggested by the Coptic community's multiple request letters, the extent of the PBS's authority was not clear to many Palestinians. Nor was it always clear to PBS and other government officials. As a result, managing religious broadcasts was complicated by the various departments' claims of authority.

While allocating broadcasting hours required the coordination of several offices, the managerial challenges it engendered were logistic. They presented ordinary challenges rather than signaling crises. For the PBS and the mandate government, the far stickier management issue proved that of the weekly services and their "sermons"—which were given at Christian, Jewish, and Muslim services, on holidays as well as in ordinary weeks. Most parts of each community's weekly services were fairly structured, following a set pattern that varied little from week to week. In their formalism and their focus on ritual practice, they would have raised no red flags for the PBS. But the sermon portion of each weekly service presented two major concerns. First, PBS administrators worried about the religious content of these sermons; that is, they worried that clerics would take advantage of the wider radio audience and use their sermons as opportunities for conversion or would offend members of other faiths by proclaiming theirs the only true one. Second, government officials in particular were apprehensive that clerics would use these sermons to comment on current events or express political opinions about the future of Palestine. What appeared to be the only foolproof solution was to ask priests, rabbis, and imams to submit copies of their sermons for prebroadcast censorship, as others invited to speak on the radio were required to do.

To address these concerns the PBS's general practice during the 1930s was to avoid broadcasting sermons. The post–World War II administrative reorganization changed this. Assistant Director Rex Keating, who had come to the PBS from the Egyptian Broadcasting Service, noted in a letter to the chief secretary that "there was considerable discussion as to the advisability of including the sermon in each broadcast" but that "eventually Mr. Samuel decided that it was desirable"—hinting that some station personnel would have preferred to continue with the previous policy.[15] (Keating and Samuel, while evidently respecting one another as colleagues, nevertheless disagreed on many aspects of PBS administration.) The dissenting administrators had explained their reservations, and they reached a compromise of sorts: "Samuel ruled that the PBS should not press for the broadcast of any sermon, but that in the event of . . . the religious body concerned [requesting] to include it, [the PBS] should insist on the sermon being submitted in manuscript form for PBS censorship."[16] In other words, the PBS would not actively seek to broadcast sermons. However, if and when a religious community asked the station to broadcast a sermon, the PBS required the text to be submitted for prebroadcast censorship. It would broadcast the delivered sermon while verifying it against the submitted copy, so station engineers could cut the feed in the event of any major deviations.

Perhaps unsurprisingly this compromise proved less than satisfactory to religious community leaders. In the same letter of complaint regarding the imposition of the Anglican Bible, the Latin patriarchate protested the sermon censorship. On several occasions at various denominations' churches, the Latin patriarchate noted, "the Radio authorities have cut off completely the service, beginning with the sermon, since they claim that the text should be submitted beforehand to the censor." The letter described this as "improper," and asked, "What right or capacity have the PB[S] staff to censor the contents of a Christian Message?"[17] This question is an important reminder that while the PBS may have considered itself mandated to promote religion and morality in general, individual religious communities objected to its power to determine the extent of their participation on air. "The attitude adopted by the Latin Patriarch," Keating stated in a memo to the chief secretary, was "fairly representative of the general resentment of the religious bodies."[18] This may have been more true of Palestine's Christian communities, as the government archives do not include evidence of Jewish or Muslim community complaints about censored sermons.

Yet returning to the PBS's prewar policy, for example, by cutting away from services before the sermon began, seemed equally likely to meet with religious authorities' disapproval. Although he called this suggestion "advisable," Keating cautioned, "in the event of such a decision being taken, criticism from the various religious bodies may be expected." In response, the chief secretary initially directed the PBS to return to its earlier policy and stop broadcasting all sermons. However, by December 1946 Samuel had persuaded him to reconsider, with the result that the PBS returned to Samuel's policy of broadcasting sermons when asked. "The normal rule should be that sermons are intended for the congregation in the place of worship concerned and not for the general listening public," the director stated in a station memo. "But if the religious community concerned specifically ask for the sermon to be broadcast, permission may be given . . . on the understanding that a) the speaker understands that he will be addressing an audience which includes many persons not members of his own congregation . . . and

b) it will be necessary for him to submit the script of the sermon in advance."[19] The first provision was intended to minimize the impact of the second: by reminding clerics not to say anything that could offend members of another faith, the precensorship changes—and the potential for confrontation—might be minimized.[20]

Samuel concluded his memo with a personal comment: "It should be made clear to the religious authorities concerned that it is distasteful to me that any member of this Department should have to ask for the scripts of sermons." However, he explained, "in the present state of tension in Palestine, we cannot afford to take any risk." From the mandate government's perspective, clerics' irritation at prebroadcast censorship was easier to manage than an outbreak of religiously inspired violence, particularly as the situation in Palestine worsened.[21] Samuel's description of the PBS as a "Department" rather than a station emphasized its connection to the mandate government. Although housed in its own building, the PBS remained officially part of the Post Office, and PBS employees were government employees.

The issues surrounding weekly services extended beyond what was (or was not) broadcast: the most contentious one was staffing, which further indicated the static produced by overlapping bureaucracies. The Chief Secretary's Office had instructed government departments, including the PBS, to give employees "their" day of rest, meaning that Christians had Sunday off, Jews had Saturday, and Muslims had Friday. As a result, the station used employees of other faiths when recording a weekly service. Although well intended, this policy proved impractical in Palestine's tense postwar atmosphere. In December 1946 a representative for Palestine's Supreme Muslim Council wrote to the chief secretary:

> We are informed that on Friday, the 29th November 1946, the Palestine Broadcasting Service sent a non-Muslim employee [*muwadhdhaf min ghair muslimeen*] to announce the broadcast of the Friday prayer from Al-Aqsa Mosque, a fact which caused some resentment amongst a considerable number of the worshipers.[22]

The representative, an eminent Palestinian named Amin Abdul Hadi, had also contacted Director Samuel directly. This was another case in which the PBS's multiple jurisdictions proved confusing to both Palestinians and personnel.

Samuel agreed with Abdul Hadi's criticism, noting that he had raised the staffing question with the chief secretary earlier that year. The problem evidently lay with the Post Office, which had understood the "day of rest" as an absolute prohibition, whereas the chief secretary had merely prohibited the *habitual* scheduling of employees on their day of rest. Since the Post Office provided the PBS's engineers, its interpretation of the day of rest instruction as a total prohibition had prevailed. As a result, only non-Muslim engineers worked on Fridays. After consultations between the PBS, the Post Office, and the Chief Secretary's Office, the Post Office instructed its staff that "only Muslim engineers should go into the Mosque on Fridays," with the same principle applying to other faiths.[23] In this case, the issue might be described less as one of managing religious expressions on the air than of overmanaging a multifaith staff. The religious controversy here arose from the government's efforts to respect its employees' faiths, but the Post Office's literal interpretation of the day of rest principle had negative repercussions when applied to the PBS.

Holidays: Newsworthy Broadcasting

The third management issue concerned holiday programs, which were numerous. The mandate state recognized the holidays of all three Abrahamic faiths, including those marked by denominational differences, such as Eid al-Fitr and Easter, which different sects of each faith celebrated on different days. While holiday broadcasts appear to have been included in the annual allocation of religious broadcasting hours, they often required more airtime than ordinary services. Easter broadcasts generally included a Saturday vigil as well as services on Easter Day, and sometimes Good Friday and the following Monday. During Ramadan and Passover, the holiday broadcasts were spread over a longer period, with the station's daily broadcasts changing to accommodate readings and calls to prayer. For example, the PBS's schedule during Ramadan 1940 included three breaks in the evening program: one for *maghreb* prayer, one for *'aisha'* prayer, and one for a reading from the Qur'an.[24] *Falastin* praised these broadcasts and reported approvingly on the station's Eid al-Fitr broadcasts in a front-page article, noting that they made it possible for "the entire world" to hear the Eid prayer given at Al-Aqsa Mosque. "The Eid program was an *eid* in itself," the paper proclaimed in its headline.[25] Interestingly, the newspaper used religious language throughout this article—as in its description of Al-Aqsa as blessed by God. The phenomenon of a Christian-owned newspaper

القسم العربي في محطة الإذاعة

برنامج العيد الحافل كان عيداً بنفسه

كان برنامج العيد في محطة الإذاعة الٔقدس صيبه اسناد شؤوه الى العرب ،
الفلسطينية حيداً بنفسه مع فيه العالم كه وحسن اختيار الفريق الذي يتولى ادارته
صلاة العيد من المسجد الاقصى الذي بارك وقد استطاع هذا القسم العربي ان يبلغ
الله حوله . وقد كان من بركات الله هل في الاشهر الاخيرة من ضروب التحسين
الناس ان يبلغ بهم التقدم الى حد ات وكفاية حاجات الجهور وتمبدأصباب
يصل مضمن الاقصى الشريف فسيم تبذيه ، وترقية ذوقه وشموره ، و ما لا
اخوانهم في اعضاء العمود وبشار كونهم بكاد ينقصها بلغه في ذلك ادبوهصر

Figure 4.2. "The Arabic Section on the Broadcasting Station," *Falastin*, November 3, 1940, p. 1.

describing a Muslim holiday and religious site from a Muslim perspective should serve as a reminder that religious identity, particularly between Arab Palestinian communities, was more nuanced and complex in this period than is sometimes assumed. Calls to put aside communalism and focus on shared beliefs or religious tolerance may have served political ends, but they were not mere window-dressing for the Palestinian national cause.

Holidays might have appeared likely to produce the most controversial religious broadcasts. Easter celebrations, for example, highlighted not only the fundamental theological difference separating Christianity from Judaism and Islam but also the splits between Christian sects. But holiday broadcasts caused almost no controversy. Instead, what they excited was interest, in the form of news coverage. The Palestinian papers took a steady and sustained interest in the PBS's holiday broadcasts. For example, the *Palestine Post* in April 1937 announced how the PBS would mark Orthodox Easter:

The Eastern services of the Greek Orthodox Church, from the Church of the Holy Sepulcher, and two subsidiary programs will be transmitted . . . tomorrow and Sunday. A gramophone recital of Greek music and songs will be broadcast from the studios from 11:25–11:55 tomorrow night, to be followed by a broadcast till 12:40 A.M. from the Church of the Holy Sepulcher of the Greek Easter Midnight Mass which will be celebrated by His Beatitude the Patriarch Elect.

The article continued by noting the broadcasts for other Christian sects:

> The Armenian Eastern Morning Mass, presided over by His Beatitude the Armenian Patriarch, will be radiated from the Church of the Holy Sepulcher from 7:30–8:30 on Sunday morning, the Greek Easter program being completed with studio readings from the Easter Gospel by the Rt. Rev. the Coptic Bishop, in Coptic; the Rt. Rev. the Syrian Orthodox Bishop, in Syriac, and the Very Rev. Superior of the Abyssinian Convent, in Amharic.[26]

Like many program-focused articles, this one was short but detailed. The mandate government facilitated this coverage: *Falastin* noted that its article announcing the 1936 Easter broadcasts originally came as an announcement from the Government Printing Office,[27] indicating again how the PBS's work interwove with that of other government departments. However, newspapers also expressed their own interest in these programs, discussing holiday broadcasts in their listener's columns without government prompting. After the 1940 Ramadan calls to prayer, the *Palestine Post*'s "Listener's Corner" had commented approvingly, "Nothing could be more impressive than the voice of the muezzin through the silence of the night." It praised these broadcasts religiously and artistically: "The PBS has made it possible for all Muslim listeners with a radio set to listen to the call to prayer from a sheikh whose clear diction and voice leave nothing to be desired."[28] In addition to informing listeners of upcoming broadcasts, these review-style pieces reaffirmed to Palestinian listeners that all faiths' religious broadcasts merited praise.

The press coverage also signaled something more. The *Palestine Post*'s 1937 Easter article indicates the complex logistical task that the mandate government had assigned the station by including religious broadcasts in its purview. For the PBS the greatest challenge they posed was the hours of extra work required to orchestrate lengthy, multisite live broadcasts. The Orthodox Easter broadcasts alone included a mix of services, readings, and songs, with masses by two separate Orthodox communities—requiring broadcasting setups in different parts of the Church of the Holy Sepulcher—and studio readings by representatives of three others, in a total of five languages. Managing all this, whether in terms of logistics, language, or intracommunal disagreements, was a major undertaking—one that PBS staff repeated for the Gregorian Easter, as well as for each major Jewish and Muslim holiday.

Religion on the Radio: A Lasting Legacy?

By making the PBS responsible for meeting the "claims of religion" in 1936, the mandate government turned on-air religious expression into a management project that lasted for the next sixteen years. The PBS's experience with religious broadcasts was a complex one that engaged it in decisions and negotiations that directly affected Palestine's Muslim, Jewish, and Christian communities. Putting religion on the radio in mandate Palestine gave the PBS and other government departments a new authority over these religious communities: the authority to regulate their access to this part of the public sphere. It also required a massive investment of time and energy, for individual officials and for the bureaucratic apparatus, and it frequently engendered confusion over the degree to which the PBS could be considered an autonomous station or a government department.

The Palestinian context added to these challenges, with religious identities used to bolster political claims and religious communities competing for preferential access to and control over government institutions. More fundamentally, putting religion on the radio in Palestine helped transfer to the region a British concept of radio as a public good overseen by the government. It also helped transfer a British sense of what kind of public should be served by the national station—a religious, moral one—and what role radio should play in reinforcing public morality through religious broadcasts.

At the same time, the PBS's religious broadcasting and the issues it raised point to the station's growing value as a national institution and to the increasing tensions between its Arabic and Hebrew sections—tensions that escalated into open hostilities after World War II. The next chapter examines these tensions and the four crises that erupted around the PBS during the later years of the mandate.

CHAPTER 5

Claiming the PBS: Whose National Radio?

'Ajaj Nuwayhid and Ibrahim Tuqan found that working opposition-ally within the colonial structure of the British mandate allowed them to use the PBS as a means of supporting a nationalist modernity for Arab Palestine. However, this was only one possible Arab community response to the station. When the station was first established, it was by no means certain that Palestine's Arab community would accept, respond to, and even identify with the station. After all, from all external appearances the PBS was a "colonial institution," created and controlled by the colonialesque mandate British state. According to Frantz Fanon, one of the few Middle East and North African colonial theorists to consider broadcasting,[1] Palestinians should have either ignored or fought against the station—the two responses he considered characteristic of Arab and Berber Algerians' response to Radio Alger. They should not have tuned in as listeners or found positions of genuine authority and leadership within its administration.

Fanon dedicated a chapter of his well-known work *A Dying Colonialism* to Radio Alger, in which he criticized the station for broadcasting primarily to the colonial audience and on subjects considered inappropriate by Algerian Muslim listeners. He argued that Algerians rejected the station and radio in general because they considered Radio Alger a colonial tool and because most were too poor to afford receiver sets. Instead, Fanon said, Algerians began to purchase receivers and listen to the radio only when the first national Arab stations began broadcasting in the late 1940s, and even then they listened to Radio Alger only for its broadcasts of popular music and not for news or other programming that bore a French colonial influence. According to Fanon, Algerians transformed their radio listening habits into signs of nationalist solidarity during the Algerian war, when the French Algerian government made listening to the Voice of Fighting Algeria (*La voix de l'Algérie combattante*, translated as "The Voice of Free Algeria" in the English edition of Fanon's book) and even possessing a radio set criminal acts. In Fanon's analysis, the colonial station Radio Alger existed for Algerians only as an institution that they first ignored due to the cost of radio receivers, the primarily French-language broadcasting, and the European programming and subsequently rejected. The Palestine Broadcasting Service, however, was not rejected by either community. Instead it was fought over by the Arab and Zionist Jewish communities, part of each group's broader demand for recognition of theirs as the sole "natural" claim to Palestine. Their contestations reveal the degree to which British officials assigned to the top leadership positions had in reality only confused and partial control over the station, its staff, its programming, its records and recording instruments, and its physical plant.

The proof of the degree to which the PBS became established as an institution meaningful to both the Arab and the Jewish communities in Palestine lay in the contestations of the Arabic and Hebrew service staff and station listeners over whose "national" radio station the PBS was. At the same time, they reflected the maturation of the station as a complicated but authentic state institution with a focus on entertainment programming and a professionalized approach to copyright and royalty fees, as well as labor concerns. This chapter first addresses these financial issues and then analyzes the ways in which national contestations manifested themselves with respect to the station. At four moments during the PBS's existence it became the site of critical tugs-of-war, illustrating the ways in which arguments over radio control reflected station personnel and community leaders' larger concerns over the state, and fate, of Palestine. In these tugs-of-war it was Jewish members of the PBS and the broader community who tended to push the envelope. Arab Palestinians demonstrated much less willingness to antagonize their fellow PBS employees and limited themselves to protests. The PBS's British staff, so influential in other areas of station administration, often watched from the sidelines—or looked on one another with suspicion.

First, the controversy that materialized over the station's on-air identification indicated the readiness of each community to identify with the PBS from its earliest days of operation. Second, a 1944 petition to rescind the prohibition on playing "ha-Tikvah" demonstrated the degree to which the station became caught up in broader Arab-Jewish struggles for official British recognition of national symbols like anthems. Third, the Jewish press and community leaders' use of receiver license statistics to argue for more equitable broadcasting hours suggests the degree to which the station struggled to meet the sometimes conflicting expectations of its audience and the mandate government that funded it. This connected with two related issues: the community's desire for short-wave broadcasting and a second transmitter for the PBS. Fourth and finally, the station's ultimate split into Kol Israel and the Hashemite Jordanian (Palestine) Station in 1949, with most of the PBS Jewish staff continuing as Israeli broadcasting authority staff and many PBS Arabic staff running the new Jordanian station, illustrates the degree to which the radio staff themselves had become politicized by the end of the mandate. Issues of "whose national radio" started with the literal claiming of the station's name, continued with the playing of "national" anthems and the use of audience statistics to claim broadcasting hours, and ended with the physical carving up of the station as the mandate state collapsed.

Copyrights and Royalties

Financial concerns underlay a number of PBS decisions—and influenced the quality and variety of the station's programming for all listeners. The number and kind of gramophone records was an issue that occupied both station administrators and listeners. The issue of copyright and royalty payments, on the other hand, was equally important for administrators but almost invisible to listeners. Copyrights and royalties had concerned government officials from the PBS's earliest stages, with BBC officials brought in for consultation on these issues. While describing copyright laws in Palestine as "not known," one official stated that "sooner or later, arrangements will have to be made either with the Performing Rights Society or a similar body for ad hoc or annual payments to cover the use of copyright music and other material." He noted that the BBC paid 5 percent of its net license revenue to the Performing Rights Society, suggesting that the PBS might be able to reach a similar agreement.[2] Revised BBC comments submitted the following year suggested that the cost might be much less, as long as the station relied on local talent. "If the programs are to contain a considerable proportion of native music," the later report stated, "it should be possible to negotiate copyright payments on a lower scale."[3]

In either case, arrangements with the Performing Rights Society covered only live performances. As the BBC official noted, "the right to use commercial gramophone records for broadcasting purposes in Palestine will probably need careful negotiation with the gramophone companies," which held the rights to their recordings. He cited a recent BBC initiative to record programs and sell the recordings "at the rate of L5 for an hour's program and L3 for half an hour's program, with the right to broadcast three times."[4] In other words, broadcasting gramophone recordings, which had been envisioned as a substantive portion of PBS broadcasting, would require negotiating with each gramophone record company as well as negotiating for the number of times each record could be broadcast. This transformed record purchasing from a one-time concern to an ongoing cost, creating an issue that continued to occupy PBS administrators' minds after the station was up and running.

By the mid-1940s copyright and royalty payment issues had been ironed out, but this did not mean that they had been in any way reduced. In fiscal year 1946–1947, copyright fees and royalties accounted for 13 percent of the PBS's overall operating budget: roughly LP6900 of LP53,000.[5] These payments were scaled in accordance with the station's broadcasting hours and the number of radio set licenses, meaning that their prominence in the budget would never diminish. These contracts appear to have been negotiated on a yearly basis, which became increasingly difficult after 1946. For example, in early 1948 the station director offered the Society of Authors, Composers, and Music Publishers (ACUM), established by Jewish Palestinian artists, LP500 for the mechanical copyrights of the ACUM works that the station had used in the previous quarter. This amount was based on the station librarian's estimate since, as Samuel noted, "Broadcasting House has been evacuated," leaving staff unable to compile a specific list of works recorded.[6]

Even as the station endured the final months of mandate rule—which would also prove to be its final months as a station—station administrators continued to pay copyright fees and include them in their 1949 budgets. As part of this process, they continued their negotiations with the Performing Rights Society, ACUM, and the various record companies. It was not that station administrators were unaware of the situation but that to them copyright payments were not side issues. They were essential to the station's continued functioning and to administrators' understanding of the station as one that abided by international norms of intellectual property. From the early references to BBC experiences with copyrights to the concern among station administrators even in 1948 to pay the station's "assessable" performance hours, these developments suggest the institutionalization in Palestine of European concepts of intellectual property rights. They also suggest that concepts of transparency, fair play, and rule of law continued to hold meaning even in almost impossible circumstances.

Labor Relations and Contract Negotiations

If copyrights and royalties addressed the labor of those who produced the recorded music and the compositions broadcast on the PBS, another major issue developed around the station's in-house and freelance musicians. By the mid-1940s the list of musicians employed by the Hebrew section alone reached nearly ten single-spaced pages. It included a list for permanent musicians and for "casual" musicians; for orchestras, choirs, institutions, and impresarios; for scriptwriters, critics, and translators; for singers of Hebrew songs and classical singers; for Bible cantors and "Eastern melodies"; for pianists (subdivided into soloists and accompanists) and for instrumental soloists; for conductors and for Palestinian composers; and finally for Music section staff.[7]

Their numbers had grown as the PBS moved away from its initial reliance on records and toward the greater use of live broadcasts, musical and otherwise. With this growth came a rise in the number of contract negotiations and labor disputes, as well as a set of related issues. How should the station deal with freelance musicians' instruments, which those rehearsing daily wished to store at the PBS? If it allowed them to store their instruments there, was it also responsible for preventing other musicians from using them, as a symphony drummer assumed in a complaint issued in 1947? What about cases in which property was stolen? Similarly, the increased number of musicians led to increasingly complex labor negotiations, as musicians competed—or collaborated— for higher wages.

The incredible growth in the number and kind of musicians employed by the PBS, as well as the related issues of labor relations and contract negotiations, reflected the professionalization of musicians in Palestine. This process included immigrants and natives, Arabic, English, and Hebrew speakers. On the Arabic side, 'Ajaj Nuwayhid again played an instrumental role, requiring musicians hired by the Arabic section to learn to read music and to develop other professional skills. On the Yishuv side, musicians worked to establish the same professionalism of hiring and contracts as they had enjoyed—or wished that they had enjoyed—in Europe. The net result was to more solidly ground notions of professional status for musicians and to establish principles of contract and labor negotiation—despite the PBS's tendency to remain very firm on wages.

None of these three issues emerged in a vacuum. What ties them together, beyond their connection to music broadcasts, is money. Budgetary limitations led government officials to pressure the PBS to economize from the beginning, and budget concerns continued to dominate throughout its lifetime. The archives hold files dedicated to issues as small as which office should pay for a L10 charge—an amount far less than the cost of a battery-operated radio at the time.

The money questions, while often deeply bureaucratic, are not trivial. They connect with logistical issues of shipping and availability (for gramophone records) and foreign payments (for musicians and recording companies) that highlight the evolving nature of state relations in the Middle East during the mandate period, as well as the additional challenges wrought by World War II. They highlight the financial and logistical underpinnings of the mandate state, suggesting that the controversies that arose developed against a backdrop of financial concerns that underlay the mixture of anxiety and administrative power that was the mandate state.

Station On-Air Identification

The PBS began operations on March 31, 1936. Before one week had passed, the station was the subject of controversy, and over a basic issue: its name. Formally, the station was known as the Palestine Broadcasting Service. The problem lay in the way in which the station, and thus Palestine, was identified on the air. Evidently no protocols had been established regarding station identification, although the ordinary practice of the day was to announce "This is City X calling" or "This is Station Y." During the PBS's inaugural broadcast, the Hebrew section announcers introduced the station as Kol Eretz Israel: the Voice of the Land of Israel. (As discussed in chapter 1, "Eretz Israel" refers to the biblical land of Israel.) The following week saw protests and counterprotests issued to the government, extensive press coverage, and claims on all sides that popular indignation had been aroused.

On April 6 the *Palestine Post* published a blistering editorial. The paper blamed the editors of *al-Liwa'*, an Arabic-language Islamic paper with a small but elite following,[8] for what the *Post* described as *al-Liwa'* capitalizing on the station identification issue, using it to push the mandate government to prohibit "Eretz Israel" in any official setting.

> It might as well be admitted that Arab journalists are, in some ways, skillful propagandists. There is skillful propaganda of a sort which, at its best, represents a half truth as the whole truth, a particle of fact as entire fact. A less complimentary and a less euphemistic name might be found for this sort of misrepresentation, but then the discriminating reader can supply his own substitutes. He might, if he chooses, substitute "unscrupulous" for "skillful" and "lies" for "propaganda." But by whatever name [one uses]. . . it must be admitted that Arab journalists had got hold of something greatly to their tastes when they picked out of the ether the words *Eretz Isra'el* in the Hebrew translation of the High Commissioner's speech inaugurating the Broadcasting Service last Monday—picked it out and tortured and worried it until the usual thing happened: Those responsible for pacification pacified the recalcitrants by inflicting a gross insult upon the Jewish listeners to the Palestine Broadcasting Service's Hebrew programs.[9]

The *Palestine Post* was not the only organization to protest. The Vaad Leumi, the National Council or executive authority of the Jewish community in mandate Palestine, which enjoyed official recognition by the mandate government, sent a delegation to meet with the High Commissioner.[10] Ultimately, these protests led the PBS to issue a new protocol regarding station identifications: all announcers would use "Jerusalem." Thus the Arabic broadcasters announced "This is Jerusalem" (Huna al-Quds) and the Hebrew announced "[This is] the voice of Jerusalem" (Kol Yerushalayim), while the English section used "[This is] Jerusalem calling." The words *Eretz Israel* were not to be used on the air, although the abbreviation AY, pronounced "aye" or "Aleph Yod," for the first letters of *Eretz* and *Isra'el*, was allowed. (This abbreviation appeared on all currency printed during the mandate, so government permission for its employment at another state institution, the PBS, was not without precedent.)

Like many controversies during the mandate period, this one was settled with a compromise created and enforced by the government authorities, fully satisfying no one. Yet as controversies went, this one was fairly mild: *Falastin* reported on the story but did not take it up as a cause, and after a few letters to the editor published in various papers the issue lost steam.[11] As "A Britisher," the writer of the final letter published on the subject noted, "We all accept 'Jerusalem calling,' but it is a pity this wasn't done at the very beginning."[12] By the time Nuwayhid became involved with the station, broadcasters seem to have been allowed some leeway with respect to how they identified the station, at least during special occasions. "During holiday and religious festival programs, the [Arabic] broadcaster . . . began at the opening of the airwaves to raise his voice in proclaiming 'this is the city of 'Umar' or 'this is the land of the Isra'' and the Mi'raj' and the expression 'this is Jerusalem' remained in use at the same time."[13]

From time to time in subsequent years the issue would flare up again, whenever someone from the PBS referred to Eretz Israel on the air. Arabic newspapers would note these mentions but do not seem to have made them the foundation of larger complaints. It may be that the reason the issue did not fester was because station administrators regularly reaffirmed its position on the PBS's on-air identification. For example, the station's October 1946 "Planning Committee Meeting" included a discussion of "opening announcements," regarding which the minutes stated that the PBS's English-language broadcasts should begin with "This is Jerusalem, Good evening every one," and end with "This is the Palestine Broadcasting Service, etc."[14]

For Palestinians of all nationalities and affiliations, the matter of whether to use Eretz Israel on the air was merely one in a series of battles fought over the right to claim Palestine as either a Zionist or an Arab national space. For the PBS, however, it was something more. The controversy was the first indication that the PBS was more than merely a "colonial" station—that it was seen not (or at least not only) as an agent of the mandate regime but as a valuable institution whose identity—and consequent capacity to help form a national culture—might be claimed by either side. After all, by the 1930s, the golden age of state radio, having a radio station was considered a key attribute of a nation-state. As a potentially national radio in a potentially national state, the PBS was an institution that was fought over from the beginning.

National Anthems and "ha-Tikvah"

What evoked strong passions was the desire of Vaad Leumi and some Hebrew service personnel to broadcast "ha-Tikvah" (The Hope), a musical piece described alternately as an anthem of hope for the Jewish people and as the Jewish national anthem—a desire that manifested itself as a flashpoint at several moments during the station's life. During its early years the PBS had no policy regarding "ha-Tikvah" specifically. The station's general policy was to play no national anthems, whether during regular or special occasion broadcasts—although "exceptions have been made for the British anthem . . . on special occasions," stated a confidential memo written by the station's Music section controller, German Jewish refugee and composer Karl Salomon, and sent to the controller of the combined English-Hebrew section. "This decision was, of course, not well received by Jewish listeners; but under existing conditions it was the only possible decision." [15]

"ha-Tikvah" and "Jewish National Music"

The "ha-Tikvah" issue emerged in the context of a broader Jewish community discussion about what might constitute "Jewish music" and what role the PBS, along with other cultural institutions, should play in supporting its development. The *Palestine Post* had raised the issue from the early days of the PBS, describing a "selection of Offenbach melodies" played the previous weekend. "We have here a perfect specimen of music which we instinctively feel to be specifically Jewish," the paper said, "without there being any suggestion of Hasidic dances or anything of the kind." "Offenbach is Jewish," the editorial continued, "and very noticeably so, in his style of expression and . . . musical witticisms."[16] The *Palestine Post*'s editorial was picking up on one of Yishuv's nation-building projects, creation of a Jewish national music, which had become an increasingly important issue by the 1920s. Musicians and political leaders alike debated what constituted Jewish music. How European? How "Oriental"? Should it be religious or have some relationship to a cantor's prayers? Was it enough simply that the composer be Jewish? Did location matter: would music composed in Palestine be more authentically Jewish?

The debate produced a range of ideas. As Jehoash Hirshberg has noted, opera was proposed by some for its ability to "catalyze" developments in more popular music and for its emphasis on language.[17] While folk music was popular—"The musical scene in Palestine in the 1920s was almost exclusively dominated by members of the Society for Jewish folk music"[18]—the *Palestine Post*'s disparaging reference to Hasidic dances suggests the view of classical enthusiasts. While those who preferred classical music frequently complained about the quality of the PBS's live broadcasts, its studio orchestra was "officially committed from the outset to the dissemination of national music, whether composed in the Diaspora or by local composers."[19] In this context the playing of "ha-Tikvah" in any PBS broadcast became an issue larger than that of the piece itself.[20]

"ha-Tikvah" and the PBS

Playing "ha-Tikvah" on the PBS became part of a broader issue—that of playing it in any official mandate government milieu and thereby giving the "Jewish national anthem" the stamp of government approval. In April 1938 Chief Secretary Battershill circulated a secret memo to Palestine's district commissioners and department heads as well as the officers in charge of Britain's armed forces—a memo intended to clear up what Battershill characterized as "uncertainty" regarding when military and civilian British government bands should play "ha-Tikvah" and how British government personnel should behave when the piece was played. Government bands were forbidden to play the piece "on official and state occasions" and permitted to do so on "other public and private occasions" only if certain conditions were met. The British national anthem had to be played first, and the permission of the presiding government authority had to be obtained in advance. The memo stated:

> Permission will normally be granted if the occasion is a purely Jewish festival or entertainment, and one at which there is good reason to suppose that the non-British part of the audience will be entirely or almost entirely Jewish, and the playing of the Hatikvah will be unlikely in consequence to cause offense to the public or to non-Jewish members of the audience. In other cases permission will be refused.

On those occasions when permission was granted, the memo stated, "courtesy (though not right)" indicated that British military and government personnel should remain standing but reminded them that they were only required to stand for the British national anthem.

However, during World War II the PBS began broadcasting the anthems of allied nations, which opened the way for supporters of "ha-Tikvah" to revisit the issue. By this point, the winds had shifted with respect to the Yishuv's relations with the British government. After the publication of the 1939 White Paper, many Zionists felt betrayed by the

British—and began to believe that confrontation rather than cooperation was the only sure way to bring about a Jewish state. At the same
time the crushing of the Palestinian resistance after the 1936–1939 re-
volts left the Arab community weak and disorganized, with an ineffec-
tual and often fractured leadership. The combination of weakness and
feeble leadership prevented them from mounting much resistance to Yishuv attempts to secure increased recognition of nation-state symbols
like the national anthem.

By the early 1940s the issue of playing "ha-Tikvah" on the PBS had
been raised again. A letter to the editor in *Haboker*, translated into English for the *Review of the Palestine Press*, a government circular, criticized the station for not playing "ha-Tikvah" during a recent Pentecost
program. "It is a strange phenomenon that our national anthem 'Ha-
tiqva' is not being broadcast in the various programs of the Hebrew
Hour," the excerpt began. It closed by asking, "Why do the Poles and
the other Allied Nations terminate their daily programs over the PBS
with their national anthem?"[21] That the letter was translated into English for government circulation—a letter that explicitly connected the
playing of "ha-Tikvah" to playing the national anthems of other nation-
states allied to Britain—says something about the potential if not the
actual tensions that the issue raised.

Karl Salomon, head of the PBS's Music section, was among the "ha-
Tikvah" supporters, and in his November 1944 memo he advocated reconsidering the decision to ban "ha-Tikvah" from the PBS's broadcasts
and at least to allow the instrumental version to be broadcast. He suggested that the first broadcast be timed to mark Vaad Leumi president
Chaim Weizmann's seventieth birthday, on December 4, 1944. Salomon noted that the PBS's policy regarding anthems had changed, "in-
sofar as the anthems of many of [British] allies have been broadcast on
several occasions." While the "Jewish people" were not a political ally,
Palestine's "Jewish Brigade," Salomon argued, was. "There is no doubt
that at every official function in the Jewish Brigade 'Hatikvah' will be
played in addition to 'God Save the King,'" he wrote. "It seems . . .
strange that in a broadcast connected with the Jewish Brigade 'Hatikvah' should be eliminated."[22]

In response to the argument he anticipated—that no Jewish state existed, nor did Zionism represent all Jews, making "ha-Tikvah" an anthem neither of a nation-state nor of a nation—Salomon changed his
reasoning. "If we read the text . . . we find that this song is not intended
to be the anthem of an existing state." He argued that the piece was a

"song of hope" with no political character—and that the tune, an adaptation of an Eastern European folk song, was even less so. On these grounds, he requested permission to broadcast the instrumental version "on very special occasions."[23] Permission was not granted, perhaps because the chief secretary disagreed with Salomon's conclusion that "nothing in this song . . . could offend any non-Jewish people living in this country."[24]

Edwin Samuel and "ha-Tikvah"

In May 1945 Edwin Samuel was appointed director of the PBS. Samuel, the son of Viscount Herbert Samuel, mandate Palestine's first High Commissioner, was a longtime British civil servant and Palestine resident who had served as chief censor during World War II.[25] Samuel had hoped for a promotion to director of education but was advised that appointing a Jew to that position was politically untenable.[26] His work in the censor's office and his involvement in the PBS's "Brighter English League"[27] broadcasts of the late mid-1930s, however, made his appointment to the PBS an attractive choice from the British home and mandate governments' views.[28]

Although Samuel was considered neutral by the British mandate government, his father had been known as a supporter of Zionism both before and after his tenure as High Commissioner, during which he laid the foundations for the mandate state's fostering of a Jewish "national home" in Palestine. Moreover, Edwin Samuel's wife, Hadassah Goor (Grasovsky), was from a prominent Zionist family and was active in Palestine's Zionist community. Yet the Arab community in Palestine appears to have seen Samuel as a fairly neutral figure during his initial years as a civil servant—although during his tenure as PBS director both the Arab and the Yishuv community came to view him as wholly partisan. For example, 1930s *Falastin* articles referred to him as "Mr. Samuel," the paper's standard designation for British men. By the end of the mandate, *Falastin* referred to him as "Adon Samuel," using the Hebrew designation, as it did for other Zionists.

Regardless of whatever commitment to neutrality Samuel might personally have made, the Zionist community saw his appointment as director as a means of ensuring that its interests were looked after. As Samuel noted in his memoirs, the Jewish Agency and the Vaad Leumi had been concerned from the founding of the PBS that "Jewish rights" be protected and had persuaded the mandate government to recognize the authority of a Jewish advisory committee to review the PBS's attention to Hebrew broadcasting. "As I was Jewish myself," Samuel wrote, "I did not need to be told what were Jewish interests. In fact, I was by now sufficiently trusted—not only by the Jewish national bodies but also by the Jewish press—as to make an advisory committee really unnecessary."[29] Within a year of his appointment, the playing of "ha-Tikvah" on the air came to the fore as a Jewish interest.

In late March 1946 the PBS prepared to celebrate its ten-year anniversary. At a dress rehearsal for a tenth anniversary concert scheduled to be played at the YMCA the same evening, several members of the PBS Orchestra, whose musicians were largely Jewish, stated that they would not play "God Save the King," the British national anthem, if they were not allowed to follow it with "ha-Tikvah."[30] After Samuel came to the YMCA and met with the orchestra, promising to look into the possibility of playing the piece in the future, the concert was played as scheduled. Samuel followed this incident by requesting documentation on "the previous practice, indicating when 'Hatikvah' was played, when it was not played, . . . and the occasions about which there is now ground for discussion" during a meeting with the PBS Orchestra committee the following day.[31]

Salomon responded with a memo describing the occasions on which the PBS Orchestra had played "ha-Tikvah" without the piece being broadcast on the radio station. All were occasions in which the orchestra played in a "Jewish" setting ("when the PBS Orchestra played at the Hebrew University"; "when the PBS Orchestra played in Tel Aviv") or in military camps outside Palestine during World War II ("when the Orchestra played in Military Camps, where Jewish soldiers were present"). Salomon stated that "the members of the Orchestra were never very happy about this [restriction on playing "ha-Tikvah"]" and that "the reaction of the Jewish public is similar to that of the Orchestra." He cautioned that "with the increased political tension, the dissatisfaction of the Jewish majority of the audience might one day be expressed in a rather unpleasant way." After acknowledging that he "personally share[d] the views of the Orchestra," he expressed his hope for a solution "in line with Government policy as well as with the feelings of the musicians [of whom] all but one are Jews, and that of the Jewish public."[32]

After broaching the idea of revisiting the ban on "ha-Tikvah" during his monthly meeting with Chief Secretary J. V. W. Shaw, Samuel sent a secret memo outlining his reasons for reconsidering the ban around

April 6. Meanwhile, he had already announced publicly that the prohibition on broadcasting "ha-Tikvah" might be lifted. "The removal of the PBS ban on the Jewish National Anthem is being considered, the Hon Edwin Samuel, Director of Broadcasting, said last night," the *Palestine Post*'s "Listener's Corner" noted on March 31—the day after the PBS's ten-year anniversary.[33]

Samuel's argument regarding the playing of "ha-Tikvah" hinged on the Jewishness of the audience. The PBS Orchestra's YMCA concert had been one of a series called "Music Calling." "From personal observation," Samuel noted, "very few Arabs, if any, attend these concerts. . . . [T]he overwhelming majority of the audience is Jewish." The YMCA was not a "Jewish" setting in the same sense as the Hebrew University; in fact, YMCA officials seem to have been utterly disinclined to permit the playing of "ha-Tikvah." Instead, Samuel was arguing that the Jewishness of the setting depended on the audience. Those who were listening were those whom the PBS Orchestra should address, and by extension, those who were not present and not listening—the Arabs missing from the "Music Calling" audiences—could not be offended by the playing of a Jewish song for a Jewish audience.[34]

Whether due to the YMCA's refusal or the mandate government's, it does not appear that the latter's policy regarding the playing or broadcasting of "ha-Tikvah" changed. No period newspaper articles praise (or criticize) the appearance of the piece in PBS broadcasts, and no memoirs list it as an accomplishment (or a failure). Nor does the British home government seem to have considered it an issue worthy of discrete attention—that is, no file on "ha-Tikvah" can be found among the Colonial Office documents housed at the British National Archives. The documents cited above were taken from a file created by the PBS's Music section. This file appears to have been compiled in 1946, when playing "ha-Tikvah" on the air became an issue supported by Salomon and Samuel. The translated *Haboker* excerpts suggest that the issue had resonance within the broader Zionist community, but it is difficult to argue that this became a major point of contention between the Arab community and the Yishuv. The extant documents mention the Arab Palestinian community only tangentially, suggesting that "ha-Tikvah" proponents saw their antagonist in this instance as the British mandate government. In this case, claiming the PBS and its orchestra as national institutions was a claim made against the mandate government's reluctance to permit the playing of a "national" anthem—a classic site of nationalist and anticolonial struggles articulated in the Palestinian context.

Licenses and Listeners' Rights

Samuel's argument regarding "ha-Tikvah" rested on the fact that the concert series' audience was largely Jewish. Starting in 1939, a similar "proof" was advanced by Jewish community leaders when arguing for increasing the weekly broadcasting time for the Hebrew section. Determining the allocation of broadcasting hours for each language section was a political as well as logistical challenge that the PBS had faced from its earliest days on air. There were several ways of conceptualizing how to best divide the broadcasting hours. Democratically speaking, those who listened to the station arguably had the greatest rights to it: their license fees paid for its programming, and their interest in the station made it relevant to the community. Alternatively, as a state-owned public institution, one might expect that station broadcasts would serve the population of largest size. Finally, as a British mandate government station, one might expect the PBS to serve British government interests first and foremost. In the early years of the PBS this last was indeed the case. The Foreign and Colonial Office officials involved in creating and funding the station were acutely concerned with securing Palestinian Arab loyalty in the tense political situation of the late 1930s. Arabic programming thus dominated the PBS schedule, comprising 60 percent or more of weekly broadcasting hours.

The Jewish community seems to have initially accepted this balance of programming, for two reasons. First, community leaders concurred with the government's assumption that the Arab population was more likely to rebel against Britain in the event of political unrest in Europe. Government officials' fears regarding the susceptibility of Arabs to anti-British propaganda broadcast from the Italian station Radio Bari dovetailed with Zionist arguments regarding the backward state of Palestinian Arab culture. The more "advanced" Jewish population, participating in rational, enlightened Western culture, required less government attention because it was less likely to rebel or otherwise pose a threat—a self-serving assumption that for a time suited both government and Yishuv. The second reason reflected the Jewish population's greater interest in tuning in to European and other international stations. Many Palestinian Jews were relatively recent immigrants whose radio listening habits reflected their continuing cultural orientation to Europe. Hence the *Palestine Post*'s wireless schedules in the early and mid-1930s listed programming for over ten European stations.

However, the anti-Semitic turn in Central and Eastern Europe that led many Jews to immigrate to Palestine during the 1930s discouraged them from maintaining German, Austrian, Polish, and so on, as their primary identities. Their increasing identification with Palestine as a national home led to their growing preference for the PBS—particularly its musical and theatrical broadcasts, which reflected Yishuv debates over what constituted a Jewish national culture. At the same time, Jewish community leaders hoped that the Palestine station would reach out to Jews in Europe, encouraging immigration. As a result, they had pressed the mandate government to operate the PBS on short-wave rather than medium-wave frequency. Even at the station's inauguration, Dr. Abraham Katznelson, who had served on the original Program Advisory Committee as a Vaad Leumi representative, noted, "To the waves that carry the speech of all nations . . . is being added the Hebrew wave that is to carry to every corner of the Yishuv." And, he added, "in the future also to every corner of the Diaspora." What was it that this wave would carry? It was, he continued, "the message of Jerusalem."[35] Getting that message out beyond the limited reaches of medium-wave broadcasting, however, would prove to be a challenge that pitted Jewish community leaders against British mandate officials.

Wavelength Issues

The mandate government had agreed to the creation of a medium-wave broadcasting station, the most cost-effective means of reaching listeners throughout the territory. Medium-wave transmissions could be received by the least expensive radio sets, allowing the greatest possible number of Palestinians access to the broadcasting service. Short-wave broadcasts, while capable of reaching much greater distances, required more costly radio receivers—those likely to be owned by cosmopolitan urbanites interested in tuning in to European stations or the BBC Empire Service but not by lower-middle- or working-class Palestinians, and certainly not by villagers. The decision in favor of medium-wave broadcasting, however, was met with dismay by many in the Yishuv.

Much of this dismay was linked to Palestine's special status: supporters were eager that the station be able to reach an overseas audience. The *Palestine Post*, an enthusiastic advocate of short-wave broadcasts from the early 1930s, continued criticizing the government's decision all through the planning stages, including this editorial, published the day before the PBS went on the air:

> [Restricting the station's power] will prevent foreign countries which we feel sure are eager to hear the authentic voice of the land from lis-

tening to Palestine's emissions. . . . We would urgently plead that as soon as the new organization has got into stride those who are in charge of its technical administration may see their way to extend the accessibility of our broadcasting service to the world at large. This country has held a place of its own in the history of humanity since the very origins of civilization. It is our common hope that it may still have a message of more than local import in the present phase of civilization, of which the world enriching service of broadcasting is one of the most characteristic features.[36]

As the years passed and the position of Eastern and Central Europe's Jews deteriorated, Yishuv leadership began to promote short-wave broadcasting for another reason. Short-wave broadcasting in Hebrew was seen as a means of encouraging Diaspora Jews to come to Palestine. The tight immigration quotas that the British mandate and home governments imposed on Palestine following the 1936–1939 Arab revolt and the 1939 White Paper, however, meant that British officials proved increasingly intractable regarding the request to expand the PBS to the shortwave.

Although the number of radio licenses sold each year was increasing by the mid-1930s, the station's launch in March 1936 had engendered a dramatic and sustained increase in the number of Palestinian radio receiver licenses. The licenses, which cost 500 mils each, were required for each radio set, regardless of the number of listeners, and were renewable annually; subscribers paid their fees to the Post Office and received a registration slip in return. The government regularly published statistics on the number of license holders, which were printed as news articles in the local press. Jewish-owned radio licenses accounted for much if not most of this growth. (As radio license applications were accepted in Palestine's three official languages, determining the communal identity of each was done by combining the number of radio set licenses filled out in Hebrew with the number of English-language licenses with "Hebrew" names.)[37] By the end of 1936 the *Palestine Post* began breaking down the aggregate number by communal group. In an article published on December 9, the paper noted that in the eight months since the PBS began broadcasting the Post Office had issued approximately 4,500 new licenses. Of these, it specified, "about 3,100 applications or about two thirds were in Hebrew, 1,100 in English and about 300 in Arabic."[38]

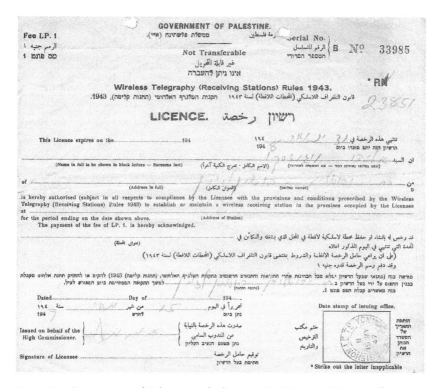

Figure 5.1. Government of Palestine radio license, 1947. Source: Private collection.

Although the *Post* did not specify license holders' communal identities in all its articles on the subject, it did so in many. The critical decision that the *Post* made was not that of tracking licenses by community but that of publishing them as news. The two numbers—the aggregate and the particular—told very different stories: the first, that of a steadily growing overall interest in radio; and the second, that of the Jewish community's disproportionately higher radio set ownership. The *Palestine Post* employed this second story to argue that the PBS was most often listened to and best appreciated by the Jewish community.[39] (*Falastin* also published license figures but generally folded them in with other Post Office statistics.)[40] That Hebrew-speaking and/or Jewish Palestinians purchased radio set licenses in disproportionately higher numbers was not in doubt, as the 1947 radio set license above indicates. What this meant in terms of Arab Palestinian radio interest, however, was debated.

Individuals in the Jewish community appear to have been cognizant of "the power of numbers" from early on. One of those who opposed the proscription on "Eretz Israel," for example, suggested that Jewish license holders and station personnel protest against the government's decision and that "if satisfactory results are not forthcoming, licensees ought to return their licenses . . . and participants in the programs should refuse to take part in them."[41] In 1939 the Vaad Leumi picked up this argument and presented it to the mandate government. In response to the PBS administration dissolving the Program Advisory Committee, which included representatives from each Palestinian community, the Vaad Leumi petitioned the chief secretary for control over Hebrew section programming. At the same time, it requested that the PBS "assure the Hebrew program a full share in the schedule of broadcasting hours and of the expenditure, in accordance with the proportion of Jewish license holders to the general total." The problem was that while Jews made up four-fifths of the PBS audience and through their license fees provided the greatest financial support to the station, the Hebrew section received less than a third of station airtime. The *Palestine Post*, which reported the story, explained:

> The Jewish share in the general programmes [is] in inverse ratio to the number of wireless licenses, and therefore their contributions to PBS revenue. While Jewish listeners constitute at least 80 per cent of the licensed public, the Vaad Leumi states, the Jewish share in the broadcast programmes [is] no more than 30 per cent, and even the larger part of that time [is] given over to general musical programmes jointly shared with the English Hour.[42]

With the onset of the war later that summer and the resultant overhaul in the station's administration and programming,[43] further discussion of the Vaad Leumi's petition faded. As a historical document, its significance lies in its demand that the community that paid the largest proportion of license fees should enjoy the greatest airtime—an argument that the Zionist community made regarding state taxes and government services generally. This was a call for the PBS to be a market-driven public station, in the sense that it should serve the listeners who funded it.

Mandate authorities might well have dismissed the Vaad Leumi's use of statistics to argue for increased funding and programming hours for the Hebrew section even without the outbreak of war, using the logic of the station's model, the BBC. The BBC's ability to sustain itself with radio license fees derived from the much greater percentage of the British population that took radio licenses. The far fewer listeners in Palestine meant that this revenue made up only a small portion of the PBS's operating budget. Mandate government funding paid the rest. Thus the democratic logic that those whose money constituted the lion's share of the station budget should have the greatest influence over its programming in fact would have supported the status quo.

In a talk given to London's Royal Institute of International Affairs in mid-1946, PBS Director Edwin Samuel laid out the PBS's situation in Palestine with respect to audience size, composition, and allocation of broadcasting hours. He noted:

> There are 60,000 licensed sets, and this number is being increased by about 20,000 a year. This increase is largely due to the backlag from the war. From the language in which the applicants make out their license forms it is easy to determine what is the racial origin of listeners. Recent figures show that four-fifths of the listeners are Jews; about one-third of the Jewish community of Palestine—now about 600,000 to 700,000— are "wired for sound." About one-tenth of the Arab population can listen: this lower proportion is due not so much to the fact that they are not interested as to the lack of electricity supply. . . . The listening public thus consists of one-third of the Jewish community, one-tenth of the Arab community, and what are politely called "others"—British, Armenians, Greeks, etc.[44]

In 1946 the population of Palestine was approximately 1.9 million. Even assuming that ten persons listened to each licensed radio set, a rather high number for most countries of Palestine's wealth and education, only one in three Palestinians would have been listening to the radio. Differential listener-to-set ratios prevailed in Palestine's communities, however, with Arab Palestinians presumed to have a higher ratio thanks to the village sets. While the overall low rate of listening is striking, the vast gulf between listenership among the Jewish and Arab populations is even more so: 80 percent of Jews in Palestine were licensed radio listeners, while only 10 percent of Arabs were. Samuel acknowledged the difficulties of allocating broadcasting hours in such a skewed situation:

> That provides us straight away with the difficult problem of how we are to distribute our time. There is a minority community with a majority of listeners. However, we work on the assumption that we have a

periphery of listeners who are Arabic speaking in other countries of the Middle East, such as Syria, Lebanon, Transjordan, Egypt, and Iraq. We thus provide a fifty-fifty service.[45]

Nor would the argument that the listeners' preferences should determine station programming have proven successful. The BBC's mission, often described as to educate and elevate, placed station administrators in a paternal role vis-à-vis listeners, with the responsibility to improve their minds and cultural sensibilities. Programs were selected in accordance with what BBC officials felt the audience "needed" rather than with what it wanted. PBS officials (as well as government officials) shared this paternalist view. Despite pressures to democratize, the PBS remained a station whose programming held out the possibility of promoting a national culture but whose structure insisted on the promotion of two national cultures, under a mandate government that refused to let either flower into an independent nation-state. As a result, the station's allocation of programming hours reinforced the separatist nature of the mandate government in Palestine, encouraging the development of a deeply unintegrated cultural system to match the already entrenched separatism in the political and economic realms.

Claiming the Spoils

The PBS became the target of anti-British and antimandate terrorist activities from relatively early on. In late spring 1939 the station moved from its first home in the Palace Hotel to its own buildings on Queen Melisande's Way; an article in *Jerusalem Radio*, a short-lived government-subsidized special supplement to the *Palestine Post*, noted that "the security aspect has not been neglected and suitable steps have been taken to safeguard the building and the apparatus as well as artists and staff visiting the premises."[46] On August 3 three bombs went off in quick succession during the broadcasting of the Children's Hour. One bomb damaged the control room, another damaged a hallway, and a third, placed under the announcer's desk, wounded and ultimately killed two PBS staffers: the "Children's Hour" announcer, a Jewish immigrant from South Africa named Mae Weissenberg, and the control room officer, an Arab named Adib Mansour. A third employee, Gabriel Dimitropoulous, suffered mild injuries.

The explosion was front-page news in the Palestine papers and was reported in the *Times of London* as well.[47] "Fortunately no children

Figure 5.2. PBS Hebrew "Children's Hour" broadcast, no date (1936–1939).
Source: G. Eric and Edith Matson Photograph Collection, Prints and Photographs
Division, Library of Congress, LC-DIG-matpc-22422.

were present, as is often the case, when they ask to be allowed to listen
to the broadcasting of the program," the *Times* noted. Children were
often but not always used in the program; at other times adults played
the needed roles.

The effects of the bombing were deep and far-reaching. John Melkon Rose, a half-English, half-Armenian Palestinian who with his two
sisters used to participate in the "Children's Hour" broadcasts, mentioned the bombing in the memoir he wrote over fifty years later.[48]
Heather Fairley Teague, who knew both victims from her work as a
children's book reviewer for the PBS, heard the bomb and was called to
comfort Weissenberg in the hospital. She wrote her parents in England:

> I had passed my First Aid Certificate thing and was attending a lec-
> ture on home nursing at the Government Hospital when a purler of a
> bomb explosion rattled the windows. Everyone gave a weak smile and
> pretended it was a road-making blast. Seven minutes later there was an-
> other; we still pretended, but I had a curious tense feeling. Another two
> minutes, and there was a colossal bang. We still continued with our lec-
> ture. Presently some of the class signaled to me that a man was call-
> ing to me from the road. I rushed down. Mae Weissenberg, the woman
> I work with on the children's hour, had been hurt, and had asked for
> me to come to her. Her husband was away in Tel Aviv. I went. Her legs,

from the knees down, were pretty badly smashed up. They had placed three bombs in the PBS—one under her announcing desk, one in the hall, one in the control room. She was very brave, very quiet, and showed no sign of hysteria at all. It was difficult to believe she was so badly shattered.

Teague remained with Weissenberg until the hospital took her in to surgery.

At the last moment her poor wretch of a husband rushed in. He had just got back from Tel Aviv, and someone had told him in the street. John [Teague's husband] was wildly searching for him in the car. They let him in to see her in the operating theatre for a few minutes. We waited and waited. Oh! What a wait. She was in there an hour and a quarter. The injuries were worse than they had at first supposed, and the doctor talked of amputation of one leg—but otherwise she seemed all right. She was being kept under morphia so we did not see her before she went upstairs. We took the husband home with us to be near the telephone. About 11 I telephoned the night sister. She was doing well—had been conscious and sent her love to us. At two the telephone rang. She was worse—could we come up. We staggered out on one of those heartbreaking night rushes—trying desperately to beat time. She was dead when we got there—shock.

Teague and her husband were brought into Weissenberg's hospital room to see her body. Teague described Weissenberg's face as peaceful but found that this brought little comfort.

She was only 25, and my heart is bitter—bitter against the inhuman swine who must have know what they were doing and to whom, unless the time on the bomb went wrong. We kept the husband with us until after the funeral. If you have never seen a Jewish funeral you cannot understand what an appalling day that was. I can never forget it. She was a South African by birth—young, intelligent, gay and charming.[49]

The station's broadcasts continued, with announcers initially broadcasting from the emergency studio in Ramallah, on the transmitter grounds, and subsequently from the Jerusalem Post Office until the PBS headquarters was repaired. A smaller and possibly unrelated ter-

rorist attack occurred the following week, when a man threw a bomb at
the police officer stationed in front of the station headquarters; the po-
liceman suffered minor injuries, and the station was unharmed.[50] After
this incident, no further bomb attempts occurred, and media coverage
of the original attack died down. Aside from an article in *Falastin* that
mentioned that a Jewish employee of the English section had been arrested in connection with the bombing, no culprits appear to have been
found.[51]

Aside from one failed attempt by eight Hebrew-speaking men to take
over the Ramallah transmitting station in May 1944,[52] no major terrorist attacks targeting the PBS occurred during the war. But starting in
1946, the attacks resumed. On January 20 the *Palestine Post* reported
the blowing up of the electrical substation located near the PBS headquarters: "Three heavy explosions shortly after 8:15 last night were followed by sharp automatic and rifle fire in various parts of the city. . . .
Further explosions were heard about an hour later and again at 10:45."[53]
The government declared a curfew; the PBS, whose transmitter in Ramallah ran off the same substation, went off the air. The following day,
the *Post* explained what had really happened, quoting an official government communiqué: "On the night of the 19th January armed Jews
attempted to blow up the studios of the [PBS] in St. Paul's Road [the
road adjacent to Queen Melisande's Way] Jerusalem."[54] The paper described the attacks as "outrages," but their near-success appears only to
have encouraged future attacks.

By 1946 the Palestine mandate government's refusal to support either the Palestinian Arab or Zionist vision of a national culture for Palestine had become visibly irrelevant. Both communities were actively
engaged in preparing for an independent state—preparations most notably characterized by ongoing skirmishes and paramilitary attacks
throughout the territory. For the PBS, this meant frequent attacks on
the broadcasting house and the transmitting station, as well as attempts
by various Jewish guerrilla organizations to storm the station. Police
guards were posted; when these proved ineffective, Arab Legion troops
(the Jordanian military, then under British control) were stationed
there. Minutes taken from meetings of various PBS departments show
the extent to which security became an increasing concern, with personnel assigned rotating shifts as "duty officers."

As the security situation deteriorated after the UN Partition Plan
and the British plan for withdrawal were announced, Jerusalem was di-

vided into various security zones. PBS staff members were issued passes to cross these zones in station cars and/or under escort, but the Jewish staff soon refused to come to the studio, explaining that they feared the Arab Legion troops and the dangers of crossing through Arab sections of the city.[55] They petitioned for the Hebrew and Music sections to be relocated to the Jewish neighborhood of Rehavia, where new broadcasting studios were erected. Edwin Samuel approved the request:

> By the middle of December [1947], I had to evacuate all Jewish and British staff from Broadcasting House, which was situated on the edge of the Arab quarter of Musrara. The Hebrew and music sections and the Jewish part of the administrative staff were regrouped around temporary studios in Rehavia: the English section worked wholly from branch studios in Security Zone A; the Arabic section and the Arabic part of the administrative staff continued to work at Broadcasting House under Arab Legion protection, with reserve studios and offices at Ramallah. These were for use on days when the firing at Sheikh Jarrah was too intense for Arab buses to bring in those members of the Arab staff who lived in or who had moved to Ramallah.

These security measures meant that, as Samuel noted, "the only place where British Arabs and Jews still met was in the Public Information Office to which we transferred our three news rooms."[56] The PBS began to fracture physically, ending whatever history of intercommunal cooperation had existed. Again British station administrators like Keating could do little more than watch; their intervention, even where possible, made a negligible difference.

In January 1948 the separation of the Hebrew and Music sections from the Arabic section was further solidified by the decentralization of PBS program planning, which left each section largely in charge of its own programs. By March, Samuel was overseeing the division of the station's financial affairs, since it had become increasingly difficult for station controllers to access funds from banks located outside their particular zone. Samuel explained:

> Imprest Account No. 1 with Barclay's Bank for LP 3000 will in future be controlled by Mr. A. Nashashibi, the Controller of Arabic Programs.
> Imprest Account No. II for LP 2000 has now been opened in Barclay's Bank (Western Branch) and will be controlled by Mr. M. Zlotnik, the Controller of Hebrew Programs.

Account No. II will cover payments of the Hebrew Music, English, and News sections, except expenditures incurred by the Arabic newsroom which will be paid through the Controller of Arabic Programs.

He closed by reminding Nashashibi and Zlotnik to avoid overruns—as if financial imprudence were the largest concern preoccupying the station and Palestine's residents generally.[57]

The assistant director, Rex Keating, and other staff saw the relocation of the Hebrew and Music sections as a ploy to secure broadcasting equipment for the Haganah, as several Jewish staff were rumored to be active members of this and other paramilitary groups. That Samuel was himself Jewish only exacerbated tensions within the PBS, as station personnel on both sides perceived his sympathies to lie increasingly with the Zionist cause. Keating's diaries from the period are filled with comments about Samuel's "crooked mind" and partisanship,[58] and his memoir juxtaposes diary entries with parenthetical recollections. His assessment of the reasons for the station's split shows Samuel as an active supporter of Hebrew section attempts to carve a new Jewish national station from the PBS:

12 December [1947]: Samuel told me that the Hebrew Section were in a state of panic. The Arab Legion had been stationed at the PBS to guard it and the Jewish staff were fearful of a massacre. I suspect that something is a foot.

Commenting on this diary entry, Keating later added:

My suspicions were soon justified. Several days later the Jewish staff failed to turn up at the PBS and I found that they had been secretly transferring files, records and studio equipment to a studio already prepared in the Jewish zone of Jerusalem. I never saw them again. The PBS was now effectively split in two. Samuel, the Director, joined the Hebrew Section, while I, the Assistant Director, stayed in Broadcasting House with the Arab and English sections. The irony of the situation was the Hebrew news and programs had to pass through our central control room and thence to the transmitter at Ramallah which was in an area under Arab control. At any time the Arab technicians could have pulled the plug on all Hebrew broadcasts, but they never did. Such was their devotion to duty that broadcasting in English, Hebrew and Arabic continued to the end of the Mandate. The PBS example was quickly followed by other Departments, despite all the efforts of Government to stop them. The split became total. In effect, the incipient Israeli government was being realized.[59]

The hostility increasingly on display within the PBS mirrored that of the territory at large. While the daily gun battles, road seizures, curfews, and security zone changes continued, the PBS limped along with its insides slowly being carved away. As the mandate lurched to a close, members of the Arabic and Hebrew sections—separated physically by security zone restrictions—seem to have spent their workdays struggling both to keep the PBS on the air and to secure what broadcasting material they could for the day when the British no longer governed. Yet when the mandate did end, the PBS itself became an institution that no one wanted to claim. The concluding chapter traces the initial disavowal and ultimate recuperation of the PBS by Palestinians and Israelis alike and turns to the broader implications of the legacy of the PBS and other interwar stations around the region.

CONCLUSION

The Multiple Afterlives of the PBS

The mandate for Palestine officially ended at midnight on May 15, 1948. What did this mean for the Palestine Broadcasting Service? Like other government institutions, it had a postmandate plan intended to provide administrative continuity and uninterrupted service—a plan soon overtaken by events. The station's footprint remained: the buildings and transmitter were still there and continued to broadcast on the same frequency, but the station's name, identity, and personnel changed. Physically, the station split: the broadcasting house, located in West Jerusalem, ended up in Israeli hands; the Ramallah transmitter, which had been taken by the Arab Legion, came under Jordanian control.

In Jerusalem, Hebrew section personnel provided the technical and administrative continuity that the PBS's postmandate plan intended. But the station's identity changed. Almost immediately it was renamed Kol Israel—Voice of Israel—one of the on-air station identifications prohibited by the mandate government and the name that the Haganah had used for its clandestine station. Since the PBS transmitters were in Jordanian hands, Kol Israel began by broadcasting from an emergency transmitter located in Tel Aviv until new ones were built. At the same time, the nascent Israeli state also began short-wave broadcasting, a project aimed at attracting Jewish audiences overseas. Like the name change, this development marked a significant break from the mandate era. British officials had consistently refused Yishuv requests for short-wave broadcasting, fearing that broadcasts to Jews abroad would put increasing pressure on Palestine's immigration quotas.

The uncertainty that prevailed during this period is evident from the disjuncture between various period documents. Readers of the *Palestine Post* might have concluded that the PBS ceased broadcasting before the mandate ended: an article published May 14 announced that "the first broadcast of the Jewish State's Radio, Kol Israel," would occur that afternoon.[1] Yet while in Jerusalem the PBS morphed from a medium-wave, mandate institution to a short- and medium-wave, national institution, *Falastin* continued to publish the PBS's Arabic program schedule through July 1949 with no mention of any changes, either in the station's wavelength or in its name. How did readers interpret the paper's silence on the dramatic changes taking place on the ground with respect to radio broadcasting in Palestine? Were these programs relayed through Kol Israel's transmitters in Jerusalem? Were they broadcast from the former PBS transmitters in Ramallah?

The few documents that remain from this period give no indication; nor do they indicate whether the two sections of the former PBS continued to cooperate in any way. This ambiguity disappeared in 1949: first in April, when *Falastin* began to publish "Ramallah Radio" programs, and more definitively in August, when it began to publish those of the "Hashemite Jordanian (Palestine) Station." Both stations broadcast from the PBS's Ramallah transmitter and used the same frequency as the PBS. The new station operated with former PBS staff but with fewer broadcasting hours and a much-reduced budget—and it broadcast only in Arabic.

Although the *Palestine Post* and *Falastin* offer some sense of the changes taking place on the ground in Palestine, neither tells the full story. Did the PBS cease to exist when Kol Israel came on air? Did it cease to exist when Ramallah Radio began broadcasting on its medium-wave frequency? Or did it end when the International Broadcasting Union recognized the Israeli station? When juxtaposed, the different narratives of the PBS's end highlight the ambiguity of what "end" meant in this case, and the importance of recognizing that the PBS's influence did not end in 1948 or even 1949. Understanding "and then what happened," whether as a recounting of the station's aftermath or its afterlife, is integral to understanding the PBS's long-term impact on Palestinian and Jordanian (and Israeli) broadcasting. What these multiple narratives highlight is the degree to which the PBS in its organization and operations had reinforced the separatism that characterized mandate governance as a whole.

In the immediate aftermath of the mandate, Israelis and Palestinians alike appear to have chosen to draw no connection between later stations and the PBS. This would appear to support a Fanonian argument that the PBS functioned primarily as a colonial institution—an in-

Figure C.1. Radio transmitter masts in Ramallah, late 1930s. Source: G. Eric and Edith Matson Photograph Collection, Prints and Photographs Division, Library of Congress, LC-DIG-matpc-04023.

authentic and unrepresentative voice carrying no authority and against which each struggled. Yet this was not the case. Instead, one might suggest, the PBS succeeded only too well in creating two independent, autonomous, and competing institutions in its Arabic- and Hebrew-language services. By the early 1950s the PBS had been subsumed into its two successor stations in Jordan and Israel. Meanwhile, the PBS's former Arabic section personnel—like Nasser el-Din' and 'Azmi Nashashibi, 'Ajaj Nuwayhid, and Sari Nusseibeh—leveraged their tenure at the PBS to make a classic postcolonial transition from mandate fonctionnaires to members of national cadres in broadcasting or other fields. Former staff took their PBS experience with them to broadcasting stations and government service in Israel, Jordan, Lebanon, Syria, and Cyprus.

Yet the PBS's legacy developed beyond the use of its broadcasting house and transmitter, and even beyond the influence of its former administrators. In recent decades the Israeli Broadcasting Authority and the Palestinian Broadcasting Corporation have both made efforts to reclaim the PBS as a protonational station—emphasizing the importance of "their" section while minimizing or ignoring the other, as well as downplaying the British government's role. For the Palestinian side, the station is used to connect the past—the Arabic section of the Palestine Broadcasting Service—with the present, the post-Oslo Palestinian

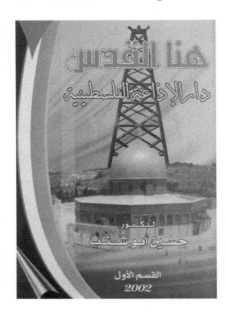

Figure C.2. The symbolically rich (but historically inaccurate) cover of Hussein Abu Shanab's *Huna al-Quds: Dar al-Idhaʿa al-Falastiniyyah 1936,* published in Palestine in 2002.

Broadcasting Corporation. The PBC's use of the old PBS transmitter in Ramallah helped reinforce this connection, at least until December 2001, when the transmitter and Voice of Palestine headquarters were destroyed by the Israeli army.

While the physical link between past and present has been destroyed, the recuperation of the PBS remains an important component of a new, post-Oslo historical memory. This memory recuperates the PBS, honoring it as the predecessor of the PBC—a state-run broadcasting corporation whose credibility as a national institution is strengthened by this longer pedigree. In doing so, it builds upon the separatism enshrined in the history of the PBS—a separatism that makes it possible for the PBC to describe itself as the inheritor of the PBS, with almost no description of the PBS's Hebrew service.

Hussein Abu Shanab's *Huna al-Quds,* published in Palestine in 2002, illustrates both visually and rhetorically the PBS's new role in Palestinian national history. The book takes its title from the PBS's on-air identification, "This is Jerusalem [calling]." Its cover depicts a remarkable scene: the PBS/PBC transmitter rising behind the Dome of the Rock, the famous Umayyad mosque that sits on the Haram al-Sharif in the heart of Jerusalem's Old City. The image is a digital creation: the transmitter, which was already destroyed by the time the book went to press, sat in Ramallah and was not visible from the Haram al-Sharif. The cover depicts a rhetorical claim, not a physical reality, that supports the historical narrative that the book recounts. The cover, like the text, presents the Palestine Broadcasting Corporation as the inheritor of the Palestine Broadcasting Service, allowing it to claim the right to broadcast from Jerusalem.

There have been similar developments in Israel, where since the mid-1970s Kol Israel and the Israel Broadcasting Authority (IBA) have worked to link Israeli state broadcasting with the Hebrew section of the PBS. In 1976 the IBA produced a television special, *Forty Years of Kol Israel*, which linked the PBS to Kol Israel, creating an unbroken historical narrative of "the station" from 1936 to 1976. The program's narrative reduced the PBS to its Hebrew and Music sections and minimized the differences in identity, administration, and scope separating the PBS's Kol Yerushalayim from the 1970s Kol Israel. Ten years later, in 1986, the Israeli Post Office (which itself inherited the mandate-era Palestine Post Office's responsibility for licensing radio sets) issued a commemorative stamp that celebrated "50 years of broadcasting from Jerusalem." Such a statement both claimed radio broadcasting from Jerusalem as an activity of the Israeli state and acknowledged that 1986 did not mark, for example, "50 years of state broadcasting from Jerusalem" or "50 years of Israeli broadcasting from Jerusalem." As with the

Figure C.3. Commemorative stamp cover issued by the state of Israel in 1986 to mark "50 years of broadcasting from Jerusalem." Source: Private collection.

PBC, it also built on the separatist model of the PBS, using it to mis-remember the station as one almost exclusively connected to Hebrew-language broadcasting.

In both cases, it is important to note the central role of Jerusalem in the reimagining of the Palestine Broadcasting Service (and, second-arily, the minimization of the importance of the transmitter and broad-casting station in Ramallah). Both communities remember the Jerusa-lem station as a national station, and its claim on Jerusalem plays into larger contestations over Jerusalem as an Israeli and/or Palestinian cap-ital. These efforts to retrospectively construct a national history for Kol Israel and the PBC from the PBS speak more to the power of imag-ined institutions than to mandate officials' intentions for the PBS. Yet at the same time they push the PBS to fulfill its promised role as a sign of statehood—a symbol of state sovereignty that reflected both the ma-turity of state institutions and the government's control of them. As a sign of statehood, the PBS could have enabled Palestinians from both communities to argue before the League of Nations that the state had achieved the necessary maturity for full independence.

Yet the PBS never worked as an uncomplicated sign of statehood. Its role in mandate Palestine was to reflect and magnify the conflict be-tween Arab Palestinians and Zionists, by concretizing and reinforcing the separatism in its operations that the mandate state facilitated in the political realm. Rather than contest or complicate this separatism, the PBS allowed it to push the expression of conflict in new directions in the broadcasting arena. Since the end of the mandate the station's role in historical memory has been further complicated by political develop-ments in Palestine and Israel that can be traced to the 1940s, as well as by television and the Internet's supercession of radio as the key broad-casting media. Whether the use of the PBS in this manner will provide common ground for cooperation or for further conflict between Pales-tinian and Israeli broadcasting authorities in the years to come remains to be seen.

The PBS and Mandate Palestine

1918   British Army led by General Allenby enters Palestine, begins military administration.

1919   Paris Peace Conference assigns mandate for Palestine to Great Britain.

1920   Nabi Musa / Jerusalem uprisings; High Commissioner Herbert Samuel arrives in June.

1921   Amin al-Husseini appointed Grand Mufti and later head of the British-created Supreme Muslim Council, the official representative of the Muslim community in Palestine.

1922   Vaad Leumi (Jewish executive) recognized as official representative of the Jewish community in Palestine.

1929   "Wailing Wall" uprisings; Shaw Commission and Hope-Simpson Reports on Jewish immigration and land purchases.

1930   Passfield White Paper incorporates Shaw and Hope-Simpson recommendations (later disavowed and never enacted as policy).

1931   Irgun Zvai Leumi (IZL) founded as Zionist national military.

1932   Istiqlal (Independence) Party founded as Palestinian nationalist, pan-Arabist party.

1933   Palestine obtains broadcasting frequency at International Broadcasting Union's Lucerne Conference.

1936   Palestine Broadcasting Service (PBS) begins broadcasts in March, with BBC staff in top administrative positions; Arab revolt begins in April; general strike April–October.

1937   Arab revolt continues in rural areas; PBS establishes village broadcasting initiatives and broadcasts "Talks to Farmers"; Peel Commission Report; Radio Bari spurs BBC Arabic and extra PBS news broadcasts.

1939   Arab revolt ends; MacDonald White Paper limits Jewish immigration to 5,000 over five years and restricts land sales; PBS broadcasts continue and radio set license sales increase.

1939   World War II begins; PBS restructured under tighter government control and censorship.

1941   'Ajaj Nuwayhid named controller of PBS Arabic section.

1945   World War II ends; PBS restructured and Edwin Samuel named director; PBS obtains second transmitter, and illegal Jewish broadcasting resumes.

1946   Anglo-American Commission of Inquiry recommends one state, neither Jewish nor Arab, with 100,000 Jews admitted from Europe; Britain announces intent to end the mandate.

1947   United Nations Special Committee on Palestine submits Partition Plan recommending a two-state solution with Jerusalem under international governance; General Assembly approves. Jewish Executive accepts the plan; Arab Palestinians do not.

1948   PBS staff assigned to various Jerusalem security zones, with the Hebrew and Music sections broadcasting from Rehavia. Britain ends the mandate for Palestine on May 15; civil war erupts; PBS splits as Israel takes the Broadcasting House in Jerusalem and Jordan takes the Ramallah transmitter.

Notes

Introduction

1. "Balfour Declaration 1917," Yale Law School, Avalon Project Documents in Law, History, and Diplomacy, http://avalon.law.yale.edu/20th_century/balfour.asp. Last accessed Mar. 15, 2012.

2. The Husayn-McMahon correspondence, which recorded the negotiations between Great Britain and Sharif Husayn between 1914 and 1916, included the Meccans' commitment to revolting against the Ottoman Empire and British promises of funding, support for an independent Hijaz, and support for an independent Arab state with unspecified territorial boundaries. Among Arabs, the Husayn-McMahon correspondence was taken as a sign of British untrustworthiness when news broke of British-French negotiations to divide the Levant into British and French territories, as captured in the Sykes-Picot Agreement of 1916.

3. "San Remo Resolution," Apr. 24, 1920, accessed via the Council on Foreign Relations' "Essential Documents," www.cfr.org/israel/san-remo-resolution/p15248. Last accessed Mar. 15, 2012.

4. Assaf Likhovski, *Law and Identity in Mandate Palestine* (Chapel Hill: University of North Carolina Press, 2006), pp. 21–23.

5. Population statistics vary; the lower numbers here come from Likhovski, *Law and Identity*, and the higher ones from Amos Nadan, *The Palestinian Peasant Economy under the Mandate: A Story of Colonial Bungling* (Cambridge, MA: Harvard University Press, 2006). The *Survey of Palestine* gave the population as 649,048 in 1922 and as 1,673,071 in 1944. *A Survey of Palestine Prepared for the Information of the Anglo-American Committee of Inquiry* (Jerusalem: Government Printer, 1946), 141.

6. "Palestine Broadcasting Begun," *Palestine Post*, Mar. 31, 1936, p. 8

7. Ibid.

8. The Berne-based International Broadcasting Union (Union Internationale de la Radiodiffusion), which held several regulatory conferences in the 1920s and 1930s, assigned frequencies. See *Documents de la conférence eu-*

ropéenne des radiocommunications Lucerne (Berne: Bureau International de l'Union Télégraphique, 1933).

9. See, e.g., Douglas Boyd, "Development of Egypt's Radio: Voice of the Arabs under Nasser," *Journalism Quarterly* 52, no. 4 (1975): 645–653; Louise Bourgualt, *Mass Media in Sub-Saharan Africa* (Bloomington: Indiana University Press, 1995). Other studies include Mordechai Avida, "Broadcasting in Israel," *Middle Eastern Affairs* 3, no. 1 (Nov. 1952): 321–327; Leslie John Martin, "Press and Radio in Palestine under the British Mandate," *Journalism Quarterly* 26, no. 2 (June 1949): 186–193 (Avida had worked for the Hebrew section of the PBS and continued to work at its successor, Kol Yisrael, and Martin was an American who had grown up in Palestine); Douglas Boyd, "Hebrew-Language Clandestine Radio Broadcasting during the British Palestine Mandate," *Journal of Radio Studies* 6, no. 1 (Winter 1999): 101–115; Derek J. Penslar, "Radio and the Shaping of Modern Israel, 1936–1973," in *Nationalism, Zionism, and Ethnic Mobilization of the Jews in 1900 and Beyond*, ed. Michael Berkowitz (Leiden: Brill, 2004) (focuses on post-1948 developments in Israeli radio broadcasting but begins with a summary of the history and impact of the PBS's Hebrew section); Eytan Almog, "A Wireless Broadcasting Station in Palestine: The First Hebrew Radio Station in the World," *Qesher* 20 (Nov. 1996) [Hebrew]; Tamar Liebes and Zohar Kampf, "'Hello! This Is Jerusalem Calling': The Revival of Spoken Hebrew on the Mandatory Radio (1936–1948)," *Journal of Israeli History* 29, no. 2 (2010): 137–158. See also Danny Kaplan's study on the production of national time via Israeli radio broadcasting: Danny Kaplan, "The Songs of the Siren: Engineering National Time on Israeli Radio," *Cultural Anthropology* 24, no. 2 (May 2009): 313–345; Douglas Boyd, *Egyptian Radio: Tool of Political and National Development* (Lexington, KY: Association for Education in Journalism, 1977); Edmund de Schweinitz Brunner, "Rural Communications Behavior and Attitudes in the Middle East," *Rural Sociology* 18, no. 2 (June 1953): 149–156.

10. See Asa Briggs, *The History of Broadcasting in the United Kingdom*, 3 vols. (London: Oxford University Press, 1979); Asa Briggs, *The BBC: The First Fifty Years* (Oxford: Oxford University Press, 1985); Peter Partner, *Arab Voices: The BBC Arabic Service, 1938–1988* (London: BBC External Service, 1988). See also Gerard Mansell, *Let Truth Be Told: 50 Years of BBC External Broadcasting* (London: Weidenfeld & Nicolson, 1982); Christian Brochand, *Histoire générale de la radio et de la télévision en France*, 2 vols. (Paris: Documentation Française, 1994); Susan Smulyan, *Selling Radio: The Commercialization of American Broadcasting, 1920–1934* (Washington, DC: Smithsonian Institution Press, 1994); Robert McChesney, *Telecommunications, Mass Media and Democracy: The Battle for Control of U.S. Broadcasting, 1928–1935* (New York: Oxford University Press, 1993); Alice Marquis, "Written on the Wind: The Impact of Radio during the 1930s," *Journal of Contemporary History* 19 (1984): 385–415; Callum A. MacDonald, "Radio Bari: Italian Wireless Propaganda in the Middle East and British Counter-Measures," *Middle Eastern Studies* 13, no. 2 (May 1977): 195–207. For British influence on Indian radio development, see Partha Sarathi Gupta, *Radio and the Raj, 1921–1947* (Calcutta: Center for Studies in Social Sciences and K. P. Bagchi, 1995).

11. W. J. Baker, *A History of the Marconi Company* (London: Methuen, 1970). For studies in related fields, see Oliver Read and Walter Welch, *From Tin Foil to Stereo: Evolution of the Phonograph* (Indianapolis: H. W. Sams, [1959] 1977); Sue Bowden, "Household Appliances and the Use of Time: The United States and Britain since the 1920s," *Economic History Review* 27, no. 4 (Nov. 1994): 725–748; Daniel Headrick, *The Invisible Weapon: Telecommunications and International Politics, 1851–1945* (New York: Oxford University Press, 1991); Claude S. Fischer, *America Calling: A Social History of the Telephone* (Berkeley: University of California Press, 1992). Friedrich Kittler's *Gramophone, Film, Typewriter* (Stanford: Stanford University Press, 1999) was also helpful.

12. Jacob Metzer, *The Divided Economy of Mandatory Palestine* (Cambridge: Cambridge University Press, 1998), p. 215.

13. See, e.g., Ami Ayalon, *Reading Palestine: Printing and Literacy, 1900–1948* (Austin: University of Texas Press, 2004); Mustafa Kabha, *The Palestinian Press as Shaper of Public Opinion, 1929–1939: Writing up a Storm* (Edgeware, U.K.: Mitchell Vallentine, 2007).

14. As was common in the region, a "growing readership" did not mean a mass readership. Although literacy rates and living standards increased during the mandate, Arabic newspapers in particular reached only a minority of the adult Arabic-speaking population. Readership rates among the Yishuv were proportionately higher although distributed across several publication languages. Overall, circulation statistics appear low relative to the size of the population: in 1946 a government survey put the circulation of two major newspapers, *Falastin* and the *Palestine Post*, at 8,000 and 20,000, in a population of roughly 1.9 million. Palestinian newspapers formed a public sphere but one that favored the prosperous, the literate, and the urban. See *A Survey of Palestine, Prepared for the Information of the Anglo-American Committee of Inquiry* (Jerusalem: Government Printer, 1946), Sec. 25: List of Newspapers Published in Palestine, 1346–1355.

15. "Radio in Yemen," *Falastin*, May 17, 1935, p. 8. The article noted that the three receivers would be housed in the palaces of Imam Yahya and Crown Prince Sayf al-Islam Amir Ahmed and in the house of Sayyid Abdullah al-Wazir.

16. This transition to state-owned radio stations largely excluded the United States, whose radio broadcasting policies developed along a different trajectory. Canada and the Latin American states, however, developed extensive and deeply rooted state broadcasting systems. See, e.g., Joy Elizabeth Hayes, *Radio Nation: Communication, Popular Culture, and Nationalism in Mexico: 1920–1950* (Tucson: University of Arizona Press, 2000).

17. The 1920s saw the establishment of small, one-man stations all over the world—not only in Europe and the United States. Most broadcast music or news and commentary provided by their operators, with limited broadcasting hours. Although numerous, they were often short-lived. Of the more than one hundred amateur stations operating in Egypt during the 1920s, for example, most had ceased broadcasting by 1930, leaving space for the Egyptian State Broadcasting Service to begin broadcasting in 1934. See Boyd, *Egyptian Radio*, p. 3.

18. According to Derek Penslar, Abramovitch obtained his license after eight years. Derek Penslar, "Transmitting Jewish Culture: Radio in Israel," *Jewish Social Studies* 10, no. 1 (2003): 1–29. The Yishuv and the British mandate government clashed throughout the mandate over the issue of short-wave broadcasting to Jewish communities in Europe, which the Zionist leadership hoped—and the government feared—would draw larger numbers of Jewish immigrants.

19. For the telegraph's impact on the Ottoman Empire, see Roderic Davison, "The Effect of the Telegraph on the Conduct of Ottoman Foreign Relations," in *Decision-Making and Change in the Ottoman Empire*, ed. Ceasar Farah (Kirkville: University of Missouri Press, 1993); Eric Rogan, "Instant Communication: The Impact of Telegraph Communications at the Syrian Periphery," in *The Syrian Land: Processes of Integration and Separation: Bilad al-Sham from the 18th Century to the Mandatory Period*, ed. Thomas Philipp and Birgit Schaebler (Stuttgart: Steiner, 1998), pp. 113–128. For the impact of the telegraph on European foreign policy, see Stephen Kern, *The Culture of Time and Space, 1880–1919* (Cambridge, MA: Harvard University Press, 1986).

20. William Hudson to the President of the Radiocommunications Conference, May 26, 1933. *Documents de la conférence européenne des radiocommunications Lucerne, Mai-Juin 1933*, p. 355.

21. CO/733/266/7, Report of Broadcasting Committee, Dec. 23, 1933.

22. Ibid.

23. The 1931 census gave the total population at 1,033,314. See Edward Hagopian and A. B. Zahlan, "Palestine's Arab Population: The Demography of the Palestinians," *Journal of Palestine Studies* 3, no. 4 (Summer 1974): 32–73.

24. "Harnessing the Air," *Palestine Post*, July 5, 1934, p. 2. The *Post* credited the original idea of a Palestine broadcasting station to C. F. Strickland and an unnamed "Jewish journalist" who had floated the idea in 1925.

25. E. David Goitein, "This Is Jerusalem Calling: Desiderata for a Palestine Broadcasting Corporation," *Palestine Post*, Dec. 28, 1934, p. 5.

26. E. David Goitein, "Free Expression of Opinion: Desiderata for a Palestine Broadcasting Corporation," *Palestine Post*, Jan. 6, 1935, p. 3.

27. E. David Gotein, "A Well-Run Broadcasting Station: Music, Drama, and Entertainment," *Palestine Post*, Jan. 9, 1935, p. 3.

28. "Broadcasting Station Opening in November: Government Announces Program Schedule," communiqué published in the *Palestine Post*, July 7, 1935, p. 1.

29. "Palestine Is on the Air: What the New Broadcasting Service Will Do," *Palestine Post*, July 12, 1935, p. 3. Given Egypt's much larger population (roughly 14.5 million), the low ratio still translated into roughly 10,600 radio receiver licenses.

30. CO 733/308/12, High Commissioner Arthur Wauchope to Under-Secretary of State W. G. A. Ormsby-Gore, July 3, 1936.

31. See "BBC Officer for Palestine/Adviser on Program Broadcasts," *Palestine Post*, Sept. 4, 1935, p. 1. Rendall's secondment was intended to be temporary.

32. See "Mr. C. B. McNair, PBS Director," *Palestine Post*, Jan. 19, 1939, p. 6; and Colonial Office internal memo dated June 16, 1941, CO 733/442/2.

33. Arabic section staff members were also sent to Cairo for training. ʿAzmi Nashashibi traveled to Cairo to study the station's operations after World War II.

34. "Sub-Directors Chosen for Radio Station," *Palestine Post*, Dec. 24, 1935, p. 5.

35. "Appointment to the Broadcasting Service," *Palestine Post*, Feb. 14, 1936, p. 8.

36. "'Jerusalem Calling' in English, Arabic, Hebrew: Palestine Broadcasting Began: High Commissioner Outlines Aims of PBS," *Palestine Post*, Mar. 31, 1936, p. 1. *Falastin* also reported approvingly on the station's inaugural broadcast, but its brief article focused almost exclusively on the Arabic broadcasts.

37. Hajj Amin al-Husseini, the scion of an eminent Palestinian family, was appointed to the new position of "grand mufti" by High Commissioner Herbert Samuel in 1921, when al-Husseini was twenty-eight. As grand mufti, he also oversaw the Supreme Muslim Council, a British creation charged with overseeing religious courts and entrusted with the administration of nearly all Palestine's *waqfs*, or religious trust funds. While al-Husseini had been an anti-British activist prior to his appointment, he was a fairly noncontroversial figure until the Wailing Wall riots of 1929, when he presented himself as a defender of Islam and Palestinian rights. His activism continued, and in 1937 he fled Palestine after being stripped of his official positions, later moving to Nazi Germany, where he gained notoriety as a Nazi propagandist.

38. For a thoughtful, oral history–based anthropology of this period, see Ted Swedenburg, *Memories of Revolt: The 1936–1939 Rebellion and the Palestinian National Past* (Fayetteville: University of Arkansas Press, 2003). For an analysis of the long-term impact of the general strike and the revolt on the Palestinian nationalist movement, see Rashid Khalidi, *The Iron Cage: The Story of the Palestinian Struggle for Statehood* (Boston: Beacon Press, 2006).

39. See, e.g., "The Condition of Palestine on the Radio: Intercession of Arab Monarchs and Martial Law," *Falastin*, Oct. 1, 1936, p. 1. The negotiations ended the general strike, which facilitated the uprisings' subsequent diffusion through the countryside.

40. The Permanent Mandates Commission was the League of Nations body charged with overseeing the progress of all mandate territories, which it did primarily by requiring mandate powers to submit annual reports and to participate in annual review meetings.

41. League of Nations Permanent Mandates Commission Minutes of the 29th Session, Geneva, May 27–June 12, 1936, Report of the Commission to the Council, *League of Nations Publications VI.A, Mandates 1936*, p. 62.

42. *Report of the Committee on the Development of the Palestine Broadcasting Service*, Government of Palestine, Oct. 20, 1936, p. 3. The ISA holds a copy of this report in its PPI (Palestine Publications Index) files (no number).

43. FO 395/557, High Commissioner Arthur Wauchope to Secretary of State (Colonial Office) W. G. A. Ormsby-Gore, Jan. 10, 1938.

44. "Man to Man," *Palestine Post*, July 6, 1936, p. 6.

45. Ibid.

46. For urbanization statistics, see *Survey of Palestine*, p. 697. For the image of the fellah as the "symbolic representative of the cultural and historical continuity of the Palestinian people," see Swedenburg, *Memories of Revolt*, p. 22.

Chapter 1

1. John N. Tleel, *I am Jerusalem* (Old City, Jerusalem: Privately published, 2000), 16.

2. Susan J. Douglas, *Listening In: Radio and the American Imagination* (New York: Random House, 1999), "historicize," p. 28, and "Radio listening . . . ," p. 26.

3. Thus, for example, the May 17, 1935, article in *Falastin*, "Radio in Yemen," which as noted above reported the Yemeni government's purchase of three telegraph machines and three radios.

4. Beirut's Radio Orient as well as smaller, more ephemeral Levantine stations in Damascus and Baghdad began broadcasts later in the decade. In the 1930s European Jews turned to Central and Eastern European stations, which featured prominently in the radio program schedules published in the *Palestine Post*, but by the early 1940s the paper had stopped printing these schedules.

5. What is more difficult to determine is the *way* in which people listened. It is commonly assumed, for example, that women listened while doing housework (ironing in the morning and sewing in the evening)—perhaps the first step toward the radio as background listening practice common today. Even if this listening practice is historically proven, numerous other questions remain. Did men also occupy themselves with other tasks while listening to evening news programs? Did groups of people gathered to listen chat with one another while doing so? Did people talk *to* the radio? When an invitation was extended to listen to a broadcast, was the host expected to repeat that invitation for the life of the serial, talk series, or broadcast program? Were invitees expected to bring gifts? All these questions suggest avenues for future research.

6. Douglas, *Listening In*, p. 24.

7. Victoria de Grazia, Introduction to *The Sex of Things: Gender and Consumption in Historical Perspective*, ed. Victoria de Grazia and Ellen Furlough (Berkeley: University of California Press, 1996), p. 4.

8. Elizabeth Frierson, "Cheap and Easy: the Creation of Consumer Culture in Late Ottoman Society," in *Consumption Studies and the History of the Ottoman Empire, 1550–1922*, ed. Donald Quataert (Albany: SUNY Press, 2000), p. 246.

9. Timothy Burke, *Lifebuoy Men, Lux Women: Commodification, Consumption, and Cleanliness in Modern Zimbabwe* (Durham: Duke University Press, 1996), p. 5.

10. Ibid., 7.

11. Relli Shechter, "Reading Advertisements in a Colonial/Development

Context: Cigarette Advertising and Identity Politics in Egypt, c. 1919–1939," *Journal of Social History* 39, no. 2 (Winter 2005): 483–503.

12. Ibid., p. 500. He states that the emergence of "democratized" markets in some cases did not occur until the early mid-1970s, when regional prosperity was produced by a surge in oil prices, but notes that this periodization requires further research to be conclusively stated.

13. Victoria de Grazia, *The Culture of Consent: Mass Organization of Leisure in Fascist Italy* (New York: Cambridge University Press, 1981), p. 155.

14. Roland Marchand, *Advertising the American Dream: Making Way for Modernity, 1920–1940* (Berkeley: University of California Press, 1985), p. 64.

15. *Survey of Palestine*, p. 148.

16. Everett Rogers, *The Diffusion of Innovations*, 4th ed. (New York: Free Press, 1995). Rogers's diffusion curve is often referred to as an S-curve, which is the shape the graph takes from 0 percent to 50 percent, the point at which half the population has adopted the innovation. Seen in its entirety (innovators/early adopters/early majority/late majority/laggards), however, the graph is a bell curve.

17. Ibid., p. 1.

18. Malcolm Gladwell, *The Tipping Point: How Little Things Can Make a Big Difference* (Boston: Back Bay Books, 2002).

19. D. L. LeMahieu, *A Culture for Democracy: Mass Communication and the Cultivated Mind in Britain between the Wars* (Oxford: Clarendon Press, 1988), p. 234.

20. Although research for this chapter included a survey of several Arabic newspapers, the two newspapers employed for supporting source material and macro-analyses here are *Falastin* and the English-language *Palestine Post*. *Falastin* started publishing from Jaffa in January 1911, under the direction of Isa and Yusuf al-Isa. By the mid-1930s and 1940s it had become the second largest circulation Arabic paper in Palestine, after *al-Dif'a*, and arguably the most influential. The *Palestine Post* began publishing from Jerusalem in December 1932, under the direction of Gershon Agronsky, an American immigrant. As the sole English-language paper published in Palestine, the *Palestine Post* enjoyed a broader—i.e., cross-community—circulation than any other paper. Because its readership included British officials in Palestine's mandate government, the paper appears to have enjoyed or at least claimed a certain "paper of record" status. The *Palestine Post* became the *Jerusalem Post* in 1952, under which name it continues to publish today. A brief but useful summary of the Palestine press, which focuses on the *Post*, is Martin's "Press and Radio in Palestine under the British Mandate." (Martin lived in Palestine during the late mandate period, working in some capacity as a print journalist.) See *A Survey of Palestine*, Sec. 25: List of Newspapers Published in Palestine.

21. Kevin Martin, "Enter the Future! Exemplars of Bourgeois Modernity in Post-World War II Syria" (Ph.D. diss., Georgetown University, 2005), pp. 47–48.

22. "Radio Corporation of America / Camden, New Jersey, USA / NOTICE," *Palestine Post*, Jan. 29, 1937, p. 10.

23. "To all radio buyers in Jerusalem and suburbs," RCA Victor Radios notice, *Palestine Post*, Apr. 1, 1937, p. 14. The phrasing of this notice may shed light on whose ad it truly was. In the late 1930s Edwin Samuel, future director of the PBS (1945–1948), was hired by the station as the anonymous but erudite "President of the Palestine Brighter English League." As president, Samuel broadcast weekly talks on the finer points of the English language, aimed at educating ESL speakers. Station listeners could "join" the League by mailing a token fee to the PBS broadcasting house; the fee covered mailing costs for summaries of each Brighter English broadcast. Samuel seems to have viewed his role as a crusader for, if not savior of, the purity of the English language in Palestine. In his memoirs and in an oral history interview conducted a few years before his death, he referred to several of what he considered the most egregious examples of "Pinglish," or Palestinian English. Among these was the expression "I beg to inform," which Samuel considered an attempt to communicate class and education by those who (in his view) lacked both. Based on Samuel's characterization, the RCA Victor ad was more likely penned and placed by the Palestine Radio Company than by RCA directly. Again, though, the real issue was the support given by RCA to its official agent in the latter's efforts to preserve the exclusivity of the manufacturer-wakil relationship. For more on the Brighter English League, see Edwin Samuel, *A Lifetime in Jerusalem: The Memoirs of the Second Viscount Samuel* (London: Vallentine, Mitchell, 1970), pp. 173–174; and "Broadcasting in Eretz Israel," a 1976 interview conducted by Aryeh Sachs and Mordechai Avida (né Zlotnik), Harman Institute of Contemporary Jewry, Oral History Division, #(133) 3, catalog #0047523. "Eretz Israel," as discussed in chapter 5, was the termed used by Zionists for the biblical land of Israel. In Hebrew-language communications, the mandate state was described as "Palestina," with the letters *aleph* and *yod* following in parentheses. The aleph stood for the first letter of the word *eretz* (like *ard* in Arabic, a word meaning "land"), while the yod stood for the first letter of Israel. See "Philco Radio & Television Corporation," *Palestine Post*, Apr. 1, 1937, p. 13; Apr. 6, 1937, p. 6.

24. "Warning," American Household Equipment Company (Belgium) for Matalon Brothers, *Falastin*, May 30, 1939, p. 6; and "Announcement," June 2, 1939, p. 4. The June 2, 1939, announcement is either a sincere correction or a hedge against libel. It repeats the statement regarding Mazin and Musa and then states, "We did not intend [*lem naqsud*] in the announcement published previously to touch the honor [*sharaf*] of the two men mentioned above."

25. For ads featuring these men as Airline agents, see *Falastin*, Apr. 18, 1937, p. 4 (Badiʿ Musa), and May 7, 1938, p. 5 (Shukri Rizk).

26. "WARNING," J L & B Haissman ad, *Palestine Post*, Sept. 12, 1938, p. 2.

27. See "Radio Minerva," Kovalsky & Sons Minerva radio ad, *Falastin*, Mar. 25, 1934, p. 12; June 6, 1934, p. 7; June 8, 1934, p. 2.

28. See "Silence! Listen to the Siera Super," Rabinowicz, *Falastin*, Jan. 5, 1936, p. 4; and "Listen the Siera Super Is Playing," Rabinowicz, *Palestine Post*, Jan. 2, 1936, p. 6; Jan. 7, 1936, p. 6; Jan. 8, 1936, p. 8.

29. "The 1938 ZENITH RADIO," Svislotzky Brothers Zenith Radio ad, *Palestine Post*, Oct. 10, 1937, p. 8. The brand disappeared from newspaper pages during the war but reappeared in 1946 under the agency of Fritz Friedlaender, who primarily sold Pye radios but also Tesla radios, another small radio brand, from the repair shop he ran in Jerusalem. See "Zenith Radio," Fritz Friedlander Zenith Radio ad, *Palestine Post*, Aug. 30, 1946, p. 2.

30. "Westinghouse Radio," National Electricity Shop (*mahall al-kahraba' al-watani*) Westinghouse Radio ad, *Falastin, June 22, 1934*, p. 7.

31. Rashid Khalidi points out that two sets of agents could still have been selling these radio brands after the strike ended but that only the Jewish agent may have continued to advertise via the newspapers.

32. "Heartiest Congratulations!" Montgomery Ward Company Airline Radios ad, *Palestine Post*, Sept. 4, 1935, p. 8.

33. "Airline Radio," Badi' Musa and Ramadan 'Akila Airline Radio ad, *Falastin*, Apr. 18, 1937, p. 4.

34. For the Arabic agents, see "The New Hijri Year," Airline Radios ad placed by various agents, *Falastin*, Feb. 10, 1940, p. 2.

35. Either the arrival of Pye Ltd. in Palestine was a major event (though it certainly was not the first British radio brand sold in Palestine) on a slow news day or its public relations department was particularly adept, landing it a small article in the *Palestine Post*—a feat unmatched by any other radio set brand during the mandate. See "British Radios Introduced," Dec. 23, 1938, p. 9.

36. See, e.g., "PYE & AIRLINE RADIOS," Matalon Brothers Pye & Airline radios ad, *Palestine Post*, Jan. 8, 1939, p. 2; and "Airline American Radio Pye English Radio," Airline & Pye radio ad placed by various agents, *Falastin*, Feb. 13, 1940, p. 4.

37. See for example "Why are all wireless sets available in every radio shop immediately on the spot," P. Schiglik Pye Radio ad, *Palestine Post*, July 5, 1946, p. 4. For Fritz Friedlaender as Pye agent, see "Zenith Radio / Fritz Friedlaender / sole agent in Jerusalem for 'PYE' RADIOS," Fritz Friedlaender Zenith Radio ad, *Palestine Post*, Aug. 8, 1946, p. 2.

38. The history of Protestantism in Palestine and the specific connection between Anglican evangelism and British government efforts to develop Anglican and then Jewish protégés in Palestine to gain political leverage vis-à-vis the Ottoman government is covered in Alexander Scholch, "Britain in Palestine, 1838–1882: The Roots of the Balfour Policy," *Journal of Palestine Studies* 22, no. 1 (Autumn 1992): 39–56. The article is a posthumous extraction and adaptation from his work *Palestine in Transformation, 1856–1882: Studies in Social, Economic and Political Development*, which the Institute for Palestine Studies reprinted in late 1992. Another good general source is Abdul Latif Tibawi, *British Interests in Palestine, 1800–1901: A Study of Religious and Educational Enterprise* (Oxford: Oxford University Press, 1961). Much of the biographical information given here on T. S. Boutagy is taken from the multipage obituary published in *Falastin*: see "Théophile Boutagy in God's Custody," Nov. 25, 1944, p. 2.

39. Biographical and family information is taken from the "Genealogy Re-

port of Boutros Boutagy 22 Nov 05," a document created by Edwin (Eddie) Palmer, nephew of Émile, Gordon, and Charles, for the private Boutagy family website.

40. This information is taken from a translation of excerpts from Théophile Seraphim Boutagy's memoirs, originally written in 1941, made by Juliette Allam and other family members. The translated excerpt is available through the private Boutagy family website. The original memoirs are in the possession of the family of Hilda Boutagy, T. S. Boutagy's youngest daughter. An addendum of "additional notes" at the end of the translation gives the family name as Boujajy, changed by the Reverend Seraphim's father, Boutros, to Boutagy, pronounced with a "dark" *taa*, and further emended by T. S. Boutagy's brother Shukri to Boutagy with a "light" *taa*. This information stands in contrast to that available elsewhere, which suggests that the family name was originally Abu Taj.

41. May Seikaly, *Haifa: Transformation of an Arab Society, 1918–1939* (New York: I. B. Tauris, 1995, rpt. 1998), p. 35.

42. Ibid., pp. 108–109.

43. Ibid., pp. 111–112.

44. The history of the Freemasons in Palestine and the Levant more generally is a fascinating topic and one deserving a more complete treatment than will be given here—not least for the large numbers of Jews and Muslims active in the organization. The lodges in Palestine during the mandate period followed a number of different rites, from the Alexandrian to the Scottish, with little consistency in practice or communication between lodges of the different orders. In 1949, after the collapse of the mandate state, the formation of the state of Israel, and the de facto truce between Israel and its neighbors had all taken place, the masters of the various lodges signed a petition that was sent to the Grand Lodge of Scotland, asking that all lodges be united under the Scottish rite and a newly created Grand Lodge of the State of Israel. Émile Boutagy signed this petition in his capacity as past master of the Lodge of Carmel. See www.roger.nicolet.co.il for more on the history of the formation of the Israeli order; for more on the Boutagys' involvement with the Freemasons, see Seikaly, *Haifa*, p. 167.

45. Peretz Cornfeld, ed., *Palestine Personalia 1947* (Tel Aviv: Sefer Press, 1947), p. xx.

46. PRO: FO 371 45422, Plan of Propaganda for Palestine 1945, May 15, 1945, p. 4.

47. ISA RG 2.16 361 20, Chief Secretary's Office—Distribution of Radio Sets in Villages, Émile Boutagy to Chief Secretary, Jan. 23, 1940, p. 2; and Émile Boutagy to High Commissioner, Jan. 23, 1940, p. 2.

48. Cornfeld, *Palestine Personalia*.

49. "Boutagy's Stores are the first founded in Palestine to present gifts to their patrons," Boutagy's Stores ad, *Falastin*, June 2, 1938, p. 5.

50. Marchand, *Advertising the American Dream*, p. 10.

51. Although refrigerators were more expensive to purchase and incurred ongoing operating costs in the form of significantly elevated electricity bills, radios and refrigerators were linked as desirable modern home purchases in other

types of advertising. A 1937 King Solomon Bank ad stated, "Housewives ask: 'Can I afford it?' What a comfortable feeling you have when you know that you can afford that electric refrigerator or that new radio because you have money in the bank. SAVE and then spend, and while you are saving, let your piastres bring you 4% INTEREST." *Palestine Post*, June 14, 1937, p. 2.

52. *Survey of Palestine*, 735. This estimate assumes an average daily wage of 200 mils for a male Palestinian laborer. The monthly wage for a government clerk with a wife and two children was 10 LP.

53. See chap. 2 for an analysis of radio set selling to Arab Palestine's rural markets.

54. In all advertisements, Arabic-language copy used the same font as the paper itself, suggesting the logistical challenges and expenses of creating Arabic type sets. Arabic-language printing presses were expensive to own and operate, in large part because of the type set; as a result, printers appear to have used the same font for all print jobs.

55. Palmolive Soap ad, *Falastin*, June 4, 1933.

56. Martin, "Enter the Future!" 12.

57. Personal communication with Shechter, Nov. 20, 2006.

58. "A New Station in Palestine for Broadcasting," Boutagy's Stores ad, *Falastin*, Oct. 3, 1935, p. 8.

59. "Boutagy's Gift Today," Boutagy's Stores ad, *Falastin*, July 23, 1935, p. 8.

60. "Very Important Announcement!" Boutagy's Stores ad, *Falastin*, Jan. 25, 1934, p. 8. See also "Wireless broadcasting and the use of radio," Boutagy's Stores ad, *Falastin*, May 27, 1934, p. 10, which ran as a full-page English/Arabic ad three days before the station opened.

61. "On the occasion of the opening of the wireless broadcasting station in Egypt," I. Kumayko Zenith radio ad, *Falastin*, June 2, 1934, p. 3. The spelling "Kumayko" is transliterated from the Arabic ad copy (*kaff wau mim alif yaa kaff wau*), as is the initial of his first name (*alif*). I presume from this orthographic awkwardness that the name is not Arab, but I have been unable to find any additional information about Mr. Kumayko or his enterprise, whose location the ad identified as 291 Jaffa Street.

62. "Listen to the Holy Qur'an every morning," Boutagy's Stores ad, *Falastin*, Feb. 23, 1935, p. 8. The ESB opened its morning broadcasts with Qur'anic recitation. Its consistent inclusion of such religious programming made the station the most Islamic-identified station, to use an awkward term, in the region. Regarding ESB programming generally, Boutagy's Stores also ran ads highlighting more secular programming. See "Listen to Miss Um Kulthoum," Boutagy's Stores ad, *Falastin*, Mar. 20, 1935, p. 3.

63. "His Majesty King George V," Boutagy's Stores ad, *Falastin*, Mar. 2, 1935, p. 8.

64. "Boutagy's Stores News," Boutagy's Stores ad, *Falastin*, Feb. 4, 1936, p. 8.

65. "Listen to the Palestine Broadcasting Station," Emerson Radio ad, *Falastin*, Apr. 12, 1936, p. 9.

66. "Reflections," *Palestine Post*, Jan. 29, 1937, p. 8.

67. Partner, *Arab Voices*, offers the best historical overview of the development of the BBC's Arabic broadcasting service. See pp. 20–22 for Partner's description of the protests the Palestine government and the Colonial Office made over the BBC's Arabic news reportage of events in Palestine, which began with its inaugural broadcast.

68. See, e.g., the "Palestine and Trans-Jordan: Examination of the Annual Report for 1936" section of the League of Nations Permanent Mandates Commission Minutes of the 29th Session, Geneva May 27–June 12, 1936, Report of the Commission to the Council [Series of League of Nations Publications VI.A. Mandates 1936] 7th meeting June 1, 1936, p. 62, in which British representatives to the League of Nations stated that the PBS's reporting of news communiqués and situation updates regarding the "disturbances" had already garnered praise from Palestinians "from different sections of the population."

69. Jewish Agency Economic Research Institute, *Statistical Handbook of Middle Eastern Countries* (Jerusalem: Azriel Printing Works, 1945), statistics 1930–1941, pp. 22–23; and 1942–1943, p. 169. The Palestinian pound had been established by the British mandate government in 1927 and was initially pegged to the British pound. During the war its value fluctuated slightly but never enough to make a substantial difference. See *A Survey of Palestine*, p. 1302.

70. "Radio Cadet and Car Radio (Radio for Car) for Sale," *Falastin*, Jan. 17, 1942, p. 2.

71. "Radios and Electrical Appliances for Sale," *Falastin*, Jan. 23, 1943, p. 2.

72. On Walsh's appointment, see the May 10, 1938, personal communication from a friend at the Colonial Empire Marketing Board with a regrettably illegible signature, ISA RG 5 1454 25. The letter congratulates Walsh on his bravery in accepting such a thankless post, an accurate description of an office whose primary relations with all Palestinians, whether industry representatives or private subjects, were either troubled or vexed.

73. Carbon of letter from Émile Boutagy to the (unnamed) newly appointed head of the War Economic Council, Nov. 23, 1943. Many thanks to Sherene Seikaly for bringing this letter to my attention; for a different contextualization of it, see her "In the Name of the Public Good," unpublished manuscript.

74. See the reminder notice "Radio Receivers in the Cars of Lebanon," *Falastin*, Feb. 15, 1940, p. 4.

75. T. S. Boutagy & Sons ad, *Palestine Post*, May 2, 1945, p. 2; and May 4, 1945, p. 6.

76. Philco radio ad placed by Ampa Ltd., *Palestine Post*, June 5, 1945, p. 4.

77. RCA radio ad placed by Palestine Radio Company, *Palestine Post*, Nov. 1, 1945, p. 2.

78. Bamia and Sharkis ad, *Falastin*, Nov. 20, 1945, p. 2.

79. Pilot radio ad placed by the 'Aoun Brothers, *Falastin*, Dec. 1, 1945, p. 2.

80. Pye radio ad placed by Mr. Shihada Sa'ada, *Falastin*, June 22, 1946, p. 2.

81. "Arabs in Israel," *Palestine Post*, June 24, 1948, p. 4.

82. "Difficult Journey," Readers' Letters, *Palestine Post*, July 4, 1948, p. 4.

83. "No Luxuries to Tax," Readers' Letters, *Palestine Post*, Mar. 3, 1949, p. 4.

84. The new Boutagy's Store was a casualty of the Lebanese civil war. This and other information about the Boutagy family after 1948 comes from personal communications with Eddie Palmer and other members of the Boutagy family.

85. Charles was kidnapped from the Windsor Hotel in Haifa. He was ultimately released, unharmed. See www.palestine-encyclopedia.com/EPP /Chapter07_7of7.htm for more information on his kidnapping; and "Merchant Arrested," *Palestine Post*, June 9, 1948, p. 1, for more on his arrest.

86. "Social and Personal," *Palestine Post*, Sept. 9, 1949, p. 2.

Chapter 2

1. *A Survey of Palestine*, p. 147. Government records such as the *Survey of Palestine* put terms like *race* and *Arab* in quotation marks; religious categories were the standard ones used.

2. John Hope Simpson, *Palestine: Report on Immigration, Land Settlement and Development* (London: His Majesty's Stationery Office, 1930), p. 65.

3. *Report by His Majesty's Government in the United Kingdom of Great Britain and Northern Ireland to the Council of the League of Nations on the Administration of Palestine and Trans-Jordan for the year 1930*, par. 39.

4. For more on these sales, see Mark Tessler, *A History of the Israeli-Palestinian Conflict* (Bloomington: Indiana University Press, 1994), p. 178.

5. Kenneth Stein, "Rural Change and Peasant Destitution: Contributing Causes to the Arab Revolt in Palestine, 1936–1939," in *Peasants and Politics in the Modern Middle East*, ed. Farhad Kamezi and John Waterbury (Tallahassee: Florida International University Press, 1991), pp. 143–170.

6. Hope Simpson, *Palestine*, p. 65.

7. Ibid., p. 66.

8. Ibid., pp. 67–70.

9. Ibid., p. 148.

10. C. F. Strickland, "The Possibility of Introducing a System of Agricultural Cooperation in Palestine" (Government of Palestine, Jerusalem, 1930), par. 2.

11. Ibid.

12. Joselyn Zivin, "The Imagined Reign of the Iron Lecturer: Village Broadcasting in Colonial India," *Modern Asian Studies* 32, no. 3 (1998): 717–738.

13. Strickland, "The Possibility."

14. The numerous other newspapers that circulated through the territory were published in Arabic, Hebrew, or other languages. The *Post* was founded as a pro-Zionist paper in 1932 by Gershon Agronsky and continued until 1952, when it was renamed the *Jerusalem Post*, under which name it continues to

publish today. Leslie John Martin, a British citizen who had lived in Palestine, described the paper as follows: "Although the policy of the paper was frankly Zionist, it wielded considerable influence in all circles in Palestine. For a long time it was the only English language daily in the country, and as such, was read not only by British government officials, who had no alternative paper, but also by the educated Arabs. It published all the government communiqués and legal notices that no Palestine resident could afford to miss. Its local news coverage was excellent, though somewhat one-sided. Little Jewish news of interest was missed, although its Arab news often seemed confined to murders, thefts, and quarrels" (Martin, "Press and Radio in Palestine under the British Mandate"). In the early 1930s, though, the *Post's* tone vis-à-vis the rural Arab population tended to be more paternal than hostile.

15. C. F. Strickland, "Village Broadcasting in Palestine: A Much-Needed Service to Rural Arabs," *Palestine Post*, July 23, 1933, p. 3.

16. "Over the Air," *Palestine Post*, July 3, 1935, p. 4.

17. "Broadcasting Station Opening in November: Government Announces Program Schedule," communiqué published in the *Palestine Post*, July 7, 1935, p. 1.

18. Ylana Miller, *Government and Society in Rural Palestine, 1920–1948* (Austin: University of Texas Press, 1985), p. 86. See also Ela Greenberg, *Preparing the Mothers of Tomorrow: Education and Islam in Mandate Palestine* (Austin: University of Texas Press, 2010).

19. Ellen Fleischmann discusses British mandate government education policies and goals in her *The Nation and Its "New" Women: The Palestinian Women's Movement, 1920–1948* (Berkeley: University of California Press, 2003), p. 37.

20. Miller, *Government and Society*, p. 88.

21. Ibid., p. 20.

22. Ibid., p. 88.

23. Douglas, *Listening In*, p. 5.

24. CO 323/1588/2, "Broadcast Programs from Jerusalem for Arab Listeners." This document was written by the Palestine government in late 1937 or early 1938.

25. Ibid.

26. FO 395/557, High Commissioner Arthur Wauchope to Colonial Office Secretary of State W.G.A. Ormsby-Gore, Jan. 10, 1938.

27. Ayalon, *Reading Palestine*. This quotation is taken from Ayalon's interview with Hajj Hasan Salim Abu ʿAql, p. 149. Ayalon spells the village ʿArʿarah.

28. CO 323/1588/2, "Rural Programs for Arab Listeners," written by the Palestine government in late 1937 or early 1938.

29. Ibid.

30. Ibid.

31. Ibid.

32. Ibid.

33. FO 395/557, High Commissioner Arthur Wauchope to Colonial Office Secretary of State W. G. A. Ormsby-Gore, Jan. 10, 1938.

34. Humphrey Bowman, "Rural Education in the Near and Middle East," *Journal of the Royal Central Asian Society* (July 26, 1939): 402–414.

35. Nadan, *The Palestinian Peasant Economy under the Mandate.*

36. "House of Commons," *Times of London*, Oct. 25, 1935, p. 7. The *Times of London* is archived online at web1.infotrac.galegroup.com.

37. MacDonald, "Radio Bari." MacDonald's article is the most frequently cited English-language source on Radio Bari and its impact. Numerous others exist in Italian, including Antonio Rossano, *Qui Radio Bari* (Bari: Dedalo, 1993).

38. MacDonald, "Radio Bari," p. 196.

39. "House of Commons," *Times of London*, Mar. 9, 1937, p. 8.

40. "House of Commons," *Times of London*, Nov. 4, 1937, p. 8.

41. Partner, *Arab Voices*, p. 5. Partner's work traces the history of the BBC Arabic Service using Foreign Office and other relevant government documents, as well as BBC archival sources and relevant newspaper articles.

42. "Truth in the Air," *Times of London*, Oct. 30, 1937, p. 15.

43. CO 323/1496/19.

44. "Special Arabic Broadcast News Service," memo dated August 28, 1937, CO 323/1496/20.

45. Partner, *Arab Voices*, p. 9.

46. Gerard Mansell, *Let Truth Be Told: 50 Years of BBC External Broadcasting* (London: Weidenfeld & Nicolson, 1982), p. 48.

47. ". . . A Snag," *Palestine Post*, Dec. 29, 1937, p. 4.

48. The critical difference for Palestine was that its mandatory power was required by the text of the League of Nations' "Mandate for Palestine" to put "into effect the declaration originally made on November 2, 1917, by the Government of His Britannic Majesty, and adopted by the said Powers, in favor of the establishment in Palestine of a national home for the Jewish people." This requirement not only distinguished it from the so-called class A mandates but also made "reconstituting [the Jewish people's] national home" in Palestine requisite for the mandate's independence. See *Mandat pour la Palestine/Mandate for Palestine*, Communiqué au Conseil et aux Membres de la Société (Geneva: League of Nations, Aug. 12, 1922), introductory remarks.

49. CO 323/1496/19, R. A. Leeper to R. V. Vernon, Apr. 1, 1937. An undated memo from the same Colonial Office file, "Broadcasting in Foreign Languages," indicated that the Committee on Arabic Broadcasting had decided against a Cyprus station on similar grounds: "The most powerful argument which decided the Committee in favor of Daventry is that while it is one thing for the metropolitan country to broadcast in foreign languages it is a vastly different matter to set up a powerful broadcasting station in a small island colony for broadcasts in a language which is not spoken in that colony; no other country has at present so far done this and the Post Office were very strongly of the opinion that for us to do so would be a blatant violation of all the accepted canons of international broadcast etiquette and decency."

50. FO 141/645/3, C. F. A. Warner, Foreign Office, London, to O. A. Scott, Baghdad, Aug. 17, 1937.

51. CO 323/1496/19, R. A. Leeper to G. T. Havard, Oct. 6, 1937.

52. T 161/1034, Liaison Office, Jerusalem. Estimates Oct. 1, 1937–Mar. 31, 1938.

53. "We do not need this or that!" *Falastin*, Jan. 7, 1938, p. 1.

54. FO 395/557, "A Report on Arabic Broadcasting in Egypt and Palestine with Special Reference to the Arabic Broadcast from London by J Heyworth-Dunne," Jan. 20, 1938.

55. Tleel, *I Am Jerusalem*, 15.

56. "Listen to Jerusalem Today," *Palestine Post*, Mar. 30, 1936, p. 1.

57. League of Nations Permanent Mandates Commission Minutes of the 29th Session, Geneva, May 27–June 12, 1936, p. 62.

58. FO 395/557, High Commissioner Arthur Wauchope to Colonial Office Secretary of State W.G.A. Ormsby-Gore, Jan. 10, 1938.

59. ISA RG 2.16 361 20, Chief Secretary's Office—Distribution of Radio Sets in Villages, file memo, May 23, 1939.

60. ISA RG 2.16 361 20, Chief Secretary's Office—Distribution of Radio Sets in Villages, Lydda District Commissioner to Chief Secretary, June 20, 1940.

61. ISA RG 2.16 361 20, Chief Secretary's Office—Distribution of Radio Sets in Villages, Government of Palestine radio set agreement, p. 2.

62. Ibid., p. 3.

63. Ibid.

64. Battershill was appointed chief secretary in 1937; he had previously been chief secretary in Cyprus, and after Palestine he would serve as governor of Tanganyika.

65. ISA RG 2.16 361 20, Chief Secretary's Office—Distribution of Radio Sets in Villages, W. D. Battershill to "my dear General," Nov. 22, 1938. The reference to the Berlin station (rather than Zeesen) is puzzling, unless for a time it broadcast certain programs in Arabic.

66. ISA RG 2.16 361 20, Chief Secretary's Office—Distribution of Radio Sets in Villages, Post Office draft version of Government of Palestine radio set agreement, p. 1.

67. ISA RG 2.16 361 20, Chief Secretary's Office—Distribution of Radio Sets in Villages, file memo, May 23, 1939.

68. ISA RG 2.16 361 20, Chief Secretary's Office—Distribution of Radio Sets in Villages, W. D. Battershill for the High Commissioner to Acting Governor, Aden, Feb. 12, 1938, p. 1. Battershill was writing in response to the acting governor's request for advice on which receiving sets were suitable for government distribution to remote locales; the latter wanted to distribute short-wave sets for Yemen's local potentates' reception of the BBC Arabic programs, a slightly different undertaking from that of the Palestine mandate government.

69. ISA RG 2.16 361 20, Secretary's Office—Distribution of Radio Sets in Villages, translation of Sheikh Amin Muhammad Hamzeh to High Commissioner, Oct. 17, 1941. Sheikh Hamzeh's handwriting is not entirely clear. I read from his words that the village will follow the emissions and broadcasts of the PBS and its talks to farmers [lit., "fellah"], rather than "experts" per se, although there are several words whose letters I cannot discern. Hence I defer to the official translation.

70. FO 395/557, High Commissioner Arthur Wauchope to Colonial Office Secretary of State W. G. A. Ormsby-Gore, Jan. 10, 1938.

71. Jehoash Hirshberg, *Music in the Jewish Community of Palestine, 1880–1914: A Social History* (Oxford: Clarendon Press, 1995), p. 214.

72. ISA RG 2.16 361 20 20, Secretary's Office—Distribution of Radio Sets in Villages, Chief Secretary to Hakotzer, Mar. 30, 1939; Hakotzer to Chief Secretary, Mar. 5, 1939 (in Hebrew, with English translation).

73. FO 395/557, High Commissioner Arthur Wauchope to Colonial Office Secretary of State W. G. A. Ormsby-Gore, Jan. 10, 1938.

74. ISA RG 2.16 361 20, Chief Secretary's Office—Distribution of Radio Sets in Villages, Postmaster General Mackay to the Chief Secretary, Dec. 16, 1947.

75. Basim A. Faris, *Electric Power in Syria and Palestine* (Beirut: American University of Beirut Press, 1936).

76. Ibid., p. 143.

77. Eveready Air Cell battery ad, *Palestine Post*, June 7, 1938, p. 4.

78. See, e.g., ISA RG 2.16 361 20, Chief Secretary's Office—Distribution of Radio Sets in Villages, Public Information Officer Owen Tweedy to Chief Secretary, Sept. 5, 1941.

79. ISA RG 2.16 361 20, Chief Secretary's Office—Distribution of Radio Sets in Villages, Émile Boutagy to Chief Secretary, Jan. 23, 1940, p. 2. The file contains a copy of the same letter addressed to the High Commissioner. The file also contains a similar letter from Émile Boutagy to the Chief Secretary, Sept. 4, 1939.

80. CO 323/1588/2, "Rural Programs for Arab Listeners," Palestine Government memo, n.d., likely written late 1937 or early 1938.

81. See, e.g., the reports in ISA RG 2.16 361 20, Secretary's Office—Distribution of Radio Sets in Villages in spring 1940.

82. PRO FO 371 /24569, cipher telegram from the High Commissioner for Palestine to the Secretary of State for the Colonies, June 15, 1940.

83. ISA RG 2.16 361 20, Chief Secretary's Office—Distribution of Radio Sets in Villages, file memo, Dec. 16, 1945.

84. In January 1934 the *Asiatic Review* published the text of an address Strickland had given to the East India Association, the *Review*'s parent organization, advocating a rural broadcasting scheme for villages in India. See C. F. Strickland, "Broadcasting for Rural India," *Asiatic Review* 30, no. 101 (Jan. 1934): 1–14.

85. See Zivin, "The Imagined Reign of the Iron Lecturer."

86. Randall Patnode, "What These People Need Is Radio: New Technology, the Press, and Otherness in 1920s America," *Technology and Culture* 44 (Apr. 2003): 285–305.

87. Reynold M. Wik, "The Radio in Rural America during the 1920s," *Agricultural History* 55, no. 4 (Oct. 1981): 340.

88. Ibid., pp. 341–343.

89. Ibid., p. 345.

90. Ibid., p. 346.

91. Edmund de Schweinitz Brunner, *Radio and the Farmer* (New York: Radio Institute of the Audible Arts, 1935), p. 5. According to the symposium proceedings editorial note, the Radio Institute of the Audible Arts was founded by Philco Radio and Television Corporation in 1934 to serve "as an informal clearing house for information on the broad cultural phase of radio" (p. 9).

92. Ibid., p. 11.

93. In a 1941 study, "Radio Comes to the Farmer," William Robinson re-examined these theories about the social impact of radio listening on rural America, including the belief that "radio exercises only a stabilizing influence upon rural people, that it tends to make them more content with living on the farm and far less prone to leave the farm for the superior advantages of the city." In his interviews with Illinois and Nebraska farmers, Robinson found that radio had little impact on persuading rural Americans, young or old, to either stay or leave the farm. William S. Robinson, "Radio Comes to the Farmer," in *Radio Research 1941*, ed. Paul Lazarsfeld and Frank N. Stanton (New York: Duell, Sloan, and Pearce, 1941), pp. 224–294.

94. Brunner, *Radio and the Farmer*, pp. 13–15.

95. Humphrey Bowman, *Middle-East Window* (London: Longman, Green, 1942), pp. 272–273.

96. "From Qaysariyya they want a radio from Boutagy," Boutagy's Stores HMV radio advertisement, *Falastin*, Dec. 1, 1936, p. 7.

97. "The most innovative radio in the world," Boutagy's Stores HMV radio ad, *Falastin*, Nov. 25, 1936, p. 7.

98. Assuming monthly payments, the February 11, 1937, ad suggests pricing of approximately 25 guineas: five at the outset, and the balance paid off in installments within the year. See "Qalqilya wants a His Master's Voice radio for the third time," *Falastin*, Feb. 11, 1937, p. 10. The English-language text of each ad showed photographs, descriptions, and prices for each model. Assuming that prices and models were accurate for Palestine as well as England, the models ranged from the 11-guinea five-valve radio advertised on February 20, 1937 (no indication of model number or electric/battery; assume medium and long wave only), through the 13-guinea five-valve super-het advertised on February 5, 1937 (also no indication whether battery or power and whether all-wave), and the all-wave AC mains 17.5 guinea model 480, available for hire purchase with an initial deposit and weekly payments of 4 shillings, advertised on February 24, 1937, to the top of the line all-wave, AC mains "autoradio" 38-guinea model 485, available for hire purchase with an initial deposit and weekly payments of 8 shillings, also advertised on February 24, 1937. These were the only four models shown in advertisements during this time period, although the February 4 for "a radio of the 14 guinea class" suggests the possibility of others. Moreover, payment rates appear to have been somewhat flexible: a February 26, 1937, ad read, "Today is the time to buy a radio" because Boutagy's was reducing monthly payments to half a guinea as a holiday promotion. (A guinea was worth one pound one shilling, or 21 shillings.)

99. "Boutagy's radio brand His Master's Voice gives life to, educates, and entertains all classes of people," *Falastin*, Feb. 4, 1937, p. 10.

100. "In al-Yajour they are blessed with a His Master's Voice radio," Boutagy's Stores HMV radio ad, *Falastin*, Nov. 26, 1936, p. 5.

101. "His Master's Voice radio is dispatched to Haneen despite the difficult roads," *Falastin*, Feb. 24, 1937, p. 11. Fakhri, the letter writer, stated that "nothing prevented you from reaching the furthest villages and farms—no mountains and no stones and no impassable roads" and continued "and thus with all right we call you Palestine's Mustafa Kamal [Ataturk?]."

102. Richard Bulliet, *Islam: The View from the Edge* (New York: Columbia University Press, 1995).

103. PRO: CO 323/1496/20, "Special Arabic Broadcast News Service memo," Aug. 28, 1937.

104. Boutagy's Stores HMV Radio ad, *Falastin*, May 5, 1940, p. 8.

Chapter 3

1. English, Music, and Engineering were the other three sections. English-language broadcasting on the PBS received much less airtime and was limited primarily to news broadcasts, talks and skits, classical music, and BBC relays. The Music section dealt with Western classical and contemporary music. The Engineering section served all four broadcasting sections on a language- and ethnicity-blind basis.

2. Hussein Abu Shanab makes a similar assessment in his history of the broadcasting station, concluding that the mandate government selected Tuqan in hope that this would either reduce his credibility with Arab Palestinians or "appease the people through state-directed political broadcasting." See *Huna al-Quds: Dar al-Idhaʿa al-Falastiniyyah 1936* (Khan Yunis: Dirasat Abhath al-Watan, 2002), p. 9.

3. Philip S. Khoury, "Syrian Urban Politics in Transition: The Quarters of Damascus during the French Mandate," *International Journal of Middle East Studies* 16, no. 4 (Nov. 1984): 507–540.

4. See, e.g., the draft letter from Malcolm MacDonald, Secretary of State for the Colonies, to the High Commissioner of Transjordan, Feb. 7, 1940, in ISA RG 2 424 T 42 40 Chief Secretary's Office: Transjordan: Control of Wireless Transmitting Apparatus. The defense regulations were published on November 24, 1939; regulations 8 and 55 dealt with wireless transmission.

5. These comments are taken from minutes at the front of the file ISA RG 2 109 1 Chief Secretary's Office: Wireless Receiving Sets, the Property of Enemies.

6. Assistant Postmaster General G. D. Kennedy wrote a series of letters to the Chief Secretary's Office in March 1941, in ISA RG 2 109 1 Chief Secretary's Office: Wireless Receiving Sets, the Property of Enemies. Kennedy was promoted to deputy postmaster general in summer 1941 and to postmaster general in 1945.

7. These comments are taken from minutes at the front of the file ISA RG 2 109 1 Chief Secretary's Office: Wireless Receiving Sets, the Property of Enemies.

8. Postmaster General to Chief Secretary, July 27, 1942, in ISA RG 2 109 1 Chief Secretary's Office: Wireless Receiving Sets, the Property of Enemies.

9. "Enemy Owned Wireless Receivers," "Schedule A" attached to Postmaster General to Chief Secretary, July 27, 1942, in ISA RG 2 109 1 Chief Secretary's Office: Wireless Receiving Sets, the Property of Enemies.

10. "Letter from Bir Sabʿa," *Falastin*, June 5, 1940, p. 4.

11. "New Licenses for Radio Receivers," *Falastin*, June 9, 1940, p. 5.

12. "From the Official Gazette," *Falastin*, Oct. 2, 1941, p. 3.

13. "Because he listened to a foreign station on the radio," *Falastin*, July 25, 1940, p. 3.

14. The Public Information Office's jurisdiction evolved over the course of the war. By 1945 cataloging the responsibilities and relationships that had accrued to it was a convoluted process. The Foreign Office's Overseas Planning Committee's 1945 "Plan of Propaganda for Palestine" described the PIO as follows: "The Public Information Office, Jerusalem, is organized as an integral part of the Secretariat of the Palestine Government, though it is housed separately. It acts also as the Palestine Office of the M.O.I., which bears much of the expenditure. Certain expenses are borne entirely by the Palestine Government, but the bulk of the budget is borne as to six-sevenths by the M.O.I., and one-seventh by the Palestine Government, with the exception of the foreign language news broadcast services, of which the expenditure is borne entirely by the Ministry. In addition to the main office at Jerusalem, there is a sub-office at Lydda in the Tel Aviv—Jaffa area, and another sub-office is being opened at Haifa. As a Department of the Palestine Government, the P.I.O. has rather wider functions than those of most M.O.I. posts abroad, e.g. the issue of Government notices, administration of press legislation and newsprint rationing, preparation of news broadcasts. The P.I.O. holds weekly press conferences and also organizes contacts between press representatives and heads of Government Departments." The report noted that "the functions of the P.I.O. include the administration of Palestine press legislation and the operation of the newsprint rationing scheme" (PRO: FO 371 45422 Plan of Propaganda for Palestine 1945, May 10, 1945, under "General Conditions").

15. Smith was writing to the Chief Secretary's Office to request permission to broadcast a live speech by Chaim Weizmann, to be given at a special meeting of the Elected Assembly of Palestine Jews, without precensorship or the use of a switch monitor. The chief secretary granted permission "as a special case personal to Dr. Weizmann," with the admonition that the permission would neither be repeated nor establish a precedent. See R. D. Smith, PBS Controller of English and Hebrew Programs, to J. V. W. Shaw, Chief Secretary, Nov. 29, 1944, and J. V. W. Shaw to R. D. Smith, Nov. 30, 1944, in ISA RG 2 365 Pol 10 44 Chief Secretary's Office: Broadcasts—Political (Individual Cases).

16. ISA RG 2 400 SF 201 45, Chief Secretary's Office, May 2, 1945, minute.

17. Abu Shanab states that Nuwayhid came from Ras al-Matn and was a partisan of King Faisal. After the Syrians were defeated at the battle of Maisaloun, he left Syria for Jerusalem. Abu Shanab, *Huna al-Quds*, pp. 119–120.

18. See Uri M. Kupferschmidt, *The Supreme Muslim Council: Islam Under the British Mandate for Palestine* (Leiden: Brill, 1987), p. 67 n. 55, where his name is spelled "Nuwayhad."

19. Weldon C. Matthews, *Confronting an Empire, Constructing a Nation: Arab Nationalists and Popular Politics in Mandate Palestine* (London: I. B. Tauris, 2006), p. 57.

20. Ibid.

21. Mark Tessler notes that the party's full name was Hizb al-Istiqlal al-

'Arabiyya fi Suriyya al-Janubiyya, the Arab Independence Party in Southern Syria. Other sources cite Nuwayhid as one of Istiqlal's founding members, noting the party's allusive connection to the independent state of Syria ruled briefly by King Faisal in 1920. Several members of the Arab Higher Committee—the executive body formed in 1936 to support and manage the general strike and other elements of the early Arab revolt—including Awni 'Abd al-Hadi, were also Istiqlal members. See also Matthews, *Confronting an Empire*, pp. 85–87.

22. Matthews, *Confronting an Empire*, p. 125.

23. See *Falastin*, Apr. 26, 1936, p. 8 (Sunday photo page); as well as two mentions in the *Palestine Post*: Apr. 24, 1936, p. 7; and July 19, 1936, p. 2.

24. British White Paper of 1939, accessed online via the Yale Law School's Avalon Project at http://avalon.law.yale.edu/20th_century/brwh1939.asp; last accessed Mar. 14, 2012.

25. Matthews, *Confronting an Empire*, p. 271.

26. Nuwayhid, *Sittun 'Amm*, pp. 256–257. Some of his friends in the Istiqlal Party supported his decision to take the controller position; others advised him against it, arguing that anyone in the opposition should not collaborate with the government.

27. Contemporary accounts provided different reasons for and dates of his leaving; in any case he died the following year after an illness.

28. CO 733 442 2 telegram, "Organization of Palestine Broadcasting Service" from High Commissioner MacMichael to the Secretary of State for the Colonies, June 5, 1941.

29. The Palestinian pound, established in 1927, was originally pegged to the British pound; although there was some slippage during the war, the two remained approximately equivalent.

30. CO 733 442 2, letter from S. E. V. Luke (Downing Street) to R. Hardie (Treasury), Sept. 5, 1941. The contract had been issued partly in anticipation of the imminent arrival of a second transmitter, and the Arabic service had been increased by 4.5 hours per week for the same reason. However, the ship bearing the second transmitter was sunk en route to Palestine, and no replacement was sent until after the war had ended. See chapter 5 for further details on the second transmitter and its impact on the station's organization and programming.

31. Nuwayhid, *Sittun 'Amm*, p. 260. For more on the Palestinian pound, see *A Survey of Palestine*, p. 1302.

32. "Weekly Program," *Falastin*, Mar. 17, 1940, p. 3.

33. "Broadcasting Corner," *Falastin*, Mar. 25, 1940.

34. Nuwayhid, *Sittun 'Amm*, p. 260.

35. Abu Shanab, *Huna al-Quds*, p. 131. The term is masculine, although in Arabic the masculine can function as a generic—more like "youth" in English than "young man."

36. Ibid.

37. See, e.g., the PBS broadcasting schedule published in *Falastin* on October 13, 1940, which lists the maghrib broadcast at 5:05 p.m. and the 'asha at 6:30. An additional Qur'anic recitation was broadcast at 10:15 p.m. "Program of the Broadcasting Authority," *Falastin*, bottom left corner, p. 1.

38. "Listener's Corner," *Palestine Post*, Oct. 25, 1940, p. 2.

39. "At the Margin of Memory/ the Arabic Section of the Broadcasting Authority / and Its Powerful Program on the Important Occasion [*'eid*] of the Birth of the Prophet," *Falastin*, Apr. 12, 1941, p. 1. On the other hand, some of *Falastin*'s laudatory articles should be read with a grain of salt: a few are so effusive that they may have come from press releases issued by the radio station. For example, a brief article announcing the special Ramadan program and accompanying issue of *Huna al-Quds* created by the PBS said that the station "has issued an especially distinguished issue of the magazine *Huna al-Quds* for the blessed month of Ramadan. It includes valuable articles which were written with special pictures for this noble month, and includes very wonderful photos and charming views of the Haram al-Sharif and the Masjid al-Aqsa." See "Special Program on the Radio and Special Issue for Ramadan," *Falastin*, Sept. 21, 1941, p. 3.

40. "Palestine Broadcasting Authority," *Falastin*, Jan. 3, 1941, p. 1.

41. See telegrams exchanged between the High Commissioner's Office and the British Ministry in Jeddah in December 1941 and 1942 (Hajj occurred in January 1942 and 1943), as well as the letter from H. C. Holmes, Public Information Officer, to Chief Secretary, Dec. 10, 1941: ISA RG 2 16 361 23. The planned broadcasts were mentioned approvingly in *Falastin*. See "Letters on the Radio to the Pilgrims in Minna," *Falastin*, Dec. 20, 1941, p. 3.

42. "Palestine Broadcasting Authority," *Falastin*, Jan. 3, 1941, p. 1. This talk was reprinted in *Hadith al-Idhaa* (Broadcast Talks), the 1942 PBS book mentioned above. Tibawi gave a number of talks for the PBS, including one titled "Education and Teaching in the Islamic Eras" (al-Tarbiya wa al-T'alīm fi al-'usūr al-Islamiya). See "Palestine Broadcasting Authority," *Falastin*, Oct. 2, 1941, p. 2.

43. "Palestine Broadcasting Authority," *Falastin*, Mar. 1, 1941, p. 1.

44. Ibid., Jan. 4, 1941, p. 1.

45. Ibid., Mar. 7, 1941.

46. Ibid., May 1, 1941, p. 1.

47. "On Radio Jerusalem," *Falastin*, Aug. 10, 1941, p. 3.

48. "Palestine Broadcasting Authority," *Falastin*, Oct. 8, 1941, p. 1.

49. Nuwayhid, *Sittun 'Amm*, p. 285.

50. "This Is Jerusalem: An Hour at the Palestinian Broadcasting House," *Falastin*, June 16, 1940, p. 4.

51. Ibid.

52. Nuwayhid, *Sittun 'Amm*, p. 261.

53. I am relying for the number, dates, and titles of these broadcasts on the PBS schedules printed in *Falastin*. The *Palestine Post* also printed the station's program schedule; it shows thirteen talks in "The New Arab House" series, lasting until March 6, 1941. However, the last four have no specific subject title and are not mentioned in the *Falastin* schedules or included among the transcripts printed in the newspaper. I believe that the *Palestine Post* schedules are misprints, due either to careless editing or to inaccurate material provided by the station, as occurred at other moments in the station's history.

54. The Foreign Office's Overseas Planning Committee's 1945 "Plan of

Propaganda for Palestine" described the state of the Arabic press as follows: "The Arabic population of a little over one million is on the whole poorly served. There are three Arabic dailies, one of which now has a London correspondent. Egyptian newspapers also circulate widely in Palestine and are believed to have a circulation equal to that of the local Arabic press. There were no local Arabic periodicals of any consequence until the Government launched 'Al Muntada.' The Arab press is chiefly concerned with local affairs. Its outlook is still parochial, but it has gained in financial stability and independence during the war and is showing signs of becoming more responsible and informed. Throughout the war the P.I.O. has sought to encourage this development by constant advice and material assistance." PRO: FO 371 45422 Plan of Propaganda for Palestine 1945, May 10, 1945.

55. The Foreign Office's Overseas Planning Committee's 1945 "Plan of Propaganda for Palestine" described wartime censorship as follows: "A strict wartime censorship is exercised by the Palestine Government. That censorship has now been transferred to the Posts & Telegraphs, thus relieving the P.I.O. from the odium attached to this work, which has been systematically exploited by the Zionists for political purposes. Political censorship aims at cutting controversy short at a point where it might lead to violence and breaches of security. No absolute stops are imposed, but certain subjects (e.g., the Jewish Brigade, the [Jewish?] State, the Mufti) are prohibited except in official utterances or news items of importance." PRO: FO 371 45422 Plan of Propaganda for Palestine 1945, May 10, 1945. The "mufti" referred to here was Hajj Amin al-Husseini.

56. Personal communication from Rashid Khalidi.

57. The *Palestine Post*'s status as the sole English-language newspaper published in Palestine and its British readership allowed it to claim a certain universality, which it supported by covering events and issues relevant to all Palestinians—though its commentary and depth of coverage reflected a Zionist view. As part of this comprehensiveness, the *Palestine Post* printed the schedules for the Arabic, English, and Hebrew sections of the Palestine Broadcasting Service in full, and its weekly "Listener's Corner" column reported and commented on the quality of the week's programming for all sections. (*Falastin*, by contrast, printed only the Arabic section's programming schedule.) On December 13, 1940, the "Listener's Column" stated, "After some selections by the Moslem Orphanage band, Mme. Salwa Sa'id gave a talk on the management of the Arab house" (p. 2).

58. See, e.g., Beth Baron's classic *The Women's Awakening in Egypt: Culture, Society, and the Press* (New Haven: Yale University Press, 1994).

59. "The New Arab House Talks," *Falastin*, Jan. 26, 1941, p. 3 (continuation of front page article).

60. Ibid.

61. Afsaneh Najmabadi, "Crafting an Educated Housewife in Iran," in *Remaking Women: Feminism and Modernity in the Middle East*, ed. Lila Abu-Lughod (Princeton: Princeton University Press, 1998), pp. 91–124; Burke, *Lifebuoy Men, Lux Women*; Jacques Donzelot, *La police des familles* (Paris: Éditions de minuit, 1977).

62. "The New Arab House Talks," *Falastin*, Feb. 2, 1941, pp. 1, 3 (continuation of front page article).

63. The role of household servants in 1940s Palestine deserves greater scrutiny, as do class striations generally. As Rochelle Davis notes in her chapter on the expansion of Jerusalem during the mandate, "an essential and yet often unmentioned aspect of the stories of these well off and middle class families is the men and women who worked for them that made such comfortable and elegant living possible. Most families employed women to clean and cook for them and men to do the gardening and other odd jobs, including raising chickens, pigeons, and rabbits for private consumption of eggs and meat. The labor pool was drawn from the urban lower middle class and poor in Jerusalem as well as the residents of the surrounding villages." See Rochelle Davis, "The Growth of the Western Communities, 1917–1948," in *Jerusalem 1948: The Arab Neighborhoods and Their Fate in the War*, ed. Salim Tamari (Jerusalem: Institute of Jerusalem Studies and Badil Resource Center, 1999), 32–66.

64. "The Muslim Woman during Ramadan" was broadcast on Oct. 4, 1940. See "Palestine Broadcasting Authority (Arabic Section) Daily Schedule," *Falastin*, Oct. 4, 1940, p. 1. The "History of Islam" series was broadcast later that winter. For a complimentary editorial on her erudition and delivery, see "The Arabic Section on Radio Jerusalem," *Falastin*, Jan. 30, 1941, p. 1.

65. See Davis, "The Growth of the Western Communities, 1917–1948."

66. "Palestinian Broadcasting Authority (Arabic Section)," *Falastin*, Nov. 5, 1942, p. 1.

67. "Books in the News," *Palestine Post*, Dec. 29, 1942, p. 4.

68. "A Woman's Voice on the Broadcasting Station," *Falastin*, Feb. 7, 1941, p. 3.

69. See Dipesh Chakrabarty, "The Difference-Deferral of a Colonial Modernity: Public Debates on Domesticity in British Bengal," in *Tensions of Empire*, ed. Ann L. Stoler and Frederick Cooper (Berkeley: University of California Press, 1997), pp. 373–400; Omnia Shakry, "Schooled Mothers and Structured Play: Child Rearing in Turn-of-the-Century Egypt," in Abu Lughod, *Remaking Women*, pp. 126–170.

70. FO 395 560, Four Questions Put to Various Officials in Palestine by Mr. Poston, Formerly Private Secretary to the High Commissioner of Palestine, with cover letter dated June 3, 1938.

71. CO 733 442 3, British Propaganda in Palestine memorandum by Ralph Poston, July 1942. Poston refers to several PBS and mandate government personnel in this memorandum; all are introduced by first and last name, and only the British officials are referred to subsequently as "Mr. [last name]." Thanks to Rashid Khalidi for pointing this out as an example of British officials' discriminatory use of first names for Arabs.

72. "Controller of Arabic Programmes Resigns," *Palestine Post*, Dec. 31, 1943, p. 3.

73. Chief Secretary's Office, May 2, 1945, minute, ISA RG 2 400 SF 201 45.

74. Ibid.

75. "Editorials of the Jewish Press," *Falastin*, Apr. 8, 1947, p. 2.

76. Edwin Samuel, Director of Broadcasting, to Wing Commander A. H. Marsack, BBC Cairo, 5.24.45, Middle East Center Archive, St. Antony's College, Oxford, Rex Keating Collection, #GB 165 0361 File 2/7/1, correspondence about obtaining new records.

77. Nashashibi had studied in London during his university days; this was not his first trip to Britain. He published an Arabic-language account of his experiences at the BBC as *From Jerusalem to London: August to December, 1946* (Jerusalem: Commercial Press, 1942); the monograph also served as his report to the PBS.

78. See Nashashibi, *From Jerusalem to London*, chap. 21, "This Is London."

Chapter 4

1. Ronen Shamir cites the Palestine Order in Council of 1922. It "enjoined the civil courts to exercise jurisdiction "in conformity with the Ottoman Law in force in Palestine on 1st November 1914," but it also stipulated that "the courts were to respect new ordinances and regulations in the future." The Order in Council also asked the courts to "adjudicate in conformity with the substance of the common law and the doctrines of equity in force in England." See his *The Colonies of Law: Colonialism, Zionism, and Law in Early Mandate Palestine* (New York: Cambridge University Press, 2000), p. 12. Assaf Likhovski argues that courts' adherence to Ottoman precedents, formal or substantive, depended on the judges' identities and affiliations. See Likhovski, *Law and Identity in Mandate Palestine*.

2. Khalidi, *The Iron Cage*, p. 63.

3. The CRAC considered religious broadcasts an integral part of the BBC's offerings, helping to explain Christianity and indicate its contemporary relevance, encourage nonchurchgoing Christians toward a more active faith, and facilitate conversion. As noted above, this emphasis on Christian teachings connected closely with the BBC's broader commitment to spreading moral values. See Asa Briggs, "Religion," in *The History of Broadcasting in the United Kingdom*.

4. Michael Bailey, "'He who has ears to hear, let him hear': Christian Pedagogy and Religious Broadcasting during the Inter-War Period," *Westminster Papers in Communication and Culture* 4, no. 1 (2007): 4–25. The quotation is from p. 131 of the 1928 handbook.

5. "Listening In," *Palestine Post*, Apr. 5, 1936, p. 6. "Listening In" described the readings above as "provid[ing] the religious element" to the week's Friday broadcasts.

6. "The Holy Qur'an on the Broadcasting Station," *Falastin*, June 13, 1936, p. 4.

7. ISA RG 15 2213 94 Public Information Office—June 12, 1945, file date, paper clipping.

8. ISA RG 2.16 361 33 Chief Secretary's Office—Censorship of Religious Broadcasts, letter from the Latin Patriarch to the High Commissioner, May 7, 1946.

9. ISA RG 2.16 361 33 Chief Secretary's Office—Censorship of Religious Broadcasts, comments, June 4, 1946.

10. ISA RG 2.16 361 33 Chief Secretary's Office—Censorship of Religious Broadcasts, letter from the Chief Secretary to the Latin Patriarch, June 6, 1946.

11. ISA RG 2.16 361 33 Chief Secretary's Office—Censorship of Religious Broadcasts, letter from PBS Assistant Director Rex Keating to the Chief Secretary, May 22, 1946.

12. ISA RG 2.16 361 28 Chief Secretary's Office—Government Publicity—Broadcasting of Public Ceremonies, letter from the Greek Coptic Patriarchate to the Chief Secretary, Dec. 17, 1946.

13. ISA RG 2.16 361 28 Chief Secretary's Office—Government Publicity—Broadcasting of Public Ceremonies, letter from PBS Director Edwin Samuel to the Chief Secretary, Jan. 29, 1947.

14. ISA RG 2.16 361 28 Chief Secretary's Office—Government Publicity—Broadcasting of Public Ceremonies, letter from PBS Director Edwin Samuel to the Chief Secretary, Mar. 6, 1947.

15. ISA RG 2.16 361 33 Chief Secretary—Censorship of Religious Broadcasts.

16. ISA RG 2.16 361 33 Chief Secretary's Office—Censorship of Religious Broadcasts, letter from Assistant Director Rex Keating to the Chief Secretary, May 22, 1946.

17. ISA RG 2.16 361 33 Chief Secretary's Office—Censorship of Religious Broadcasts, letter from the Latin Patriarch to the High Commissioner, May 7, 1946.

18. ISA RG 2.16 361 33 Chief Secretary's Office—Censorship of Religious Broadcasts, letter from Assistant Director Rex Keating to the Chief Secretary, May 22, 1946.

19. ISA RG 2.16 361 33 Chief Secretary's Office—Censorship of Religious Broadcasts, station memo from Director Edwin Samuel, Dec. 5, 1946.

20. These new provisions were shortly put to the test, when Jerusalem's Anglican bishop submitted a sermon with "sentiments asserting the paramountcy of the Christian religion" that PBS personnel feared would offend non-Christians. He was given a choice: amend his text or the PBS would cut away from the broadcast when his sermon began. See ISA RG 2.16/361/33 Chief Secretary's Office—Censorship of Religious Broadcasts, copy of letter sent from PBS staff member D.J. Smith to Director Edwin Samuel, Feb. 4, 1947.

21. ISA RG 2.16 361 33 Chief Secretary's Office—Censorship of Religious Broadcasts, station memo from Director Edwin Samuel, Dec. 5, 1946.

22. ISA RG 2.16 361 30 Chief Secretary's Office—Broadcasting of Moslem Religious Ceremonies, letter from Amin Abdul Hadi for the Supreme Moslem Council to the Chief Secretary, Dec. 1, 1946.

23. ISA RG 2.16 361 30 Chief Secretary's Office—Broadcasting of Moslem Religious Ceremonies, letter from Director Edwin Samuel to Amin Abdul Hadi, cc Postmaster General, Dec. 5, 1946; and letter from Acting Engineer in

Chief to Assistant Engineer Studios, Dec. 4, 1946. See also ISA RG 2.16 361 47 Chief Secretary's Office—PBS—Attendance on Rest Days.

24. See, e.g., "Arabic Broadcasting Program during Ramadan," *Falastin*, Oct. 4, 1940, p. 1; and daily schedules, also generally printed on the first page, throughout the month.

25. "The Arabic Section on the Broadcasting Station," *Falastin*, Nov. 3, 1940, p. 1.

26. "Broadcast of Eastern Easter," *Palestine Post*, Apr. 30, 1937, p. 8.

27. "Easter and the Broadcasting Station," *Falastin*, Apr. 12, 1936, p. 7.

28. "Listener's Corner," *Palestine Post*, Oct. 25, 1940, p. 2.

Chapter 5

1. See Frantz Fanon, *L'an V de la révolution algérienne* (Paris: La Découverte, 2001), chap. 2, "Ici la voix de l'Algérie," pp. 51–82.

2. CO 733 266 7 Comments on Report of Broadcasting Committee, no name, Feb. 20, 1934.

3. CO 733 266 7 Memo on Comments and Report of Broadcasting Committee, no name, mid-1934.

4. CO 733 266 7 Comments on Report of Broadcasting Committee, no name, Feb. 20, 1934.

5. Rex Keating to Edward Samuel, Aug. 31, 1946. Rex Keating Collection, MECA #GB165–0361.

6. Edwin Samuel to Dr. H. Goldberg [ACUM lawyer], Feb. 11, 1948, ISA RG 14 1879 24 Department of Broadcasting, 1948.

7. ISA Department of Broadcasting, Music Section, RG 14 1879 28.

8. Ami Ayalon describes a list of subscribers to *al-Liwa'* in the mid-1930s as "read[ing] like a guest list for a fancy elite event in Palestine: Husayni, Nashashibi, Dajani, 'Alami, Khalidi, Darwazah, 'Abd al-Hadi, Khatib, Tamimi, Tuqan, Zu'aytar, Rimawi, 'Anabtawi, Masri, Shawa, Bsaysu, 'Arif, and so on—making up the urban elite of Jerusalem, Jaffa, Nablus, Hebron, Gaza, and other towns." Ayalon, *Reading Palestine*, p. 90. Sarah Ozacky-Lazar and Mustafa Kabha provide more detailed information: "*Al-Liwa'a* [The Flag] was founded in Jerusalem in 1933. Its owner was Jamal al-Husseini; the editors included Emil Ghuri, Othman Qassim, and Mahmud Chirqas. The paper was a mouthpiece of the Palestinian Arab Party, which was controlled by the Husseinis. It appeared as a daily until 1939." Sarah Ozacky-Lazar and Mustafa Kabha, "The Haganah by Arab and Palestinian Historiography and Media," *Israel Studies* 7 no. 3 (2002): 58 n. 15.

9. "Between the Lines," *Palestine Post*, Apr. 6, 1936, p. 6.

10. The Vaad Leumi's official status marked a defining difference between it and Palestinian Arab organizations like the Arab Executive or the Arab Higher Committee. The British mandate government recognized as official representative institutions only those that had accepted the terms of the mandate for Palestine. The Jewish community, through the Vaad Leumi, had agreed—but

what Palestinian organization could endorse a mandate that included the terms of the Balfour Declaration? As a result, British mandate officials considered meetings with members of Palestinian organizations as ex officio sessions with private individuals. See, e.g., Khalidi, *The Iron Cage*, p. 44.

11. The *Palestine Post*'s final editorial comment on the issue treated it as a settled matter. On April 12, 1936, "The Listeners' Corner" stated merely that "the issue raised by the Arab objection to 'Eretz-Israel' being used in describing the Palestine Broadcasting Service, and the Jewish objection against the pronunciation of the initials only has been obviated during the past few days by the use of the Hebrew equivalent of 'This is Jerusalem Calling' as the introduction to programs. The term 'Al Kuds' is used in Arabic for Jerusalem" (p. 6). The column then turned to a discussion of upcoming programming, including a series of literary talks in Arabic and various orchestral pieces.

12. "Readers' Letters," *Palestine Post*, May 11, 1936, p. 2.

13. Nuwayhid, *Sittun 'Am*, p. 260.

14. See "Opening Announcements," item 210 in the Minutes of the 38th Planning Committee Meeting Held in the Director's Office October 22, 1946, ISA RG 14 1879 10 Department of Broadcasting: Music Section (1945–1947).

15. "Jewish National Anthem," confidential memo from Karl Salomon, Music section controller, to the controller of English-Hebrew programs, Nov. 27, 1944. ISA RG 14 1879 7 Department of Broadcasting: Music Section: Programs: Playing of "Hatikva," 1938–1946.

16. "Listeners Corner," *Palestine Post*, Mar. 9, 1937, p. 4.

17. Hirshberg, *Music in the Jewish Community*, pp. 69–70.

18. Ibid., p. 86.

19. Ibid., pp. 143–144.

20. For more on Jewish music in mandate Palestine, see Hannah Grad Goodman, *Jewish Music in Palestine* (New York: National Jewish Music Council, 1948).

21. Translated excerpt from *Haboker*, June 13, 1943, printed in the *Review of the Palestine Press*, with an alternate (draft?) translation included in the same file. ISA RG 14 1879 7 Department of Broadcasting: Music Section: Programs: Playing of "Hatikva," 1938–1946.

22. Confidential memo on "Jewish National Anthem" from Deputy Controller of Music Programs Karl Salomon to Controller of English-Hebrew Programs, Nov. 27, 1944. ISA RG 14 1879 7 Department of Broadcasting: Music Section: Programs: Playing of "Hatikva," 1938–1946.

23. Ibid.

24. Ibid.

25. Letter from N. J. B. Sabine of the Colonial Office's Public Relations department to R. A. Rendall of the BBC, Mar. 26, 1945. PRO CO 733 470 14.

26. Samuel, *Lifetime in Jerusalem*, chap. 10.

27. See note 80 above.

28. See, e.g., High Commissioner Gort's letter to Oliver Stanley, Secretary of State for the Colonies, Feb. 10, 1945, recommending Samuel's appointment. PRO CO 733 470 14. Samuel's religion and elevated social status meant that few other positions were open to him. "From Mr. Samuel's personal point of

view the appointment should be a happy one," a Colonial Office staffer identified as Eastwood noted in an internal comment dated March 17, 1945. "He has become rather side-tracked from the normal administrative machine and his future employment has been something of a problem"—a problem that the PBS appointment solved. PRO CO 733 470 14.

29. Samuel, *Lifetime in Jerusalem*, p. 213.

30. Draft of secret memo on "Hatikvah" from Edwin Samuel, Director of Broadcasting, to J. V. W. Shaw, Chief Secretary, following their conversation, Apr. 5, 1945. ISA RG 14 1879 7 Department of Broadcasting: Music Section: Programs: Playing of "Hatikva," 1938–1946. The PBS Orchestra was the station's official orchestra; it played pieces for the Music and Hebrew sections. The Arabic section had its own musicians and musical groups.

31. "Minutes of the eighth meeting of Mr. Samuel with the Orchestra Committee on Wednesday, the 27th March, 1946, at 9 a.m.," recorded Apr. 4, 1946. ISA RG 14 1879 7 Department of Broadcasting: Music Section: Programs: Playing of "Hatikva," 1938–1946.

32. Memo on "Hatiqwa," Karl Salomon, Music Section Controller, to Edwin Samuel, Director of Broadcasting, Apr. 5, 1946. ISA RG 14 1879 7 Department of Broadcasting: Music Section: Programs: Playing of "Hatikva," 1938–1946.

33. "PBS ban on 'Hatikva' to be reconsidered," *Palestine Post*, Mar. 31, 1946, p. 2.

34. Draft of secret memo on "Hatikvah." ISA RG 14 1879 7 Department of Broadcasting: Music Section: Programs: Playing of "Hatikva," 1938–1946.

35. "Palestine Broadcasting Begun," *Palestine Post*, Mar. 31, 1936, p. 8.

36. "Palestine on the Air," *Palestine Post*, Mar. 30, 1936, p. 6.

37. The determination of religious and/or ethnic identity through family and personal names was (and continues to be) common practice in the region. In 1941 the American University of Beirut conducted a regional poll of radio listening habits. To identify Hebrew section and Arabic section listeners, the survey team employed the same method: Post Office license applications plus name identification. See Stuart Carter Dodd, *Pioneer Radio Poll in Lebanon, Syria, and Palestine* (Jerusalem: Government Printer, 1943).

38. "Nearly 19,000 Radio Licenses / Remarkable Increase since April Last," *Palestine Post*, Dec. 9, 1936, p. 5.

39. *Falastin*, which generally published only the aggregate license statistics, used this same argument to counter British government accusations that Palestine's Arabs were succumbing to Radio Bari's anti-British broadcasts. In an article titled "Radio Licenses Are Incomparable Proof," the paper cited Post Office license statistics to argue that Palestinian Arabs were entirely uninterested in Bari—as they were uninterested in radio generally. See *Falastin*, Feb. 17, 1938.

40. See, e.g., "Post Telephone and Wireless Proceeds through the End of January 1940," *Falastin*, Apr. 18, 1940, p. 5, which mentions the number of licenses held in December 1939 and January 1940 in the final sentence.

41. "A Suggestion for Jewish Radio Listeners," *Palestine Post*, Apr. 9, 1936, p. 6.

42. "Jews Would Control Their Section of Palestine Broadcasting Service / Vaad Leumi Memorandum to Chief Secretary," *Palestine Post*, June 9, 1939, p. 1.

43. The Ministry of Information was made directly responsible for PBS programming, which expanded to include broadcasts for allied populations and troops in French, Greek, Polish, and other languages. This arrangement lasted until 1945, when the appointment of Edwin Samuel as station director marked the station's return to peacetime operations.

44. Edwin Samuel, "The Problems of Broadcasting in Palestine—A Bilingual Country," speech given at the Royal Institute of International Affairs (London), July 5, 1946. ISA RG 103 Private Papers of Edwin Samuel.

45. Ibid.

46. "Broadcasting House, Jerusalem," *Jerusalem Radio*, June 30, 1939, NA/PRO 30 94 2, New Broadcasting House, Jerusalem.

47. "Closing of Broadcasting Station after Explosion; Suspension of Broadcasting and News from Room at the Post Office; Death of Arab Engineer Mr. Adib Mansour and Burial of His Body in Dignified Ceremony" and another article including a subsection titled "Death of Jewish Broadcaster and Rescue of English Children," *Falastin*, Aug. 4, 1939, p. 1. "Explosions in PBS Studios Injure Three, Wreck Offices; Normal Broadcasts Cut Off by Time Bomb Havoc," *Palestine Post*, Aug. 3, 1939, p. 1. "Bombs Stop a Broadcast; Jerusalem Outage; Radio Station Staff Injured," *Times of London*, Aug. 3, 1939, p. 11. Neither Mansour nor Weissenberg died immediately, hence the "injured" headlines from the latter two.

48. John Melkon Rose, *Armenians of Jerusalem: Memories of Life in Palestine* (London: Radcliffe Press, 1993), p. 153.

49. Heather Teague letter dated August 9, 1939, Heather (Fairley) Teague Collection, MECA #GB165–0279, St. Antony's College Middle East Centre Archives.

50. "Bomb Thrown outside PBS Building," *Palestine Post*, Aug. 9, 1939, p. 1.

51. "Continued Investigation of the Incident at the Broadcasting Station," *Falastin*, Aug. 8, 1939, p. 5.

52. "Attempt to 'Take over' Ramallah Radio Station," *Palestine Post*, May 19, 1944, p. 1.

53. "Two Officers Killed in Repelling Attacks; Electric Station Blown Up; Curfew in Jerusalem," *Palestine Post*, Jan. 20, 1946, p. 1.

54. "Attack was Aimed at PBS Studios," *Palestine Post*, Jan. 21, 1946, p. 3.

55. See ISA RG 14 1879 25 Department of Broadcasting: Music Section: a) curfew passes, b) admission passes, c) instructions: security officer, 1946–1947.

56. Samuel, *Lifetime in Jerusalem*, pp. 247–248.

57. Memo from Edwin Samuel, Director of Broadcasting, to PBS officers, Mar. 9, 1948. ISA RG 14 1879 24 Department of Broadcasting, 1948.

58. Middle East Center Archive, St. Antony's College, Oxford, Rex Keating Collection MECA GB165–0361, Files 1/1–3, diaries.

59. Rex Keating, *The Trumpets of Tutankhamun: Adventures of a Radio Pioneer in the Middle East* (Oakley: Fisher Miller Publishing, 1999), p. 90. Keat-

ing was fairly even-handed in his skepticism about the motives of most PBS staff, and his criticisms of Samuel focused as much on what he considered the latter's lax attitude toward his working hours as to his support for the Zionist cause.

Conclusion

1. "'Voice of Israel' in Tel Aviv," *Palestine Post*, May 14, 1948, p. 3.

Bibliography

Archival sources

British Library Sound Archive

#25A1656-#25A1660 April's Children: Note: An April Fool Programme (PBS)
#25A1661-#25A1665 Funny Business: Note: A Collection of Sketches (PBS)
#25A1666-#25A1667 Cunningham, Sir Alan, High Commissioner and CIC Palestine, 1945–1948: Note: Final address/appeal to people of Palestine (PBS)
#25A1668 News Bulletins: Keating, Rex and Long, Lesley (Two extracts from PBS, Jerusalem)
#25A1669 Battle at PBS Studio
#25A1672-#25A1677 A Double Bill: Note: Two Short Plays Broadcast on PBS Light Programme.
#25A1678 10,000 Years of PBS Extracts, provided by Rex Keating
#30B4827 Rex Keating: ESB News Bulletin in English (EGYPT)
#30B4829-#30B4830 Rex Keating: St David's Day Programme (B'cast Jerusalem)
#30B4831-#30B4834 10,000 Years of PBS Extracts, provided by Rex Keating
#30B4835 Scrapbook Hebrew, 1936–1946 (Fragments from PBS Hebrew Service)
#30B4836 Sir John Shaw: Address following explosions at King David Hotel, Jerusalem

British National Archives (formerly Public Records Office)

CAB 84/19/31 Jerusalem broadcasting station (Sept. 26, 1940)
CO 323/1451/47 Palestine wireless facilities [1937]
CO 323/1496/19-CO 323/1496/20 British counterpropaganda broadcasts in Arabic (1937)
CO 323/1496/21 Broadcasting in Arabic (1937)
CO 323/1588/2 Palestine service broadcasting in Arabic (1938)

CO 323/1652/43 Palestine: Broadcasts in Arabic, 1939–1940
CO 323/1736/12 Proposed Polish wireless station to broadcast from Palestine to Occupied Poland [1940]
CO 537/1905 Broadcast news service: Palestine [1944–1946]
CO 733/266/7 Broadcasting in Palestine
CO 733/308/12 Palestine Broadcasting Service: Staff and vacancies (1936)
CO 733/442/2 Organisation of Palestine Broadcasting Service
CO 733/442/3 Mr Poston's memorandum on Palestine Broadcasting Service Staff 1942
CO 733/470/14 Reorganisation of Palestine Broadcasting Department
FO 141/645/3 BBC: includes comments on broadcasting and broadcasts in Egypt, and also from Jerusalem (1937)
FO 371/23251 Broadcasting in Palestine [1939]
FO 371/24569 Broadcasting in Palestine [1940]
FO 371/27358 Arabic broadcasts (1941)
FO 371/45422 Plan of Propaganda for Palestine (1945)
FO 371/45429 Broadcasting in Palestine [1945]
FO 371/61928 Provision of information for the Palestine Broadcasting Department (1947)
FO 371/104779 Arab media propaganda; Israeli complaints concerning press statements made by Azmi Nashashibi, Feb. 27, 1953, and material broadcast by Damascus Radio (1953)
FO 395/557-FO 395/560 Arabic broadcasts (1938)
FO 395/631-FO 395/632 Arabic broadcasts (1939)
FO 395/663-FO 395/664 German broadcasts in Arabic (1939)
FO 898/128 Propaganda activities, leaflet translations (Arabic) 1941–2
FO 953/400 Publicity material in Arabic for the Middle East (1948)
PRO 30/94/2 New broadcasting house, Jerusalem: architectural treatment to studios with photographs and news clippings from the "Jerusalem radio" and "Egyptian radio" publications (1939)
T 161/1034 COMMUNICATIONS. Telegraph: General: Proposals by Cabinet for broadcasting from Jerusalem, in Arabic, July 1937 (July 8, 1937– Apr. 19, 1941)

Israel State Archives

PPI Palestine Publications Index
RG 2 Chief Secretary's Office
RG 5 Economic Adviser
RG 9 Department of Commerce & Industry
RG 14 Department of Broadcasting, Music Section
RG 15 Public Information Office
RG 19 Colonial Audit
RG 65 Abandoned Arab Documents
RG 103 Edwin Samuel Papers

Middle East Center Archive, St. Antony's College, Oxford

Humphrey Ernest Bowman Collection, GB 165 0034
Wilfred Jerome Farrell Collection, GB 165 0104
Mrs. Heather Teague (née Fairley) Collection, GB 165 0279
Rex Keating Collection, GB 165 0361

Avraham Harman Institute of Contemporary Jewry,
Hebrew University, Jerusalem

Interview with Edwin Samuel, "Broadcasting in Eretz Israel," 1976, Oral History Division, #(133) 3, catalog #47523

Unpublished Privately Held Papers

Boutagy family papers, Edwin (Eddie) Palmer collection

Published Primary Sources
Periodicals

BBC Annual Yearbook, 1934–1949
Falastin, 1932–1948
League of Nations Mandate Reports, 1933–1940
An-Nahar, 1946–1950
Palestine Post, 1932–1950
Times of London, 1933–1948
Wireless World, 1934–1948

Memoirs

Bowman, Humphrey. *Middle-East Window.* London: Longmans, Green, 1942.
Keating, Rex. *The Trumpets of Tutankhamun: Adventures of a Radio Pioneer in the Middle East.* Basingstoke: Fisher Miller, 1999.
al-Khalidi, 'Anbara Salam. *Jawla fi al-Dhikriyat bayna Lubnan wa Falastin.* Beirut: Dar al-Nahar, 1978.
Nashashibi, 'Azmi. *Min al-Quds ila London.* Jerusalem: Commercial Press, 1947.
Nuwayhid, 'Ajaj. *Sittun 'Am ma' al-Qafila al-'Arabiya.* Prepared by Bayan Nuwayhid al-Hut. Beirut: Dar al-Istiqlal, 1993.
Rose, John Melkon. *Armenians of Jerusalem: Memories of Life in Palestine.* London: Radcliffe Press, 1993.
Samuel, Edwin. *A Lifetime in Jerusalem: The Memoirs of the Second Viscount Samuel.* London: Vallentine, Mitchell, 1970.
Tleel, John N. *I am Jerusalem.* Old City, Jerusalem: Self-published, 2000.

Contemporary Studies and Published Documents

Avida, Mordechai [né Zlotnik]. "Broadcasting in Israel." *Middle Eastern Affairs* 3, no. 11 (November 1952): 321–328.

Bowman, Humphrey. *Middle-East Window*. London: Longman, Green, 1942.

———. "Rural Education in the Near and Middle East." *Journal of the Royal Central Asian Society* (July 26, 1939): 402–414.

Brunner, Edmund de Schweinitz. *Radio and the Farmer*. New York: Radio Institute of the Audible Arts, 1935.

———. "Rural Communications Behavior and Attitudes in the Middle East." *Rural Sociology* 18, no. 2 (June 1953): 149–156.

Cornfeld, Peretz, ed. *Palestine Personalia 1947*. Tel Aviv: Sefer Press, 1947.

Documents de la conférence européenne des radiocommunications Lucerne, Mai-Juin 1933. Berne: Bureau International de l'Union Télégraphique, 1933.

Dodd, Stuart C. *A Pioneer Radio Poll in Lebanon, Syria, and Palestine*. Jerusalem: Government Printer, 1943.

Faris, Basim A. *Electric Power in Syria and Palestine*. Beirut: American University of Beirut Press, 1936.

Goodman, Hannah. *Jewish Music in Palestine*. New York: National Jewish Music Council, 1948.

Jewish Agency Economic Research Institute. *Statistical Handbook of Middle Eastern Countries*. Jerusalem: E. B. Aaronson, 1944.

———. *Statistical Handbook of Middle Eastern Countries*. Jerusalem: Azriel Printing Works, 1945.

Kestenberg, Leo. "The Palestine Orchestra in Wartime." *Musical Times* 85, no. 1220 (Oct. 1944): 303–304.

Leaver, W. R. "Science and the Voice." *Musical Times* 78, no. 1127 (Jan. 1937): 79–80.

Lewertoff, S. B. "The Palestine Orchestra." *Musical Times* 86, no. 1226 (Apr. 1945): 120–121.

Mandat pour la Palestine/Mandate for Palestine. Communiqué au Conseil et aux Membres de la Société. Geneva: League of Nations, Aug. 12, 1922.

Martin, Leslie John. "Press and Radio in Palestine under the British Mandate." *Journalism Quarterly* 26, no. 2 (June 1949): 186–193.

Martin, T. L. "More News from Palestine." *Musical Times* 51, no. 906 (Aug. 1, 1918): 358–359.

Musgrove, Cyril, and Herbert Dawson. "News from Jerusalem." *Musical Times* 59, no. 903 (May 1, 1918): 214–215.

"Music in the Making." *Tempo* 12 (Dec. 1945): 14–16.

"Musical Notes from Abroad." *Musical Times* 80, no. 1151 (Jan. 1939): 66–68.

Nathan, Robert, Oscar Gass, and Daniel Creamer. *Palestine: Problem and Promise (an Economic Study)*. Washington, DC: Public Affairs Press, American Council of Public Affairs, 1946.

Ringer, Alexander. "Musical Composition in Modern Israel." *Musical Quarterly* 51, no. 1 (Jan. 1965): 282–297.

Robinson, William S. "Radio Comes to the Farmer." In *Radio Research 1941*, ed. Paul Lazarsfeld and Frank N. Stanton, 224–294. New York: Duell, Sloan, and Pearce, 1941.

Sabaneev, Leonid, and S. W. Pring. "The Jewish National School in Music." *Musical Quarterly* 15, no. 3 (July 1929): 448–468.

Salomon, Karl. "Kol Yerushalayim: Music Programmes for Jewish Radio Listeners in Palestine." *Musica Hebraica* 1–2 (1938): 36–39.

Simon, Heinrich. *Palestine Listens to Its Orchestra: Personal Reminiscences.* New York: H. K. Advertising, 1939.

Simpson, John Hope. *Palestine: Report on Immigration, Land Settlement, and Development.* London: His Majesty's Stationery Office, 1930.

Strickland, C. F. "Broadcasting for Rural India." *Asiatic Review* 30, no. 101 (Jan. 1934): 1–14.

———. "The Possibility of Introducing a System of Agricultural Cooperation in Palestine." Government of Palestine, Jerusalem, 1930.

A Survey of Palestine, Prepared for the Information of the Anglo-American Committee of Inquiry. Jerusalem: Government Printer, 1946.

Thalheimer, Elsa. *Five Years of the Palestine Orchestra.* Tel Aviv: Palestine Orchestra, 1942.

Tibawi, Abdul Latif. *Arab Education in Mandatory Palestine.* London: Luzac & Co., 1956.

Secondary Sources

Abboushi, W. F. "The Road to Rebellion: Arab Palestine in the 1930s." *Journal of Palestine Studies* 6, no. 3 (Spring 1977): 23–46.

Abu Lughod, Lila. "The Interpretation of Culture(s) after Television." *Representations,* no. 59 (Summer 1997): 109–134. Special issue: *The Fate of "Culture": Geertz and Beyond.*

Abu Shanab, Hussein. *Huna al-Quds: Dar al-Idhaʿa al-Falastiniyyah.* Khan Yunis: Markaz Dirasat Abhath al-Watan, 2002.

Adams, Paul C. "Television as Gathering Place." *Annals of the Association of American Geographers* 82, no. 1 (Mar. 1992): 117–135.

Aitken, Hugh G. J. "Allocating the Spectrum: The Origins of Radio Regulation." *Technology and Culture* 35, no. 4 (Oct. 1994): 686–716.

Almog, Eytan. "A Wireless Broadcasting Station in Palestine: The First Hebrew Radio Station in the World." *Qesher* 20 (November 1996) [Hebrew].

Ayalon, Ami. *Reading Palestine: Printing and Literacy, 1900–1948.* Austin: University of Texas Press, 2004.

Baker, W. J. *A History of the Marconi Company.* London: Methuen, 1970.

Bailey, Michael. "'He who has ears to hear, let him hear': Christian Pedagogy and Religious Broadcasting during the Inter-War Period." *Westminster Papers in Communication and Culture* 4, no. 1 (2007): 4–25.

Baron, Beth. *The Women's Awakening in Egypt: Culture, Society, and the Press.* New Haven: Yale University Press, 1994.

Benson, Carlton. "From Teahouse to Radio: Storytelling and the Commercialization of Culture in 1930s Shanghai." Ph.D. diss., University of California, Berkeley, 1996.

Bohlman, P. V. "The Immigrant Composer in Palestine, 1933–1948: Stranger in a Strange Land." *Asian Music* 17, no. 2 (1986): 147–167.

———. "In Search of a Home: German-Jewish Musical Scholars and Scholarship, 1933–1940." *Journal of Musicological Research* 11, no. 3 (1991): 201–217.

———. *The World Center for Jewish Music in Palestine, 1936–1940*. Oxford: Clarendon Press, 1992.

Bourgualt, Louise. *Mass Media in Sub-Saharan Africa*. Bloomington: Indiana University Press, 1995.

Bowden, Sue. "Household Appliances and the Use of Time: The United States and Britain since the 1920s." *Economic History Review* 27, no. 4 (Nov. 1994): 725–748.

Boyd, Douglas. "Development of Egypt's Radio: Voice of the Arabs under Nasser." *Journalism Quarterly* 52, no. 4 (Winter 1975): 645–653.

———. *Egyptian Radio: Tool of Political and National Development*. Lexington, KY: Association for Education in Journalism, 1977.

———. "Hebrew-Language Clandestine Radio Broadcasting during the British Palestine Mandate." *Journal of Radio Studies* 6, no. 1 (Winter 1999): 101–115.

———. "Sharq al-Adna / The Voice of Britain." *Gazette: International Journal for Communication Studies* 65, no. 6 (2003): 443–455.

Briggs, Asa. *The BBC: The First Fifty Years*. Oxford: Oxford University Press, 1985.

———. *The History of Broadcasting in the United Kingdom*. 3 vols. London: Oxford University Press, 1979.

Brochand, Christian. *Histoire générale de la radio et de la télévision en France*. 2 vols. Paris: La Documentation Française, 1994.

Bulliet, Richard. *Islam: The View from the Edge*. New York: Columbia University Press, 1995.

Burke, Timothy. *Lifebuoy Men, Lux Women: Commodification, Consumption, and Cleanliness in Modern Zimbabwe*. Durham: Duke University Press, 1996.

Burnes, James. "Watching Africans Watch Films: Theories of Spectatorship in British Colonial Africa." *Historical Journal of Film, Radio and Television* 20, no. 20 (2000): 197–211.

Camporesi, Valeria. *Mass Culture and National Traditions: The BBC and American Broadcasting, 1922–1954*. Fucecchio: European Press Academic Publishing, 2000.

Chakrabarty, Dipesh. "The Difference-Deferral of a Colonial Modernity: Public Debates on Domesticity in British Bengal." In *Tensions of Empire*, ed. Ann L. Stoler and Frederick Cooper, pp. 373–400. Berkeley: University of California Press, 1997.

Chopyak, James. "The Role of Music in Mass Media, Public Education, and the Formation of a Malaysian 'National Culture.'" *Ethnomusicology* 31, no. 3 (Autumn 1987): 431–454.

Davies, Alan. "The First Radio War: Broadcasting in the Spanish Civil War, 1936–1939." *Historical Journal of Film, Radio and Television* 19, no. 4 (1999): 473–513.

Davis, Rochelle. "The Growth of the Western Communities, 1917–1948." In *Jerusalem 1948: The Arab Neighborhoods and Their Fate in the War*, ed. Salim Tamari, pp. 32–66. Jerusalem: Institute of Jerusalem Studies and Badil Resource Center, 1999.

Davison, Roderic. "The Effect of the Telegraph on the Conduct of Ottoman Foreign Relations." In *Decision-Making and Change in the Ottoman Empire*, ed. Ceasar Farah, pp. 53–66. Kirkville: University of Missouri Press, 1993.

Donzelot, Jacques. *La police des familles*. Paris: Éditions de minuit, 1977.

Douglas, Susan J. *Listening In: Radio and the American Imagination*. New York: Random House, 1999.

El-Eini, Roza I. M. *Mandated Landscape: British Imperial Rule in Palestine, 1939–1948*. London: Routledge, 2006.

Fanon, Frantz. *L'An V de la révolution algérienne*. Paris: La Découverte, 2001.

50 Years of Japanese Broadcasting. Ed. History Compilation Room, Radio & TV Culture Research Institute. Tokyo: Nippon Hoso Kyokai, 1977.

Fischer, Claude S. *America Calling: A Social History of the Telephone to 1940*. Berkeley: University of California Press, 1992.

Fleischmann, Ellen. *The Nation and Its "New" Women: The Palestinian Women's Movement, 1920–1948*. Berkeley: University of California Press, 2003.

Frierson, Elizabeth. "Cheap and Easy: The Creation of Consumer Culture in Late Ottoman Society." In *Consumption Studies and the History of the Ottoman Empire, 1550–1922*, ed. Donald Quataert, pp. 243-260. Albany: SUNY Press, 2000.

Frost, Robert L. "Machine Liberation: Inventing Housewives and Home Appliances in Interwar France." *French Historical Studies* 18, no. 1 (Spring 1993): 109–130.

Gladwell, Malcolm. *The Tipping Point: How Little Things Can Make a Big Difference*. Boston: Back Bay Books, 2002.

Goldstein, Carolyn. "From Service to Sales: Home Economics in Light and Power, 1920–1940." *Technology and Culture* 31, no. 1 (January 1998): 121–152. Special Issue: *Gender Analysis and the History of Technology*.

de Grazia, Victoria. *The Culture of Consent: Mass Organization of Leisure in Fascist Italy*. New York: Cambridge University Press, 1981.

———. Introduction to *The Sex of Things: Gender and Consumption in Historical Perspective*, ed. Victoria de Grazia and Ellen Furlough. Berkeley: University of California Press, 1996.

de Grazia, Victoria, and Ellen Furlough, eds. *The Sex of Things: Gender and Consumption in Historical Perspective*. Berkeley: University of California Press, 1996.

Greenberg, Ela. "Educating Muslim Girls in Mandatory Jerusalem." *International Journal of Middle East Studies* 36 (2004): 1–19.

———. *Preparing the Mothers of Tomorrow: Education and Islam in Mandate Palestine*. Austin: University of Texas Press, 2010.

Gronow, Pekka. *The Recording Industry: An Ethnomusicological Approach*. Tampere, Finland: University of Tampere, 1996.

Gronow, Pekka, and Ilpo Saunio. *An International History of the Recording Industry*. London: Cassell, 1998.

Gupta, Partha Sarathi. *Radio and the Raj, 1921–1947*. Calcutta: Center for Studies in Social Sciences and K. P. Bagchi, 1995.

Hagopian, Edward, and A. B. Zahlan. "Palestine's Arab Population: The Demography of the Palestinians." *Journal of Palestine Studies* 3, no. 4 (Summer 1974): 32–73.

Hamm, Charles. "'The constant companion of man': Separate Development, Radio Bantu, and Music." *Popular Music* 10, no. 2 (May 1991): 147–173.

Hayes, Joy Elizabeth. *Radio Nation: Communication, Popular Culture, and Nationalism in Mexico: 1920–1950*. Tucson: University of Arizona Press, 2000.

Headrick, Daniel. *The Invisible Weapon: Telecommunications and International Politics, 1851–1945*. New York: Oxford University Press, 1991.

Hirshberg, Jehoash. *Music in the Jewish Community of Palestine, 1880–1948: A Social History*. Oxford: Clarendon Press, 1995.

Hirschkind, Charles. *The Ethical Soundscape: Cassette Sermons and Islamic Counterpublics*. New York: Columbia University Press, 2009.

Kabha, Mustafa. "The Palestinian Press and the General Strike, April–October 1936: *Falastin* as a Case Study." *Middle Eastern Studies* 39, no. 3 (July 2003): 169–189.

———. *The Palestinian Press as Shaper of Public Opinion, 1929–1939: Writing up a Storm*. London: Mitchell, Vallentine, 2007.

Kaplan, Danny. "The Songs of the Siren: Engineering National Time on Israeli Radio." *Cultural Anthropology* 24, no. 2 (May 2009): 313–345.

Kern, Stephen. *The Culture of Time and Space, 1880–1919*. Cambridge, MA: Harvard University Press, 1986.

Khalidi, Rashid. *The Iron Cage: The Story of the Palestinian Struggle for Statehood*. Boston: Beacon Press, 2006.

Khoury, Philip S. "Syrian Urban Politics in Transition: The Quarters of Damascus during the French Mandate." *International Journal of Middle East Studies* 16, no. 4 (Nov. 1984): 507–540.

Kinnear, Michael S. *The Gramophone Company's First Indian Recordings, 1899–1908*. Bombay: Popular Prakashan, 1994.

Kittler, Friedrich A. *Gramophone, Film, Typewriter*. Stanford: Stanford University Press, 1999.

Kupferschmidt, Uri M. *The Supreme Muslim Council: Islam under the British Mandate for Palestine*. Leiden: Brill, 1987.

Lacey, Kate. *Feminine Frequencies: Gender, German Radio, and the Public Sphere, 1923–1945*. Ann Arbor: University of Michigan Press, 1996.

Larkin, Brian. "The Materiality of Cinema Theaters in Northern Nigeria." In *Media Worlds: Anthropology on a New Terrain*, ed. Faye Ginsburg, Lila Abu Lughod, and Brian Larkin, pp. 319–336. Berkeley: University of California Press, 2002.

Lelyveld, David. "Transmitters and Culture: The Colonial Roots of Indian Broadcasting." *South Asia Research* 10, no. 1 (Spring 1990): 41–52.

LeMahieu, D. L. *A Culture for Democracy: Mass Communication and the Cultivated Mind in Britain between the Wars.* Oxford: Clarendon Press, 1988.

Leslie, D. A. "Global Scan: The Globalization of Advertising Agencies, Concepts, and Campaigns." *Economic Geography* 71, no. 4 (Oct. 1995): 402–426.

Liebes, Tamar, and Zohar Kampf. "'Hello! This Is Jerusalem Calling': The Revival of Spoken Hebrew on the Mandatory Radio (1936–1948)." *Journal of Israeli History* 29, no. 2 (2010): 137–158.

Likhovski, Assaf. *Law and Identity in Mandate Palestine.* Chapel Hill: University of North Carolina Press, 2006.

Lockman, Zachary. *Comrades and Enemies: Arab and Jewish Workers in Palestine: 1906–1948.* Berkeley: University of California Press, 1996.

MacDonald, Callum A. "Radio Bari: Italian Wireless Propaganda in the Middle East and British Counter-Measures." *Middle Eastern Studies* 13, no. 2 (May 1977): 195-207.

Mansell, Gerard. *Let Truth Be Told: 50 Years of BBC External Broadcasting.* London: Weidenfeld & Nicolson, 1982.

Marchand, Roland. *Advertising the American Dream: Making Way for Modernity, 1920–1940.* Berkeley: University of California Press, 1985.

Marquis, Alice. "Written on the Wind: The Impact of Radio during the 1930s." *Journal of Contemporary History* 19 (1984): 385–415.

Martin, Kevin. "Enter the Future! Exemplars of Bourgeois Modernity in Post-World War II Syria." Ph.D. diss., Georgetown University, 2005.

Matthews, Weldon C. *Confronting an Empire, Constructing a Nation: Arab Nationalists and Popular Politics in Mandate Palestine.* London: I. B. Tauris, 2006.

McCann, Bryan. *Hello, Hello Brazil: Popular Music in the Making of Modern Brazil.* Durham: Duke University Press, 2004.

McChesney, Robert. *Telecommunications, Mass Media, and Democracy: The Battle for Control of U. S. Broadcasting.* New York: Oxford University Press, 1993.

Metzer, Jacob. *The Divided Economy of Mandatory Palestine.* Cambridge: Cambridge University Press, 1998.

Miller, Ylana. *Government and Society in Rural Palestine, 1920–1948.* Austin: University of Texas Press, 1985.

Mrázek, Rudolf. *Engineers of Happy Land: Technology and Nationalism in a Colony.* Princeton: Princeton University Press, 2002.

Nadan, Amos. *The Palestinian Peasant Economy under the Mandate: A Story of Colonial Bungling.* Cambridge, MA: Harvard University, Center for Middle Eastern Studies, 2006.

Najmabadi, Afsaneh. "Crafting an Educated Housewife in Iran." In *Remaking Women: Feminism and Modernity in the Middle East,* ed. Lila Abu Lughod, pp. 91–124. Princeton: Princeton University Press, 1998.

Nashashibi, Nasser Eddin. *Jerusalem's Other Voice: Ragheb Nashashibi and Moderation in Palestinian Politics, 1920–1948.* Exeter: Ithaca Press, 1990.

Oren, Tasha. *Demon in the Box: Jews, Arabs, Politics, and Culture in the Making of Israeli Television.* Piscataway, NJ: Rutgers University Press, 2004.

Partner, Peter. *Arab Voices: The BBC Arabic Service, 1938–1988.* London: BBC External Services, 1988.

Patnode, Randall. "What These People Need Is Radio: New Technology, the Press, and Otherness in 1920s America." *Technology and Culture* 44 (April 2003): 285–305.

Penslar, Derek J. "Radio and the Shaping of Modern Israel, 1936–1973." In *Nationalism, Zionism, and Ethnic Mobilization of the Jews in 1900 and Beyond,* ed. Michael Berkowitz, pp. 60-82. Leiden: Brill, 2004.

———. "Transmitting Jewish Culture: Radio in Israel." *Jewish Social Studies* 10, no. 1 (2003): 1–29.

Racy, Ali Jihad. "The Many Faces of Improvisation: The Arab Taqasim as a Musical Symbol." *Ethnomusicology* 44, no. 2 (Spring–Summer 2000): 302–320.

Rajogopal, Arvind. *Politics after Television: Hindu Nationalism and the Reshaping of the Public in India.* Cambridge: Cambridge University Press, 1996.

Read, Oliver, and Walter Welch. *From Tin Foil to Stereo: Evolution of the Phonograph.* Indianapolis: H. W. Sams, [1959] 1977.

Robinson, Michael. "Broadcasting, Cultural Hegemony and Colonial Modernity in Korea, 1924–1945." In *Colonial Modernity in Korea,* ed. Michael Robinson and Gi-Wook Shin, pp. 52–69. Cambridge, MA: Harvard University Press, 1999.

Rogan, Eric. "Instant Communication: The Impact of Telegraph Communications at the Syrian Periphery." In *The Syrian Land: Processes of Integration and Separation: Bilad al-Sham from the 18th Century to the Mandatory Period,* ed. Thomas Philipp and Birgit Schaebler, pp. 113–128. Stuttgart: Steiner, 1998.

Rogers, Everett. *The Diffusion of Innovations.* 4th ed. New York: Free Press, 1995.

Rossano, Antonio. *Qui Radio Bari.* Bari: Dedalo, 1993.

Rugh, William. *Arab Mass Media: Newspapers, Radio, and Television in Arab Politics.* Westport, CT: Praeger, 2004.

Sahhab, Elias. "This Is Radio Jerusalem . . . 1936." *Jerusalem Quarterly File* 20 (Jan. 2004). www.jerusalemquarterly.org/details.php?cat=4&id=196.

Sakr, Naomi. *Arab Television Today.* New York: I. B. Tauris, 2007.

Scannell, Paddy. *A Social History of British Broadcasting.* Oxford: Blackwell, 1991.

Scholch, Alexander. "Britain in Palestine, 1838–1882: The Roots of the Balfour Policy." *Journal of Palestine Studies* 22, no. 1 (Autumn 1992): 39–56.

———. *Palestine in Transformation, 1856–1882: Studies in Social, Economic, and Political Development.* Washington, DC: Institute for Palestine Studies, 1992.

Schulz, Dorothea. "Praise without Enchantment: Griots, Broadcast Media, and the Politics of Tradition in Mali." *Africa Today* 44 (1997): 443–464.

Segev, Tom. *One Palestine, Complete: Jews and Arabs under the British Mandate.* London: Little, Brown, 2000.

Seikaly, May. *Haifa: Transformation of an Arab Society, 1918–1939.* New York: I. B. Tauris, 1995, rpt. 1998.

Seikaly, Sherene. "In the Name of the Public Good." Unpublished manuscript.

———. "Meatless Days: Consumption and Capitalism in Wartime Palestine 1939–1948." Unpublished manuscript.

Shakry, Omnia. "Schooled Mothers and Structured Play: Child Rearing in Turn-of-the-Century Egypt." In *Remaking Women: Feminism and Modernity in the Middle East,* ed. Lila Abu Lughod, pp. 126–170. Princeton: Princeton University Press, 1998.

Shamir, Ronen. *The Colonies of Law: Colonialism, Zionism, and Law in Early Mandate Palestine.* New York: Cambridge University Press, 2000.

Shechter, Relli. "Reading Advertisements in a Colonial/Developmental Context: Cigarette Advertising and Identity Politics in Egypt, c. 1919–1939." *Journal of Social History* 39, no. 2 (Winter 2005): 483–503.

Shepherd, Naomi. *Ploughing Sand: British Rule in Palestine, 1917–1948.* London: John Murray, 1999.

Sherman, A. J. *Mandate Days: British Lives in Palestine, 1918–1948.* New York: Thames & Hudson, 1998.

Shuqrun, ʿAbd Allah. *Al-Idhaʿa wa al-Talfaza al-Maghribiya: Waqaʾiʿ wa Dhikriyat.* Casablanca: Matbaʿat al-Najah al-Jadida, 1999.

Smulyan, Susan. *Selling Radio: The Commercialization of American Broadcasting, 1928–1935.* Washington, DC: Smithsonian Institution Press, 1994.

Spitulnik, Debra. "Anthropology and Mass Media." *Annual Review of Anthropology* 22 (1993): 293–315.

———. "Mobile Machines and Fluid Audiences: Rethinking Reception through Zambian Radio Culture." In *Media Worlds: Anthropology on a New Terrain,* ed. Faye Ginsburg, Lila Abu Lughod, and Brian Larkin, pp. 337–354. Berkeley: University of California Press, 2002.

Stein, Kenneth. "Rural Change and Peasant Destitution: Contributing Causes to the Arab Revolt in Palestine, 1936–1939." In *Peasants and Politics in the Modern Middle East,* ed. Farhad Kamezi and John Waterbury, pp. 143–170. Tallahassee: Florida International University Press, 1991.

Swedenburg, Ted. *Memories of Revolt: The 1936–1939 Rebellion and the Palestinian National Past.* Fayetteville: University of Arkansas Press, 2003.

Taylor, Philip M. *The Projection of Britain: British Overseas Publicity and Propaganda, 1919–1939.* Cambridge: Cambridge University Press, 1981.

Tibawi, Abdul Latif. *British Interests in Palestine, 1800-1901: A Study of Religions and Educational Enterprise.* Oxford: Oxford University Press, 1961.

Townshend, Charles. "The Defense of Palestine: Insurrection and Public Security, 1936–1939." *English Historical Review* 103, no. 409 (Oct. 1988): 917–949.

Vaughan, James. "Propaganda by Proxy? Britain, America, and Arab Radio Broadcasting, 1953–1957." *Historical Journal of Film, Radio, and Television* 22, no. 2 (2002): 157–172.

Walker, Andrew. *A Skyful of Freedom: 60 Years of the BBC World Service.* London: Broadside Books, 1992.

Wik, Reynold M. "The Radio in Rural America during the 1920s." *Agricultural History* 55, no. 4 (Oct. 1981): 339–350.

Zivin, Joselyn. "The Imagined Reign of the Iron Lecturer: Village Broadcasting in Colonial India." *Modern Asian Studies* 32, no. 3 (1998): 717–738.

Index

Italic page numbers refer to illustrations.

Abramovitch, Mendel, 15, 206n18
advertising, 26, 29–75; in Arabic
press and publications, 41, 54–75;
for batteries and battery sets, 107–
108; consumer desire and, 56–
58; cross-advertising, 46–48; in
Falastin, 46–48, 53, 55–63, 65–
67, *67*; formats for, 58–61; general
strike and, 65, 66, 115–118; His
Master's Voice (HMV), 48, 52–
54, *52*, 60–61, 115, *116*; hybrid
form of, 59–61; by local agents
(*wakil*), 41; markets for, 46–48;
middle-class appeals, 39–40, 54,
57–58, 61–63; in *Palestine Post*,
46–48, 73; for "portable radios,"
70–71, *70*; Qur'an referenced in,
64, 213n62; for rural consumers,
27, 114–120, *116*, *117*; suspension during general strike, 65, 66;
suspension during World War II,
66; themes in, 61–66; T. S. Boutagy & Sons, 48–54, *50*, *51*, 60–
65; warnings about false agents,
42–45; World War II and, 66–67,
67, 71–75
aerials, 30–31
Afghani, Jamal al-Din al-, 131
agents, 40–48; "exclusive," 42, 46,
48; false, 42–46; false, warnings about, 42–45, 210n23; T. S.
Boutagy & Sons, 48–54. *See also
specific agents by name*
agriculture. *See* farmers
Airline Radio, 44–45, 47
Algeria, radio in, 168–169
amateur broadcasting, 14–15,
205n17
Anglican community, 48–49, 211n38
Arab Higher Committee, 24
Arabic language, form used in broadcasts, 86–88, 135–136
Arabic listening communities, 33–35,
124–125; diffusion curve and, 39
Arabic press, 12; advertising formats
in, 58–61; "hybrid" advertising,
58–61; print advertising in, 54–
75. See also *Falastin*; newspapers
Arabic programming on PBS, 6, 9,
17, 20, 23, 83, 92–95, 123–151;
Arabic language, form/quality of,
86–88, 135–136; Arabic news service, 118–119, 123; BBC Arabic Service, 95–99; children's programming, 136, 138; community
development and cultural identity
through, 26; Controller of Arabic
Programs, Nuwayhid's position
as, 131, 133–134; as discrete category, 86; education programs,

Arabic programming on PBS (*cont.*) 84–85, 88, 90–92; entertainment, 88–89; hours allocated to, 159–161, 182; hours of broadcasts, 86; household management, 140–145, *141*; information and practical aspects, 88, 89–90, 112; listening communities for, 33–35, 123, 124–125; message of Arab Palestinian progress, 123; modernization through, 134–136, 142; musical programming, 76, *119*, 135, 138–139, *139*, 172–173; nationalist modernity and, 122, 123–151; "New Arab House," 140–145, *141*, 147–148; Nuwayhid, 'Ajaj, and, 27, 124, 131–151; on-air identification, 175; programming categories, 88–89, 123; quality of programming, 135–140; religious holidays, programs on, 137, 164–165, *165*; religious themes, under Nuwayhid's tenure, 136–140, 151; rural populations targeted, 26–27, 76–122; Tuqan, Ibrahim, and, 22–23, *22*, 27, 76, 124, 132, 211n2; women broadcasters, 139–140, 142–144, 145–147; women's topics, 9, 140–148; World War II and, 123–134. *See also* rural audiences; rural broadcasting

Arabic section of PBS, 28, 123–151; independence of, 133, 149–150; local figures on staff, 22–23, 76, 124, 151; Nashashibi, 'Azmi, and, 27, 150–151; Nuwayhid as head of, 27, 131–151; postmandate events, 195–200; transition into Hashemite Jordanian (Palestine) Station, 170, 196; Tuqan as subdirector of, 22–23, *22*, 76, 133; World War II and, 123–134. *See also* Arabic programming on PBS; Nuwayhid, 'Ajaj

Arab Palestinians: British assumptions about, 85–88, 90, 114, 118, 121; British fears of rebellion among, 84, 93, 121; claims for PBS as "national" radio station, 169; community and identity, 26, 27; debt and "desperate position" of, 77, 78–79; general strike and, 23–25; independence movement among, 131–132; middle class, 7–8, 39–40; modernization and, 26–27; nationalism of, 26, 27, 134–151; percentage listening to PBS, 76, 124–125, 187; radio sales and distribution agents, 41–42, 46–48; rural, 76–122; tensions with Jewish community, 6–7, 23–25, 157–158, 169, 200. *See also* rural audiences; rural broadcasting

Arab Revolt (1930s), 24, 25, 121, 207n38

audience size and impact, 9–13, 182

Ayalon, Ami, 12

Bailey, Michael, 154
Balfour Declaration, 1–2
Bari. *See* Radio Bari
batteries, 107–108
Battershill, W. D., 103
battery-operated radio sets, 107–108, 117–118
BBC (British Broadcasting Corporation): BBC Arabic Service, 95–99; connections with PBS, 5, 7, 21–23, 204n10; copyright and royalty payments, 170–171; Empire Service, 33, 64, 183; as model for PBS, 6, 17, 152, 186–188; programming used by PBS, 18; religious broadcasting on, 152–154, 227n3

Bizra, Fatima (Jullnar), al-, 138–139, *139*
bombings, at PBS, 188–191, 232n47
Boutagy & Sons. *See* T. S. Boutagy & Sons
Bowman, Humphrey, 91

British Broadcasting Corporation. *See* BBC
"British Propaganda in Palestine" memo, 148–149, 226n71
Broadcasting Committee of PBS, 17–18
Broadcast Talks, 146
Brunner, Edmund, 112
Bulliet, Richard, 118
Burke, Timothy, 36–37, 144

censorship, 65–66, 75, 121, 124; during general strike (1936), 65–66, 76; of news broadcasts, 65–66, 75, 76, 121, 124, 225n55; of sermons broadcast on PBS, 161–163, 228n20
Central Religious Advisory Committee (CRAC), 154, 227n3
Chatterjee, Partha, 147
children's programming, 136, 138, *189*; bombings during, 188–189
Christians, 48–49, 211n38; rural populations of, 76
communities: imagined, 33, 34; listening, 33–35, 86, 123, 135, 208n5
consumption, 35–40; advertising focus on, 61–66; culture of, 6–7; "Euro-American" model, 35–36; mass market for, 37–40, 41; middle class and, 7–8, 26, 35–37, 39–40; radios as symbols of, 35–36
contracts: labor negotiations and, 172–173; for village radio set distribution, 101–104
Coptic community, 159–160
copyright and royalty issues, 170–172
cost of radio sets, 9, 10–11, 18, 37; free under village radio set distribution program, 101–105; installation payment program, 117, 220n98; medium-wave vs. shortwave, 18, 96, 183; rental costs, 108–109
Custodian of Enemy Property Office, 126

Cyprus, wireless station proposed for, 99

"day of rest" issues, 156–157, 163–164
de Grazia, Victoria, 35, 38
Difaʿ, al-, 55
diffusion of innovations, 39, 209n16
Dimitropoulous, Gabriel, 188
Din, Khalil Taqi, al-, 138
Din, Nasser, el-, 197
distribution program, for radio sets, 101–110, 120–121
Donzelot, Jacques, 144
Douglas, Susan, 32, 86
Duzdar, Shahina, 145
Dying Colonialism, A (Fanon), 168–169

Easter broadcasts, 164, 165–166
education programs, 88, 90–92; household management ("New Arab House") talks, 140–145, *141*, 147–148; rural broadcasting in Palestine, 84–85, 88, 90–92; rural broadcasting in United States, 111–114; "Rural Programs for Arab Listeners" memo, 91–92; Simpson and Strickland reports, 79–82; "Talks to Farmers," 20, 27, 83–85
Egyptian radio, 6, 8, 17, 26, 204n9; inauguration of, 63–64; listening community for, 33, 34
Eid al-Fitr, broadcasts on, 164
enemy sets, 125–128, *127*
entertainment, as programming category, 88–89, 112–113. *See also* music
Eretz Israel, 173–175
European Zone, 16

Falastin, 13, 55, 209n20; advertisements in, overview, 55–56, 57; advertisements in, content and examples, 58–63, *59*, 65, 70–71, *70*; advertisements in, numbers

Falastin (*continued*)
of (1934–1949), 66–67, *67*; advertisements in, post–World War II, 72–73; Christian ownership of, 55; circulation of, 141, 224–225n54; criticism of PBS Arabic music programming, 135; cross-advertising in, 46–48; Easter broadcast announcements, 166; front-page coverage for "New Arab House" talks, 140–143, 145, 147, 148; reaction to fears of Radio Bari, 99–101; reputation of, 55; rural customers, commitment to, 120; support for Nuwayhid's programming, 137, 142, 147, 224n39; T. S. Boutagy & Sons advertisements in, *50*, 53–54, *60*; warnings about false agents, 44; women's broadcasts, coverage of, 140–143, 145, 147
false agents, 42–46
Fanon, Frantz, 168–169
farmers: British fears of uprisings by, 84, 93; British view of, 83–85, 114, 121; "desperate position" of, 77–79; education programs for, 79–81, 84–85, 90–92; in India, programs for, 80; laws affecting, 78; migration to urban areas, 79–80, 110; Simpson and Strickland reports on, 78–82; as target for PBS broadcasts, 4–5, 23, 26–27, 76–122; in United States, radio programs for, 111–114. *See also* rural audiences
fellahin, 83–85; "plight of," 78–79; radio advertising aimed at, 115–118, *116*, *117*. *See also* farmers; rural audiences
fetishism, 36–37
Fleischmann, Ellen, 84
Freemasons, 50, 212n44
Frierson, Elizabeth, 35–36
Fry, Stephen, 21, 22

general strike, 23–25, 207nn37–38; advertising after, 115; advertising

suspended during, 65, 66; fear of Arab uprisings after, 76; news censorship and, 76
German broadcasting, British worries about, 27, 84, 92, 109, 121
Goitein, E. D., 19–20
Golender, T., 42
Greek Coptic community, 159–160
group listening: by families, 85–86; listening communities, 33–35, 86, 208n5; loudspeakers for rural audiences, 20, 83
Guardian movement, 110–111

Haboker, 150, 178, 181
Hadi, Amin Abdul, 163–164
Hajj, broadcast references to, 137
Ha-Kotzer, 106
Hamdan, Salim, 138
Hamzeh, Sheikh Amin Muhammad, 104–105
Hashemite Jordanian (Palestine) Station, 170, 196
"ha-Tikvah," 169, 175–181; as Jewish national music, 176–177; PBS position on, 177–179; Samuel, Edwin, and, 179–181; secret memo on, 180–181, 231n30, 231n33
Hebrew-language programming, 6, 17, 20, 23; allocation of programming hours, 186; broadcast through Ramallah transmitter, 193; Children's Hour, 188–189, *189*; "ha-Tikvah," playing of, 169, 175–181; listening community for, 34, 182–183; musicians, 172–173; programming categories, 123; religious holidays, programs on, 157, 164; religious programming, 156; staff for, 22, 163–164; Vaad Leumi request for control over, 186. *See also* Jewish community; Kol Israel
Hebrew section of PBS, 28; complaints about lack of independence of, 150; "day of rest" issues, 156–157, 163–164; Jewish nationalism of, 169, 175–181, 193; postman-

date events and reorganization, 195–200; relocation of, 192, 193
Heyworth-Dunne, John, 100, 101
Hirshberg, Jehoash, 105–106, 176
His Master's Voice (HMV), 48, 52–53, *52*, 54; customization of advertising, 60–61, *60*, *70*, 115, *116*, 120
Hizb al-Istiqlal (Independence Party), 131–132, 222–223n21
hostile listeners (during World War II), 125–128
household management ("New Arab House") talks, 140–145, *141*, 147–148
Hudson, William, 16, 17
Huna al-Quds (Shanab), 198–199, *198*
Husayn, sharif of Mecca, 2, 203n2
Husseini, Hajj Amin al-, 24, 131, 207n37; as Qur'an reciter, 156

immigration issues, 79, 132, 182–183; migration from rural to urban areas, 79–80, 110, 111
independence: Arab movement for, 131–132; postmandate events, 195–200; readiness for, under League of Nations mandate, 17, 98, 148, 200
Independence Party, 131–132, 222–223n21
India: rural broadcasting in, 110–111; Strickland's experiences in, 79–80, 110
information, as programming category, 88, 89–90, 112
installation requirements, 30–31
interference issues, 15–16
International Broadcasting Union, 15
international governance, for communication, 15–17
Islam: call to prayer on PBS broadcasts, 137; as common, unifying element, 136–137; scholarly broadcasts on, 137–138; Supreme Muslim Council in Palestine (British-created), 153, 156, 163

Israel: claim of Kol Israel as national station, 6, 28, 170, 195, 199–200, *199*; postmandate events, 195–200
Israeli Broadcasting Authority, 28, 197, 199
Israeli Post Office, 199
Istiqlal (Independence) Party, 131–132, 222–223n21
Italian broadcasting: British worries about, 27, 84, 92–110; Radio Bari, 92–95, 99–101, 109

Jerusalem: central role in PBS, 6, 199–200; division into political sections, 191–192; "50 years of broadcasting" stamp cover, 199–200, *199*; on-air identification for PBS, 174, 198–199, 230n11
Jewish community: allocation of broadcast hours and, 182, 186–188; boycott of PBS over broadcasts on Sabbath, 157; claims for PBS as "national" station, 169, 195, 199–200; Eretz Israel, use of term, 173–175; European station listening, 182; "ha-Tikvah" as Jewish national music, 169, 175–181; immigration, encouragement of, 182–183, 184; immigration, White Paper limits on, 132; on-air identification for PBS, 173–175; percentage of licensed radio listeners, 187; Program Advisory Committee (for PBS), 180, 183, 186; radio agents, 46–48; radio distribution program, requests to, 105–106; radio licenses, number of, 184–185, 231n37; shortwave broadcasting, promotion of, 124, 184; tensions with Arab Palestinians, 6–7, 23–25, 157–158, 169, 200; Vaad Leumi (National Council), 174, 175, 178, 179, 229n10. *See also* Hebrew-language programming; Zionists
Jordanian (Palestine) Station, 170, 196

Jullnar (Fatima al-Bizra), 138–139, *139*

Kabha, Mustafa, 12
Katznelson, Abraham, 183
Keating, Rex, vii, 161–162, 193–194
Kennedy, G. D., 126, 221n6
Khalidi, Rashid, 153
Khoury, Philip, 124
Khurshid, Qudsiyya, 145
kibbutzim, radio sets requested by, 105–106
Kol Israel, 6, 28, 170, 195; claimed by Israel as national station, 195, 199–200, *199*; *Forty Years of Kol Israel* (TV program), 199
Kumayko, I., 64

Lababidi, Yahya, 22, *22*, 156
land: immigration issues, 79, 132, 182–183; laws on, 78; sales of, 78; settlement issues, 78–79; transfers of, 132; White Paper and, 132. *See also* farmers; rural audiences
Land Disputes Possessions Ordinance (1933), 78
laws: on farmers and land, 78; on radio licenses in World War II, 128–129
League of Nations, 1, 98–99, 217n48; mandate reports to, 17, 78, 148
Lebanon, government-operated radio in, 8, 17, 34, 208n4
LeMahieu, D. L., 37–38
licensed agents, 40–48; business opportunities from radio set distribution program, 107–109; false agents, 42–46, 210n23; licensing system, 40–42; marketing by, 56–58
licenses for radio sets, 40–42, 182–194, *185*; Emergency Law on (during World War II), 128–129; fees for, 182, 184, 186–187; number of, 10–12, *11*, 18, 21, 67–68, *68*, 72–73; number of, by ethnicity/name, 184–185, 231n37; pub-

lished in newspapers, 185; special licenses during World War II, 128–129; used to identify resident "enemies," 125–126; wavelength issues, 183–188
Likhovski, Assaf, 2
listening, 33–35; hostile listeners (in World War II), 125–128; listening communities, 33–35, 86, 123, 135, 208n5; listening practices, 32; sociality of, 32–33
Liwaʾ, al-, 174, 229n8
Lubrani, Eliezer, 22–23
Lucerne conference, 15–16

MacDonald, Captain, 93
Mackay, D. H., 106
mandate government, 98–99, 217n48; British aims for, 2, 28; British legal and administrative precedents, 152; dissolution of, 191–192, 194; fear of influence of Italian and German radio stations, 27, 83, 92–110, 121, 182; initiatives for rural Arabs, 77, 101–110; Ottoman legal precedents, 152, 227n1; postmandate events, 195–200; progress reports, 24, 207n40; radio restrictions during World War II, 125–129; radio set distribution program, 101–110, 120–121; Simpson and Strickland reports, 77–82; timeline, 201–202; view of religions as a dividing factor, 152, 153. *See also* Palestine
Mansell, Gerard, 97–98
Mansour, Adib, 188, 232n47
Marchand, Roland, 38, 53
marketing of radio sets, 29–75; compared with other goods, 36–37; consumer desire and, 56–58; Egyptian radio inauguration and, 63–64; expansion of market, 37–40; markets, 46–48; mass market, 37–40, 41; pent-up demand after World War II, 73. *See also* advertising
Martin, Kevin, vii, 41, 58

Masri, Shahra, al-, 145
mass market, 37–40, 41
Matalon Brothers, 47, 108
Matthews, Weldon, 131, 132
McNair, Crawford, 21, 22
medium-wave broadcasting, 18, 96,
    97–98, 170, 183
middle class: advertising appeals to,
    39–40, 54, 57–58, 61–63; culture
    of consumption, 7–8, 26, 35–37,
    39; emergence of, 7–8; radio sets,
    associations and symbolic nature
    of, 7–8, 39–40, 54, 57–58, 75
Middle East: government-operated
    radio in, 8–9, 14, 63–64; radio
    history in, 6–14, 26, 204n9; radio
    stations, 34, 208nn3–4; radio sta-
    tions from Italy and Germany re-
    ceived by, 77, 92–110
modernization: in farming/agri-
    culture, 80, 83–85; "New Arab
    House" broadcasts, 140–145; ra-
    dio as symbol of, 35, 57, 75; for
    rural Arab populations, 77, 110,
    121; through radio/PBS, 5, 9, 13,
    27, 77, 110, 122, 134–151, 168;
    women's advancement as sign of,
    145–148
Mu'awiya ibn Abu Sufyan, 138
Mughannam, Matiel, 145
music: Arabic programming for, 76,
    119, 135, 138–139, 139; copyright
    and royalty issues, 170–172; "ha-
    Tikvah" and Jewish national mu-
    sic, 169, 175–181; labor relations
    and contract negotiations, 172–
    173; music lovers as target for PBS
    broadcasts, 4, 5, 23; music staff
    at PBS, 22, 172–173; profession-
    alism of musicians, 172–173; re-
    location of Music section, 192,
    193; storage of instruments at sta-
    tion, 172

Nadan, Amos, 92
Najmabadi, Afsaneh, 144
Nashashibi, 'Azmi, 27, 150–151, 197
Nasr, Karima, 145

Nasser, Gamal Abdel, 6, 7
national anthems, 28, 175–181
nationalism, 26–28, 123–151; Arab
    Palestinian, 26, 27, 131–132,
    134–151; claims on PBS as na-
    tional radio, 168–194, 195–200;
    Eretz Israel, controversies over,
    173–175; Istiqlal (Independence)
    Party, 131–132, 222–223n21; on-
    air identification for PBS, 173–
    175; PBS Arabic Section and,
    123–151; postmandate events,
    195–200; religious identity and,
    136–140; women's programs and,
    140–148. See also Zionists
"New Arab House" broadcasts, 140–
    145, 141, 147–148
news broadcasts: Arabic broadcast
    news-service, 118–119, 123; BBC
    Arabic Service, 95–99; British
    fears about Axis propaganda, 27,
    84, 92–101, 103, 109, 121, 182;
    censorship of, 65–66, 75, 76, 121,
    124, 225n55; eagerness of Arab
    populations for, 100–101, 110;
    Public Information Office control
    over, 129–131
newspapers: *Haboker*, 150, 178, 181;
    al-Liwa', 174, 229n8; in Mandate
    Palestine, 55, 215n14; of Nuway-
    hid, 'Ajaj, 132; reviews about PBS
    in, 12–14, 19–21. See also advertis-
    ing; *Falastin*; *Palestine Post*
Nusseibeh, Sari, 197
Nuwayhid, 'Ajaj, 27, 28, 131–151,
    133, 197; Arab nationalism and,
    131–132; background of, 131,
    222n17; as boost to PBS credi-
    bility, 124; concern for quality of
    programming, 134–140; contract
    and salary of, 134, 223nn29–30;
    as Controller of Arabic Program-
    ming, 131, 133–134; imprison-
    ment of, 132; legacy of, 148–151;
    modernist vision of, 151; news-
    papers of, 132; as pan-Arabist,
    131, 132, 134, 136–137; political
    activities of, 131–132; position

Nuwayhid, 'Ajaj (*continued*)
    at PBS, 131–134; religious broad-
    casting themes under, 136–140,
    151, 153; roles for PBS envisioned
    by, 134–135; women's program-
    ming on PBS, 140–147

on-air identification, 173–175

Palestine: history of, 1–3, 191–192;
    included in European broadcast-
    ing zone, 16; mandate state, Brit-
    ish aims for, 2, 28; mandate state,
    creation of, 1–2; middle-class cul-
    ture in, 6–7, 26, 35–40; national
    identity in, 8–9, 27, 122, 195–
    200; political impact of radio in,
    6–7, 8, 13; population growth
    in, 2–3; Protestant community in,
    48–49, 211n38; radio-listening
    audience in, 9–12; religious iden-
    tity in, 153; rural population of,
    76–77; timeline, 201–202; White
    Paper on, 132, 178–179, 223n24.
    See also mandate government
Palestine Broadcasting Service (PBS):
    allocation of broadcast hours, 155,
    159–161, 170, 182, 186–188; Ar-
    abic news services, 95–99, 118–
    119, 123; assumptions for pro-
    gramming, 85–89; audience size
    and impact, 9–13, 182, 184–185,
    186; BBC as model for, 6, 17, 152,
    186–188; BBC connections of, 5,
    7, 21–23, 204n10; BBC men at,
    21–22; BBC programming used
    by, 18; broad-based audience for,
    66, 134; Broadcasting Commit-
    tee, 17–18; censorship of news
    on, 65–66, 75, 76, 225n55; cen-
    sorship of sermons on, 161–163,
    228n20; copyright and royalty is-
    sues, 170–172; dissolution and
    split of, 170, 191–200; establish-
    ment of, 14–15, 17–23, 83; farm-
    ers and music lovers as targets, 4–
    5, 23, 77, 83–85, *119*, 120–121;

finances, division of, 192–193; fi-
    nancial concerns, 173; general
    strike and, 23–25, 207nn37–38;
    as government-operated, 8–9,
    14; history of, 1–8; initial broad-
    casts of, 1, 3–6, 23, 99; Jerusa-
    lem headquarters for, 6; Jerusa-
    lem Liaison Office for, 99; Jewish
    Program Advisory Commit-
    tee for, 180, 183, 186; labor rela-
    tions and contracts, 172–173; lan-
    guages broadcast on, 17–18, 20,
    123; legacy of, 197–200; local ac-
    ceptance of, 20, 76, 169, 175; lo-
    cal Palestinians on staff of, 22–23,
    76, 124, 133; modernization and,
    5, 9, 13, 26–27, 123–151; national
    anthems and, 175–181; national
    identity and, 28, 122, 168–194,
    195–200; newspaper/press reports
    on, 12–14, 19–21; on-air identi-
    fication, 173–175; postmandate
    events, 195–200; programming
    goals for, 18, 155, 188; propa-
    ganda vs. national institution, 8–
    14; Ramallah transmitter, 1, 3, 6,
    193, 195, 196, *197*, 198; religious
    broadcasting on, 152–167; relo-
    cation of Hebrew and Music sec-
    tions, 192, 193; terrorist attacks
    and bombings, 188–191, 232n47;
    timeline, 201–202; wartime
    changes and listening restrictions,
    128–131, 157–158; Wauchope's
    addresses on, 3–5, *4*, 23, 25, 155;
    wavelength issues, 170, 183–188;
    years of operation, 3, 6. *See also*
    Arabic programming on PBS; ru-
    ral audiences; rural broadcasting
Palestine Ministry of Information.
    See Public Information Office
Palestine Post, 19, 25, 55, 209n20,
    215n14; advertising, post–World
    War II, 73; coverage of *Broadcast
    Talks* on women's issues, 146; cov-
    erage of "New Arab House" talks,
    143; cross-advertising in, 46–48;

Eretz Israel, editorial on, 173–174; Jewish national music, editorial on, 176–177; Jewish ownership of, 55, 81; on Kol Israel as Jewish State Radio, 195–196; "Listener's Corner," 143, 166; Orthodox Easter program announcement, 165–166; short-wave broadcasts advocated by, 183–184; on Strickland report/proposals, 81–83; warnings about false agents, 42–45

Palestinian Broadcasting Corporation, 28, 197–199

Palestinian Radio Company, 47

pan-Arabism, 131, 132, 134, 136–137

Passfield White Paper. *See* White Paper on Palestine

Passover broadcasts, 164

Patnode, Randall, 111

PBS. *See* Palestine Broadcasting Service

Performing Rights Society, 170–171

Philips radios, agents for, 47

Pilot radios, 42, 72

political impact of radio, 6–7, 8, 13

Postmaster General, 16, 17, 106, 126

Poston, Ralph, 148–149

pretuned radio sets, 102–103, 108

propaganda, 8–9, 93; British fears of German and Italian radio, 27, 84, 92–95, 99–101, 103, 109, 121, 182; "British Propaganda in Palestine" memo, 148–149, 226n71; pretuned radio sets and, 102–103, 108

Protection of Cultivators Ordinances, 78

Protestant community in Palestine, 48–49, 211n38; T. S. Boutagy & Sons as part of, 48–49

public good concept, 3, 14, 121, 123, 153, 157, 167

Public Information Office, 124, 125, 192, 222n14; control over news, 124, 129–131; control over PBS

programming, 129–131, 222n14; tensions with PBS, 130–131

Pye Radio, 47, 72, 108

Qassam, Izz al-Din, al-, 23–24

Qur'an: advertisements referencing, 64, 213n62; broadcasts including, 137, 156, *156*, 224n39

radio: amateur broadcasting, 14–15, 205n17; audience, size and impact of, 9–13, 182; battery-operated vs. electric, 107–108, 117–118; decline in value of, 67; European Zone, 16; government-operated stations, 8–9, 14; history in Middle East, 6–14, 26, 204n9; importance and impact of, 6–8, 12, 13; interference issues, 15–16; international governance for, 15–17; licenses for radio sets, number of, 10–12, *11*, 18, 21; national identity, role in, 8–9, 26, 122; newness of, 29–30; private stations, 15; as a public good, 3, 14, 121, 153, 157, 167; sociality of listening, 32–33; statehood, radio stations as signs of, 16–17, 169, 173–175; technology for, 7, 37, 205n11; "user pays" principle, 10; wartime restrictions and bans, 69, 125–131. *See also* radio sets

Radio Alger, 168–169

Radio Bari, 92–95, 99–101, 109

Radio Cairo, 8, 21, 26

Radio Damascus, 8

Radio Orient, 8, 17, 34, 208n4

radio sets: advertising for, 29–75; consumer desire, marketing and, 56–58; cost of, 9, 10–11, 18, 40; distribution program, 101–110, 120–121; enemy sets, confiscation of, 125–128, *127*; installation requirements, 30–31; licensed agents for, 40–48; locations for, 31–32; manufactured outside of Palestine, 41; markets for, 37–40;

radio sets (*continued*)
    medium-wave vs. short-wave, 18,
        97–98; physicality of, 30–32; pre-
        tuned, 102–103, 108; rental of,
        108; requisitioning of (in World
        War II), 126–128; selling and
        marketing, 26–75; as signs of
        modernization and luxury, 26,
        35–36, 57, 110; size of, 30; tun-
        ing, 31; user's manual, 31; village
        radio sets, contracts for, 101–104;
        village radio sets, qualification re-
        quirements for, 101
Radio Tel Aviv, 15
Ramallah Radio, 196
Ramallah transmitter, 1, 3, 6, 193,
    195, 196, *197*, 198
RCA (Radio Corporation of Amer-
    ica), 47, 72; warning about false
    agents, 42–43, 210n23
religious broadcasting, 27–28, 152–
    167; administration and decisions
    involved, 154–157, 167; allocation
    of broadcast hours, 155, 159–161;
    Bible versions, disagreements over,
    158–159; British morals and BBC
    model, 152–154, 167, 227n3;
    Central Religious Advisory Com-
    mittee (CRAC), 154, 227n3; "day
    of rest" issues, 156–157, 163–164;
    Greek Coptic community, 159–
    160; holiday programs, 137, 164–
    167; legacy of, 167; mandate gov-
    ernment's decision for, 152–157,
    167; multifaith environment, com-
    plications of, 155–157, 159–160,
    167; overlapping jurisdictions
    and, 159–161, 163–164, 167; PBS
    commitment to, 152–154, 155,
    167; proportionally representa-
    tive scale for, 159–160; public
    good concept and, 153, 157, 167;
    Qur'an broadcasts, 137, 156, *156*,
    224n39; religions in Palestine as
    connecting factor, 136–137, 153;
    religions in Palestine as divisive
    factor, 152, 153, 154; religious
    services, 158, 159–163; religious

text readings, 156–157, *156*, 158–
    159; sermons broadcast with prior
    censorship, 161–163, 228n20;
    sermons proscribed from broad-
    casts, 153; themes under Nuway-
    hid's tenure, 136–140, 151; World
    War II, challenges after, 157–167
Rendell, R. A. "Tony," 21
rental of radio sets, 108
Rogers, Everett, 39, 209n16
Rommel, Erwin, 140
Rose, John Melkon, 189
royalty issues, 170–172
rural audiences, 5, 20–21, 25, 42,
    76–122, 187; advertising and sell-
    ing aimed at, 114–120, *116*, *117*,
    121; assumptions about, 83–
    85, 88–89; British beliefs about,
    83–85, 90, 114, 118, 121; Brit-
    ish fears of influence by Italian
    and German stations, 27, 77, 92–
    101, 103, 109, 121; "desperate po-
    sition" of Arab peasants, 77–79;
    Falastin commitment to news-
    paper delivery for, 120; loudspeak-
    ers for, 20, 83; modernization
    through radio/PBS, 7, 13, 26–27,
    77, 110; Muslims and Christians,
    numbers of, 76; percentage of Pal-
    estinians living in rural areas, 76–
    77; private purchases of radio sets,
    114; targeting by mandate govern-
    ment, 75, 77. *See also* farmers
rural broadcasting, 26, 76–122; Ar-
    abic language format, 86–88; cat-
    egories of broadcasts, 88; as a dis-
    crete programming category, 86;
    educational programming, 80–
    81, 84–85, 90–92; entertainment
    programming, 88–89; hours for,
    86; informational and practical
    programming, 88, 89–90, 112;
    mandate government goals for, 77,
    83–85; modernization through, 7,
    13, 26–27, 77, 110; radio set dis-
    tribution program, 101–110, 120–
    121; selling and advertising in,
    114–120; in United States, 111–

114, 220n93; worldwide over-view of, 110–114. *See also* rural audiences
rural migration to urban areas, 79–80, 110, 111

Sa'id, Mrs. Salwa, 140–145, 147
Salomon, Karl, 22, 23, 176; on "ha-Tikvah" controversy, 178–179, 180, 181
Samuel, Edwin, 158–160, 161–163, 179, 230–231n28; on allocation of broadcasting hours, 187–188; father of, 179; on "ha-Tikvah" issue, 179–181; wife of, 179
San Remo resolution, 1–2
school broadcasting, 90–92
Seikaly, Mai, 49–50
Seikaly, Sherene, vii, 214n73
selling radio/radio sets, 29–75; expansion of market, 37–40; false agents, 42–46; licensed agents, 40–48; markets, 46–48; mass market for, 37–40, 41; print advertising in the Arabic press, 54–75; to rural audiences, 114–120; sales and repair offices, 42; T. S. Boutagy & Sons, 48–54; World War II, sales after, 71–75; World War II, sales during, 66–71. *See also* advertising; agents; marketing of radio sets
servants, 145, 226n63
Shakry, Omnia, 147
Shanab, Hussein Abu, 198–199
Shaw, J. V. W., 180
Shechter, Relli, 37–38, 61
Shehadeh, Mary, 146
short-wave broadcasting, 96, 97–98, 170, 183
Simpson, John Hope, 78–79
Simpson report, 77–79
Smith, R. D., 129–130, 222n15
sociality of listening practices, 32–33
statehood, radio stations as signs of, 16–17, 169, 173–175
Strickland, C. F., 79–83, 110
Strickland report, 79–82

strike. *See* general strike
Supreme Muslim Council, 153, 156, 163
Svislotzky Brothers, 47
Syria, 16, 124, 138; advertisements in, 41, 47, 58

Teague, Heather Fairley, 189–190
Tel Aviv: Golender sales concessions in, 42; Svislotzky Brothers, 47
terrorist attacks on PBS, 188–191, 232n47
"This Is Jerusalem Calling": article by Goiten, 19; on-air identification of PBS, 174, 198, 230n11
Tibawi, Abd al-Latif, al-, 137–138, 146, 224n42
Tobruk, Libya, 140
Touba, Asma, 145
T. S. Boutagy & Sons, 48–54; advertisements of, 50, *50*, *51*, 53–54, 60–65, *60*; advertising aimed at rural customers, 115–118, *116*, *117*, 119–120, 121; advertising themes, 61–65; Charles V. Boutagy, 51; delivery arrangements for rural customers, 118; departure from Israel, 74–75; Émile Boutagy, 50–51, 52, 62–63, 69, 73; Émile Boutagy, letters to and responses from, 62–63, 115–117, 118; free repair for life of radio, 118; Gordon Boutagy, 51, 52–53; government distribution program and, 108; His Master's Voice (HMV), 48, 52–54, *52*, 60–61, *60*, *70*, 115, *116*, 120; installation payment program, 117, 220n98; letters to, and responses, 62–63, 115–117, 118; modernity of, 50, *51*; paper and stationary of, *51*, *52*, 53; "portable radio" ads, 70–71, *70*; post–World War II business, 71–74; Qur'an references in advertising, 64, 213n62; rental of radio sets, 69; sales statistics, 66–67, 71–72; T. S. Boutagy, 49–51, 211–212n38

tuning of radio sets, 31; pretuned sets, 102–103, 108
Tuqan, Ibrahim, 22–23, *22*, 27, 76, 124, 133, 211n2; political activities of, 23, 132; resignation of, 133

United States, rural broadcasting programs in, 111–114, 220n93
"user pays" principle, 10

Vaad Leumi, 174, 175, 178, 179, 229n10; request for control over Hebrew programming, 186
villages: broadcasting aimed at, 20–21, 25, 76–122; in India, rural broadcasting programs, 110–111; loudspeakers for, 20, 83; radio set distribution program, 101–110, 120–121. *See also* rural audiences; rural broadcasting
Voice of the Arabs, 6

warnings about false agents, 42–45, 210n23
Wauchope, Arthur, *4*, 25; initial address on PBS, 3–5, *4*, 23, 155
wavelength issues, 96–98, 170, 183–188; medium-wave, 18, 95–98, 170, 183; short-wave, 96, 97–98, 170, 183
Weissenberg, Mae, 188, 189–190, 232n47
Weizmann, Chaim, 178
White Paper on Palestine, 132, 177–178, 223n24
Wik, Reynold, 111–112
women: advancement as sign of modernity, 145–148; Arab, 85, 140–145; as audience for PBS, 9, 122; *Broadcast Talks* series, 146; household management ("New Arab House") talks, 140–145, *141*, 147–148; "night of women" broadcasts, 145, 147; women broadcasters, 139–140, 142–144, 145–147; women's programming on PBS, 9, 140–148
World War II: German and Italian broadcasts and propaganda, 84, 92–110; listening restrictions during, 128–129; North Africa, military actions in, 140; number of radio licenses and, 67–68, *68*; PBS Arabic Section during, 125–134; PBS reorganization after, 157–158; radio advertising during, 66–67, *67*; radio selling after, 71–75; radio selling during, 66–71; radio set distribution program and, 109–110; radio set restrictions and confiscation, 125–129, 130; special radio set licenses during, 128–129; women's topics broadcast during, 140–145

Yishuv. *See* Jewish community
Yisrael, Agudath, 157

Zenith radios, 64
Zionists, 2, 5; British White Paper on Palestine and, 132, 177–178; Eretz Israel, 173–175; Samuel, Edwin, and, 179–181; tensions with Arab Palestinians, 6–7, 23–25, 157–158, 169, 200. *See also* Hebrew-language programming; Jewish community

Milton Keynes UK
Ingram Content Group UK Ltd.
UKHW011949090524
442389UK00014B/188